NO-FAULT INSURANCE ANTI-FRAUD LITIGATION

A Practitioner's Guide

MAX GERSHENOFF AND BARRY I. LEVY

TORT TRIAL INSURANCE

TORT TRIAL & INSURANCE PRACTICE SECTION

Cover design by Jill Tedhams/ABA Design

Printed in the United States of America.

21 20 19 18 17 5 4 3 2 1

ISBN: 978-1-63425-790-9
e-ISBN: 978-1-63425-791-6

Library of Congress Cataloging-in-Publication Data
Names: Gershenoff, Max, author. | Levy, Barry (Writer on law), author.
Title: No-fault insurance anti-fraud litigation : a practitioner's guide / Max Gershenoff, Barry Levy.
Description: Chicago : American Bar Association, [2017] | Includes index.
Identifiers: LCCN 2017016601 (print) | LCCN 2017017219 (ebook) | ISBN 9781634257916 (diskette) | ISBN 9781634257909 (pbk.)
Subjects: LCSH: No-fault automobile insurance—Law and legislation—United States. | No-fault automobile insurance—Law and legislation—United States—Criminal provisions. | Insurance fraud—Law and legislation—United States. | Actions and defenses—United States.
Classification: LCC KF1219.5 (ebook) | LCC KF1219.5 .G47 2017 (print) | DDC 346.73/0865728—dc23
LC record available at https://lccn.loc.gov/2017016601

For Our Families

Contents

About the Authors

Max Gershenoff, Esq., helps insurers prosecute and defend complex civil lawsuits against alleged no-fault insurance fraud rings, including claims under the federal RICO act. His efforts have helped create a significant body of legal authority supporting the use of affirmative litigation, and especially civil RICO, to combat insurance fraud. He also counsels automobile, property, and life insurers on claims handling practices and investigation techniques, and he works with them to develop fraud prevention, detection, and recovery plans. Mr. Gershenoff received his A.B. degree from the University of Georgia and his law degree from the Benjamin N. Cardozo School of Law at Yeshiva University.

Barry I. Levy, Esq., has been lead counsel in hundreds of complex insurance fraud cases, including many suits to recover claim payments to physicians, medical clinics, attorneys, public adjusters, and others involved in insurance fraud schemes. Mr. Levy also counsels healthcare, automobile, property, fidelity, and life insurers on claims handling practices and investigation techniques and the development of fraud prevention, detection, and recovery plans. He also represents insurers in the defense of litigation challenging claims-handling practices. Mr. Levy received his B.A. degree from the Ohio State University and his law degree from the Ohio State University College of Law.

Preface

At first blush, no-fault insurance anti-fraud litigation may seem like a narrow and prosaic topic. No-fault fraud lacks the glamor of sophisticated Wall Street swindles, its primary victims are automobile insurance companies, and the damages in any individual case are usually relatively low—rarely amounting to more than $10,000,000.

Nonetheless, no-fault insurance fraud has meaningful consequences for society. Those of us who have moved from states without a no-fault fraud problem to states where no-fault fraud is endemic can testify to large increases in our automobile insurance premiums. While increased insurance rates may not take much of a bite out of the wealthier segments of society, they make life that much more difficult for the rest of us. Indeed, no-fault insurance fraud amounts to a significant "fraud tax" on consumers, estimated at billions of dollars each year. For example, the Insurance Information Institute, an industry group, reported that in 2011 Florida drivers paid more than $650,000,000, or almost $58 per vehicle, as the result of no-fault insurance fraud.[1] The Insurance Information Institute also calculated that in New York, policyholders paid the equivalent of a $229,000,000 fraud tax on the automobile insurance policies as the result of no-fault fraud.[2]

What is more, the most typical forms of no-fault insurance fraud—such as inflated billing for medically useless or illusory healthcare services, often submitted through healthcare practices that illegally are owned and controlled by unlicensed nonprofessionals—display a cynicism and lawlessness that chip away at societal norms

---

[1] *See* Insurance Information Institute, *Fraud and Abuse in No-Fault Auto Insurance System Results in a Substantial "Fraud Tax" for Florida's Drivers*, I.I.I. Finds (March 6, 2017), http://www.iii.org/press-release/fraud-and-abuse-in-no-fault-auto-insurance-system-results-in-a-substantial-fraud-tax-for-floridas-drivers-iii-finds-120611.

[2] *See* Insurance Information Institute, *No-Fault Insurance Fraud in New York State Is Ramping Up Premiums*, I.I.I. Finds (March 6, 2017), http://www.iii.org/article/no-fault-insurance-fraud-new-york-state-ramping-premiums.

and create an environment where ever more egregious corruption is accepted. These types of fraudulent practices, in which the independent medical judgment of healthcare providers is subordinated to their pecuniary interests—or worse, the pecuniary interests of unlicensed nonprofessionals—put the public at significant risk, and they actually exacerbate the injury compensation problems that no-fault systems were intended to remediate.

Over the course of litigating hundreds of no-fault insurance anti-fraud cases, we have consistently been surprised at the limited extent to which no-fault fraud is criminally prosecuted relative to the overall prevalence of the problem. Evidently, we are not alone: More than a few federal and state court judges have asked us, from the bench or in chambers, whether our insurer-clients have made law enforcement aware of one fraud ring or another. Even when the answer is yes, prosecutors seem to have an unfunded mandate to tackle the issue, and criminal prosecutions rarely ensue.

Even state regulatory authorities, such as professional licensing and disciplinary boards, appear unable to take any significant and consistent steps to address the issue. Oftentimes, in the course of an anti-fraud lawsuit we will learn that a defendant healthcare provider previously lost his professional license as the result of some prior, fraudulent conduct. Yet, after a course of pro forma "rehabilitation," the provider successfully petitioned for the reinstatement of his license and either set up shop committing some new kind of fraud or brazenly recommenced the same type of fraud that resulted in the loss of his license in the first place.

Against this backdrop, at least at the present, automobile insurance companies are the primary actors in the fight against no-fault fraud. The primary vehicle for their action is civil litigation against no-fault insurance fraud rings. This book is intended as a general guide to no-fault insurance anti-fraud litigation from the perspective of a plaintiff-insurer, from inception through summary judgment. We should emphasize at the outset that this book is not intended as a trial manual. While some no-fault insurance anti-fraud cases occasionally do go to trial, such trials are relatively rare. Rather, the vast majority of these types of lawsuits are resolved through settlement or, less frequently, via dispositive motion practice. In any case, the potentially large number of discrete issues that could arise in a trial of a no-fault anti-fraud lawsuit, and the very fact-intensive nature of such issues, necessarily places them beyond the scope of this book.

Acknowledgments

We would like to extend our sincere thanks to Evan Krinick, Esq., for reviewing this book and providing his valuable suggestions in terms of both its structure and content. We also are grateful to Alan Rutkin, Esq., for his assistance in getting this book off the ground. Thanks are due to Sarah Forbes Orwig of the American Bar Association, whose patience in awaiting the manuscript, and helpful comments once it finally was completed, made what could have been a stressful undertaking seem like a relative breeze. Last but not least—and as the dedication suggests—we are indebted to our families for their love and support throughout the writing process and, more generally, throughout our careers.

Despite our various debts of gratitude, the views expressed in this book are ours and ours alone—as are any errors and omissions that the careful reader may detect.

1

An Introduction to No-Fault Insurance and No-Fault Insurance Fraud

By 1930, the automobile was ubiquitous in American life. In 1900, there were only 8,000 automobiles registered in the United States, but in 1930, there were over 23,000,000.[1] This dramatic expansion in automobile use, the driving public's lack of experience with the new technology, and the absence of sufficient safety features led to a similarly dramatic increase in highway accidents and fatalities.[2]

As automobile accidents increased, scholars began to observe that the traditional tort system did not fairly and adequately compensate accident victims. One of the most notable early studies was a 1932 report by the Committee to Study Compensation for Automobile Accidents, conducted under the auspices of Columbia University's Council for Research in the Social Sciences

[1] James M. Anderson, et al., The U.S. Experience with No-Fault Automobile Insurance: A Retrospective 23 (2010).

[2] *Id.*

(the "Columbia Report").[3] The Columbia Report reached several discomfiting conclusions about the viability of the traditional tort system in the context of automobile accident compensation:

i. Despite a few very high awards, the tort system generally did not fully compensate accident victims, especially with respect to more serious losses;
ii. financially irresponsible defendants typically provided no meaningful compensation to accident victims, but even financially responsible defendants did not sufficiently compensate accident victims;
iii. to the extent that accident victims were compensated to some degree, receipt of the compensation often was delayed, with attendant hardship to the accident victims;
iv. most accident victims had lower incomes and therefore were in a weaker bargaining position when it came to bargaining for compensation; and
v. there was a considerable disparity in compensation among accident victims, with some being overcompensated and others receiving inadequate compensation.[4]

The Columbia Report concluded that liability for fault should be abolished in the context of automobile accidents, and its authors posited a system of mandatory insurance similar to the workers compensation system.[5] By the late 1950s, however, no state had enacted any type of no-fault insurance law.[6]

Unsurprisingly—given the continued increase in automobile usage and a concomitant increase in automobile accidents—the inequities in the tort system became more and more apparent as

---

[3] Committee to Study Compensation for Automobile Accidents, Report to the Columbia University Council for Research in the Social Sciences (1932) (hereinafter the "Columbia Report"); *see also* Fleming James, Jr., *The Columbia Study of Compensation for Automobile Accidents: An Unanswered Challenge*, 59 COLUM. L. REV. 408 (1959) (referring to the Columbia Report as "probably the most significant contribution to the study of torts to appear so far in the twentieth century.").

[4] James, *supra* note 3, at 408–10.

[5] Columbia Report, *supra* note 3, at 15–217.

[6] James, *supra* note 3, at 410.

the 20th century progressed.[7] There were, for instance, dramatic increases in automobile-related lawsuits, healthcare costs, and liability costs between 1955 and 1970.[8]

Ultimately, in 1965, Robert E. Keeton, a law professor at Harvard University, and Jeffrey O'Connell, a law professor at the University of Illinois, published *Basic Protection for the Traffic Victim: A Blueprint for Reforming Automobile Insurance*, which generally is considered to be a landmark on the road to widespread enactment of no-fault insurance laws.[9] Keeton and O'Connell's diagnosis of the problems with the tort system was substantially similar to the conclusions in the Columbia Report, inasmuch as they sought to address (i) general undercompensation of accident victims, especially with respect to more serious injuries; (ii) overcompensation for minor injuries; (iii) delays in compensation; (iv) high administrative costs; and (v) perverse incentives for dishonesty amongst both accident victims and tortfeasors.[10]

In place of traditional tort liability, Keeton and O'Connell proposed—in essence—mandatory first-party automobile insurance through which drivers would insure themselves, coupled with the abolishment of the fault-based tort system to the extent of that first-party coverage.[11] To buttress their recommendations, Keeton and O'Connell included a model statute in their proposal as well as an actuarial opinion to demonstrate that the proposal would result in cost savings.[12]

In 1971, Massachusetts became the first state to enact a no-fault law.[13] In keeping with the exceptional influence of Keeton and O'Connell, the leading advocate for the Massachusetts statute was

---

[7] Anderson, *supra* note 1, at 28–30.

[8] *Id.*

[9] *See*, e.g., *Id.* at 35 (referring to Basic Protection for the Traffic Victim: A Blueprint for Reforming Automobile Insurance as a "landmark work"); Florida Senate Committee on Banking and Insurance, *Report on Florida's Motor Vehicle No-Fault Law* 6 (2005) (noting that Keeton and O'Connell "were instrumental in developing the concept of no-fault insurance in the mid-1960's").

[10] Robert E. Keeton & Jeffrey O'Connell, Basic Protection for the Traffic Victim: A Blueprint for Reforming Automobile Insurance 2–3 (1965).

[11] *Id.*, at 5, 273, and *passim*.

[12] *Id.* at 299–339.

[13] Gary T. Schwartz, *Auto No-Fault and First-Party Insurance: Advantages and Problems*, 73 S. Cal. L. Rev. 611 (2000).

Michael Dukakis—then a state legislator—who had been one of Keeton's students at Harvard Law School and who liaised frequently with Keeton as he pushed the no-fault law through the Massachusetts legislature.[14] Thereafter, during the early-to-mid 1970s, at least 16 states adopted some sort of no-fault insurance law.[15] However, no state has adopted a no-fault law since 1976, and several states—namely Colorado, Connecticut, Georgia, and Nevada—have repealed their no-fault laws.[16]

Currently, 12 states have a no-fault law, specifically Florida, Michigan, New York, New Jersey, Pennsylvania, Hawaii, Kansas, Kentucky, Massachusetts, Minnesota, North Dakota, and Utah. While there are considerable variations among the no-fault laws in each of these states, they can broadly be classified by the degree to which the respective systems permit or abolish tort liability and—assuming tort liability is permitted—the type of threshold an injured party must meet before tort liability is permitted.

In this context, it is worthwhile to note that no state has adopted "pure" or "absolute" no-fault laws, meaning a system that totally abolishes recovery in tort in exchange for unlimited or near-unlimited coverage for economic loss.[17] Indeed, Keeton and O'Connell themselves did not recommend a pure no-fault system and instead proposed the type of "modified" or "hybrid" no-fault system that currently is in place in every state with a no-fault law, because they believed that a pure no-fault plan would be "doomed to founder as unable to muster the necessary widespread political support."[18] In a hybrid system, first-party insurance benefits for economic loss are provided regardless

---

[14] *Id.* at 612, n. 3.

[15] ANDERSON, *supra* note 1, at 2. However, some contend that a larger number of states enacted no-fault laws. *See*, e.g., ROBERT H. JOOST, AUTOMOBILE INSURANCE AND NO-FAULT LAW §§ 2:18, 2:19 (2d ed. 1992) (positing that 25 states enacted some type of no-fault law).

[16] Memorandum from the N.D. Legis. Council Staff on No-Fault Insurance in Other States 1 (Nov. 28, 2005) (observing that Pennsylvania—like Colorado, Connecticut, Georgia, and Nevada—repealed its no-fault law, but then adopted another no-fault law).

[17] Schwartz, *supra* note 13, at 616. It is worthwhile to note that Michigan comes closest to a pure no-fault system, inasmuch as a Michigan accident victim can recover unlimited amounts for medical expenses and it is very difficult to sue in Michigan for noneconomic loss. *Id.* at 619; *See also* N.D. Legis. Council Staff, *supra* note 16, at 1.

[18] KEETON & O'CONNELL, *supra* note 10, at 164, n. 52.

of fault and the right to sue for noneconomic loss, such as pain and suffering, is permitted only after an injured party meets a statutory threshold.[19]

There are, generally, two types of statutory thresholds in place among states with no-fault laws: "verbal" thresholds and "monetary" thresholds.[20] In monetary threshold states, an accident victim must suffer damages exceeding a particular dollar amount—$2,000, $10,000, and so on—before she will be permitted to bring a tort suit. Currently, Hawaii, Kansas, Kentucky, Massachusetts, Minnesota, North Dakota, and Utah have monetary thresholds.

By contrast, verbal threshold states require an accident victim to have suffered an injury that can be described in a particularized way before the victim can sue in tort. At present, Florida, Michigan, New Jersey, New York, and Pennsylvania have verbal thresholds. There is a fairly wide disparity among the verbal thresholds that have been adopted by verbal threshold states. As a general matter, however, in verbal threshold states a party must suffer death or a serious injury such as dismemberment, serious disfigurement, a broken bone, or the like before he will be permitted to pursue tort recovery.[21]

While no-fault insurance regimes vary somewhat among states, there are common elements among most no-fault insurance systems that create similar perverse incentives for similar types of fraudulent conduct. For instance, healthcare expenses are the most common type of economic losses that the no-fault laws were designed to address. As a result, most no-fault insurance systems permit injured parties to assign their right to receive no-fault insurance benefits to healthcare services providers in exchange for treatment.[22] Then, the healthcare services providers can submit their bills directly to—and obtain payment directly from—automobile insurance companies. This makes

---

[19] Schwartz, *supra* note 13, at 617; N.D. Legis. Council Staff, *supra* note 16, at 1.

[20] Anderson, *supra* note 1, at 12; Schwartz, *supra* note 13, at 617.

[21] *See*, e.g., N.Y. Ins. Law § 5102 (defining the "serious injury" threshold to include such things as—among other things—death, dismemberment, significant disfigurement, or a fracture); Fla. Stat. § 627.737 (setting forth a verbal threshold of death, significant and permanent loss of an important body function, other types of permanent injuries, and significant and permanent scarring or disfigurement); MCLS § 500.3135 (death, serious impairment of body function, or permanent serious disfigurement).

[22] *See*, e.g., 11 N.Y.C.R.R. § 65-3.11; N.J. Stat. § 39:6A-4.

perfect sense, so far as it goes. After all, an accident victim might not have sufficient funds on hand to pay for critical or acute care in the immediate aftermath of an automobile accident. By extension, without the comfort of knowing that they could bill insurance companies directly, healthcare providers might be disinclined to provide much-needed services.

However, the interplay between this type of no-fault insurance reimbursement system and the tort thresholds described above often is a critical driver of fraudulent no-fault claims submissions. For example, corrupt healthcare service providers that engage in no-fault insurance fraud often are in league with personal injury attorneys, who refer insureds to the healthcare providers with the understanding that (i) the healthcare providers will purport to provide medically unnecessary or illusory "treatments" to the insureds based on false contentions in the healthcare providers' treatment reports and billing and that the insureds suffered serious injuries in their automobile accidents, thereby (ii) permitting the insureds to contend that they meet the tort thresholds and permitting the personal injury attorneys to file tort cases on behalf of those insureds. All of the participants in this type of scheme—which is widespread—profit. The healthcare providers profit because they get to bill insurers for medically unnecessary and illusory treatments. The insureds and the personal injury attorneys profit because they get to prosecute tort claims.

What is more, for this type of no-fault reimbursement system to work, it is not sufficient to permit healthcare services providers to take assignments of no-fault benefits from insureds and then to directly bill automobile insurance companies for their services. Such an arrangement, on its own, would permit insurance companies to deny, delay, or reduce payments to healthcare services providers via endless challenges to the medical necessity of the underlying services, the cost of the underlying services, and so on. The result would be the worst of both worlds—not only would automobile accident victims be precluded from suing in tort, they also would be unable to obtain medical treatment because healthcare providers would be disinclined to enter or remain in the market.

As a result, state no-fault laws include provisions requiring expedited handling and prompt payment of no-fault insurance claims. For example, New York, Michigan, North Dakota, and Florida, among other states, generally require insurers to pay no-fault claims within

30 days of receipt.[23] In New Jersey, insurers generally must pay claims within 60 days of receipt.[24]

Not only do no-fault states normally require expedited claims handling, they also—as a general matter—set other certain standards of conduct that automobile and other insurers must follow when handling claims. For instance, North Dakota, Pennsylvania, Kansas, and various other no-fault states require insurers to attempt in good faith to effectuate prompt, fair, and equitable settlements of claims submitted in which liability has become reasonably clear.[25] Along similar lines, New York admonishes insurers to "not treat the applicant [for no-fault insurance benefits] as an adversary."[26]

What is more, state no-fault regimes impose significant penalties on insurers that fail to process claims within the requisite time frames. Minnesota, for example, generally permits recovery of 15 percent annual interest on overdue payments.[27] Kentucky permits recovery of 12 percent annual interest on overdue claims, but if the "delay was without reasonable foundation," the rate climbs to 18 percent.[28] North Dakota, New Jersey, and other no-fault states permit recovery of interest at the judgment rate.[29] New York permits recovery of 2 percent interest per month on tardy claims and—like Massachusetts and most other no-fault states—also permits claimants to recover attorneys' fees incurred in securing payment on claims.[30] In Kentucky, a prevailing claimant can recover attorneys' fees if the insurer's delay or denial was "without reasonable foundation."[31]

Insurers have every reason to be wary of these types of interest and attorney fee provisions because they often face a stacked deck in the event that an insured—or, more commonly, the insured's healthcare provider assignee—moves aggressively to recover on a disputed claim.

---

[23] *See* N.Y. Ins. Law § 5106; 11 N.Y.C.R.R. § 65-3.8; Fla. Stat. § 627.736; MCLS § 500.3142; N.D. Cent. Code, § 26.1-41-09.

[24] *See* N.J. Stat. § 39:6A-5.

[25] *See*, e.g., N.D. Cent. Code § 26.1-04-03; 40 P.S. § 1171.5; K.S.A. § 40-2404.

[26] *See* 11 N.Y.C.R.R. § 65-3.2.

[27] *See* Minn. Stat. § 65B.54.

[28] *See* KRS § 304.39-210.

[29] *See*, e.g., N.D. Cent. Code, § 26.1-41-09.

[30] *See*, e.g., N.Y. CLS Ins. § 5106; ALM GL ch. 90, § 34M.

[31] *See* KRS § 304.39-210.

In New Jersey, New York, and Hawaii, for instance, no-fault insureds or their assignees can submit virtually any dispute regarding no-fault benefits to arbitration.[32] Minnesota requires no-fault disputes to be submitted to arbitration in cases where the claim at issue amounts to $10,000 or less.[33]

Although the arbitral rules vary from state to state, they normally provide for a very expedited procedure, with limited opportunities for insurers to prove their defenses. For instance, New York's no-fault arbitration regulations vest the arbitrator with considerable discretion in determining whether or not evidence is relevant or material and—by extension—whether or not an insurer is entitled to discovery.[34] The result, as a practical matter, is what the Second Circuit has described as "an expedited, simplified affair meant to work as quickly and efficiently as possible" where "[d]iscovery is limited or non-existent."[35] In New Jersey, the only document discovery that a healthcare provider is required to provide in the context of a no-fault collections arbitration is "a written report of the history, condition, treatment, dates and costs of such treatment of the injured person. . . ."[36] The arbitration rules in Minnesota and Hawaii contain similar limitations on discovery.[37]

What is more, state no-fault regimes often force insurers to bear many of the arbitration costs, which can be high relative to the amount of the underlying claim. In New York, for example, the State Department of Financial Services has designated the American Arbitration Association ("AAA") as the body that is responsible for the administration of the no-fault arbitration process. In every individual case where an insurer is named as a respondent by a healthcare provider seeking payment on a no-fault claim that the insurer has denied, the insurer is required to pay AAA a mandatory, nonrefundable fee.[38] As a no-fault proceeding progresses through the arbitral process, the insurer-respondent is subject to additional fees regardless of the size

[32] *See* N.J. Stat. § 39:6A-5.1; N.Y. CLS Ins. § 5106; HRS § 431:10C-213.

[33] *See* Minn. Stat. § 65B.525.

[34] *See* 11 N.Y.C.R.R. § 65-4.5.

[35] Allstate Ins. Co. v. Mun., 751 F.3d 94, 99 (2d Cir. 2014).

[36] *See* N.J. Stat. § 39:6A-13.

[37] *See*, e.g., HRS § 658A-17; Minn. No-Fault Arb. R. 12.

[38] *See* 11 N.Y.C.R.R. § 65-4.1, *et seq.*

of the underlying no-fault claim, whether the case is meritorious, or whether the applicant ultimately withdraws the claim at any stage during the process.[39] These fees typically amount to several hundred dollars per case. By contrast, the healthcare provider–claimants are required to pay only a comparatively nominal filing fee.

In Minnesota, where the AAA also administers the no-fault arbitration process, insurers must pay a $130 filing fee when they are named as respondents in no-fault arbitration, whereas the claimants' filing fee is only $35.[40] Moreover, if the arbitration proceeds, an insurer may be required to pay up to $300 in arbitrator's fees.[41] While these additional fees may be assessed against the claimant at the direction of the arbitrator, as a practical matter the insurers generally are obligated to pay at least half of the arbitrator's fees. Similarly, in New Jersey, insurers generally must pay arbitration fees of at least $200 when they are named as respondents in no-fault collections arbitration.[42] Hawaii splits no-fault arbitration fees equally between claimants and insurer-respondents "unless otherwise allocated by the arbitrator," which means that unless the insurer can demonstrate that a claim is completely without color, it will be saddled with at least half of the fees.[43]

Insurers also can find themselves at a procedural disadvantage in states without compulsory no-fault arbitration, as local courts respond to clogged no-fault dockets by "leaning" on insurers to forego important discovery and settle their cases. One study from the Florida Insurance Consumer Advocate observed that tens of thousands of no-fault collections lawsuits had been filed against insurers in Florida county courts and that the number of suits appeared to be increasing exponentially.[44] In New York, where no-fault claimants have the option of resorting either to arbitration or to the courts, local judges have lamented the situation in their decisions. One New York City Civil Court judge opined that "the Legislature's current no-fault system

---

[39] *Id.*

[40] *See* Minn. No-Fault Arb. R. 39–40.

[41] *Id.*

[42] *See* N.J. No-Fault PIP Arb. R. 23–26 (2013).

[43] *See* HRS § 431:10C-213.

[44] *See* Office of the Insurance Consumer Advocate, Report on Florida Motor Vehicle No-Fault Insurance 36 (2011).

threatens to engulf the state judiciary into a swamp of unresolved and tangled questions."[45] Another made reference to the "overflowing dockets of no-fault first-party benefits cases" and called for the legislature to impose a solution.[46]

In addition, some no-fault insurance states have what amount to preclusion rules, which effectively eliminate or restrict an insurer's ability to contest a no-fault claim in a subsequent arbitration or lawsuit unless the insurer processes the claim within a relatively short time period. In New York, for example, there is a so-called "30-day rule," which provides that most of an insurer's defenses to a no-fault claim—including most defenses based on fraudulent misrepresentations by the healthcare provider–claimant—will be precluded if the insurer does not process the claim within 30 days.[47] In New Jersey, if an insurer precertifies treatment proposed by a healthcare provider—and insurers generally are required to handle precertification requests within a very short 72-hour time period—the insurer typically will be precluded from challenging a resulting claim based on lack of medical necessity unless the insurer can show that the precertification request involved fraud or misrepresentation.[48]

---

[45] Universal Acupuncture Pain Servs., P.C. v. Lumbermens Mut. Cas. Co., 195 Misc. 2d 352, 353 (N.Y. Civ. Ct. 2003).

[46] Socrates Psychological Servs., P.C. v. Progressive Cas. Ins. Co., 7 Misc. 3d 642, 645, fn. 1 (N.Y. Civ. Ct. 2005).

[47] *See*, e.g., Fair Price Med. Supply Corp. v. Travelers Indem. Co., 9 Misc. 3d 76, 78 (N.Y. App. Term 2005), *aff'd* Fair Price Med. v. Travelers, 42 A.D. 3d 277 (N.Y. App. Div. 2d Dep't 2007), *aff'd* Fair Price Med. Supply Corp. v. Travelers Indem. Co., 10 N.Y.3d 556 (N.Y. 2008) ("[A] defense based on a provider's fraudulent scheme to obtain no-fault benefits is precluded by defendant's untimely claim denial."). It is, however, important to emphasize that while the "30-day rule" may preclude an insurer's defenses to an allegedly fraudulent no-fault claim, it does not preclude a subsequent action by the insurer to recover fraudulently-obtained no-fault insurance benefits. *See*, e.g., Fair Price Med. Supply Corp., 9 Misc. 3d at 79–80 ("[A]n insurer precluded from defending a claim based on provider fraud is not without remedy; after paying such a claim, the insurer, for example, may have an action to recover benefits paid under a theory of fraud or unjust enrichment . . . and it may seek criminal sanctions for insurance fraud and obtain restitution. . . ."); *see also* Allstate Ins. Co. v. Mun., 751 F.3d 94, 101 (2d Cir. 2014) ("The weight of New York authority holds that the 30-day process . . . does not constrain later insurer actions seeking recovery for fraud.").

[48] *See* N.J.A.C. 11:3-4.7(g).

The totality of these circumstances creates a powerful incentive for automobile insurers to pay no-fault claims as they are submitted, or to settle disputed claims before trial or before an arbitral process concludes, except in the relatively rare event that the insurer can obtain and present proof of fraud to the court or arbitrator. Because corrupt healthcare services providers are fully aware of these circumstances, they also create powerful, perverse incentives for no-fault insurance fraud.

All of this is not to say that insurers lack at least some means to investigate suspected fraud and to delay payment of suspect claims during the pendency of such investigations. Toward this end, automobile insurance companies generally maintain in-house investigators dedicated to ferreting out fraudulent claims.

In New York, for instance, automobile insurers generally are required by law to maintain "special investigations units" that are "responsible for investigating information on or cases of suspected fraudulent activity and for effectively implementing fraud prevention and reduction activities. . . ."[49] Kentucky, New Jersey, and Florida law impose similar requirements.[50] In Kansas, special investigation units ("SIUs") are encouraged, but not required, inasmuch as automobile and other insurers are required to have "antifraud initiatives reasonably calculated to detect fraudulent insurance acts" that "may include" investigators.[51] Along similar lines, Minnesota requires insurers to implement anti-fraud claims but does not specifically require SIUs.[52] Pennsylvania requires automobile insurers to implement anti-fraud plans that include, among other things, specific procedures to "review claims in order to detect evidence of possible insurance fraud and to investigate claims where fraud is suspected."[53]

Whether or not state law requires anti-fraud plans in general or SIUs in particular, automobile insurers develop anti-fraud plans and employ investigators in every no-fault state. The required qualifications can vary considerably from state to state and from insurer to

49 *See* N.Y. CLS Ins. § 409.

50 *See* KRS § 304.47-080; N.J.A.C. 11:16-6.4; Fla. Stat. § 626.9891.

51 *See* K.S.A. § 40-2,118.

52 *See* Minn. Stat. § 60A.954.

53 *See* 75 PA. Cons. Stat. § 1812.

insurer, and even those states that impose specific requirements for members of insurer SIUs cast a fairly wide net.

In New York, for example, an individual may qualify as a special investigator if she has either (i) an associate's or bachelor's degree in criminal justice or related field, (ii) five years of insurance claims investigation experience or professional investigation experience with law enforcement agencies, or (iii) seven years of professional investigation experience involving economic or insurance-related matters.[54] In New Jersey, special investigators must have either: (i) a bachelor's degree, (ii) an associate's degree plus a minimum of two years' experience with insurance-related employment, (iii) a minimum of four years of experience with insurance-related employment, or (iv) a minimum of five years of law enforcement experience.[55] Kentucky does not impose any particular educational or experience requirements on special investigators, and Florida simply requires that insurers provide appropriate training to employees in their SIUs.[56]

As a result, insurer SIU investigators can vary widely in background and—by extension—in investigative methodology. Many SIUs recruit personnel from other departments in the insurance companies, such as claims departments, where routine claims handling can give the employees an instinct for spotting fraudulent claims. Investigators with a claims background may use a data-driven, claims-handling approach to identifying fraud, for instance by tracking suspicious claims volume, billing for unusual types of healthcare services, and minor accidents that result in substantial medical billing. This type of investigator often is particularly strong in flushing out billing for medically unnecessary or illusory services.

Some SIUs seek out personnel with a law enforcement background, such as retired police officers. These types of investigators may take a "shoe-leather" approach that relies less on claims data and more on site visits to suspect healthcare practices, witness interviews, and the like. Investigators who take this approach may be strongest when dealing with frauds involving the illegal corporate structure or management of a healthcare practice, billing for healthcare services

---

[54] *See* N.Y. CLS Ins. § 409.

[55] *See* N.J.A.C. 11:16-6.4.

[56] *See* 806 KAR 47:030; 69D-2.003, F.A.C.

that never were provided in the first instance, staged-accident rings, and other types of schemes where the proof commonly is obtained by "boots on the ground." Both types of investigators have their strengths, and—obviously—there are plenty of investigators who combine both approaches.

Though insurers maintain SIU departments, certain factors limit insurers' ability to effectively investigate no-fault insurance fraud. The first and most obvious issue is that SIU investigators are not law enforcement officials. They cannot obtain search warrants and cannot issue subpoenas except through counsel in the context of some ongoing civil litigation. As such, SIU investigations generally are limited in their means to claims data analysis, site visits to suspicious healthcare offices; witness interviews; review of publicly available information such as corporate documents, licenses, online databases, and the like. In addition, and as discussed above, most states enjoin insurers to handle claims in good faith and to refrain from treating claimants as adversaries. These provisions can seem to be in tension with the concomitant statutes requiring insurers to maintain SIU units and to investigate suspicions of fraud.

Oftentimes, insurers' investigations of suspected no-fault insurance fraud rings are limited by a practical inability to share information with, and obtain information from, other insurance companies. There are many reasons why it is in the interests of insurance companies to cooperate with one another in investigating suspect healthcare providers, yet there are equally compelling reasons why this does not always occur.

On the one hand, insurers may have suspicions regarding a healthcare provider's billing but lack the "complete picture" necessary to plead a viable complaint. For instance, if an insurer has only 25 percent of the market in a given state, yet routinely receives billing for five or six hours of healthcare services per day from a single chiropractor in that state, it is a fair bet that the chiropractor is billing for services he is not actually providing. This is because, if the insurer has only 25 percent of the market, there is reason to expect that the five or six hours of chiropractic services billed to that insurer by a single chiropractor per day represents only 25 percent of the overall billing that the chiropractor submits per day to every insurance company in the market. Obviously, the chiropractor is not working 20 to 24 hours per day. Even so, it is at least possible—if not plausible—that the suspicious chiropractor only treats customers of a single insurer on any given day. In order to prove otherwise, the insurers within the market should have a way to compare notes.

Along similar lines, an insurer may notice that a suspicious physiatrist routinely submits billing for range-of-motion tests that report identical test data across 15 percent of her patients. These identical data, while improbable, are not necessarily impossible. However, if the insurer could demonstrate that other insurance companies likewise received a critical mass of billing from the same physiatrist that reported the same identical test data, its case against the physiatrist would be substantially stronger. In order to do so, the insurers would—again—have to compare notes.

In some cases, an insurer may investigate a fraudulent healthcare provider and leverage the results of its investigation to obtain a release of the provider's claims. However, because the investigation and consequent release are insurer specific, the provider is able to continue to defraud other insurers within the market who are unaware of the fraud. In this context, inter-insurer investigative cooperation could put the fraudulent provider out of the fraud business across the board.

Even so, there are a number of reasons why such cooperation can be elusive. As discussed above, many SIU departments recruit from within their insurance companies, oftentimes from claims departments. As a result, SIU investigators may have a long tenure with a single company and, by extension, may lack extensive contacts in SIU departments at other companies. While inter-insurer SIU conferences provide some opportunity for information sharing, such conferences occur infrequently. Even if they occurred with greater regularity, the opportunities to develop productive cooperative relationships at such events is rather limited—not least because such cooperation can require corporate approval, which can take time and resources to obtain, to the extent that it can be obtained at all.

Moreover, insurers understandably may be reluctant to share the results of their investigations with their competitors, especially if they anticipate that the investigation could lead to litigation against a suspicious healthcare provider. The insurer that is first to file a lawsuit to recover fraudulently obtained no-fault insurance benefits generally will be in the best position to actually recoup money. Conversely, insurers that file later may find that the well has run dry because the provider has gone out of business, secreted or dissipated its ill-gotten gains, and so forth.

One way in which insurers share investigative information is through the National Insurance Crime Bureau (NICB). The NICB is a not-for-profit organization with a membership that includes virtually every major property and casualty insurance company in the United States, and its stated mission is to "lead a united effort of insurers, law enforcement agencies and representatives of the public to prevent and combat insurance fraud and crime through data analytics, investigations, training, legislative advocacy and public awareness."[57] Formed in 1992 from a merger of the National Automobile Theft Bureau, which helped insurers investigate vehicle thefts, and the Insurance Crime Prevention Institute, which investigated various types of insurance fraud, the NICB performs a number of useful services for insurers. These services include gathering information regarding suspicious claims, analyzing the data, and issuing bulletins to the NICB's constituent insurer-members. Since the NICB obtains much of its information regarding suspicious claims from its insurer-members and then shares the information across its membership, the organization can serve as a kind of networking platform for SIU investigators and claims departments.

While the NICB serves a useful function, it may not be able to provide the sort of specific information that would permit an insurer to actually plead a complaint, let alone the kind of complaint that would meet the heightened fraud-pleading requirements. For example, insurers that have developed truly valuable evidence of fraud through their in-house SIU investigations may prefer not to share it.

Different varieties of no-fault insurance fraud—like any fraud—evolve over time; nonetheless, they can be broken down into their most prevalent current forms. These include, on the broadest level, claims containing misrepresentations as to the corporate structure or legitimacy of the healthcare provider-claimant, claims containing misrepresentations regarding the medical necessity of the pertinent services, claims containing misrepresentations as to whether the pertinent services were provided in the first instance, and claims that misrepresent the reimbursement to which a healthcare provider is entitled in connection with a given service.

---

[57] *See* National Insurance Crime Bureau, Vision and Mission (March 6, 2017), https://www.nicb.org/about-nicb/vision_and_mission.

2

Identifying Corporate Structure Fraud

The most common type of corporate structure fraud involves a healthcare practice that is ineligible to collect no-fault benefits because it secretly and unlawfully is owned or controlled by unlicensed individuals or entities, yet it falsely represents that it is properly licensed and eligible.

A. Prohibitions Against Unlicensed Ownership of Healthcare Practices

While there are some exceptions that generally are not applicable in the context of no-fault insurance claims—for instance, hospitals, ambulatory surgery centers, and so on—state laws generally prohibit unlicensed individuals or entities from owning or controlling healthcare practices. This typically is accomplished in several ways.

For instance, ownership of professional corporations or other professional entities is normally limited by law to individuals who are licensed in the underlying professions.[1] What is more, some state licensing boards expressly prohibit professional practice arrangements that amount to partnerships between licensed and unlicensed individuals or entities. For example, the New Jersey Board of Medical Examiners has promulgated a "professional practice structure" regulation that in most circumstances prohibits physicians from partnering with, or being employed by, unlicensed individuals or entities.[2] Other states prohibit unlicensed ownership of healthcare practices through the "corporate practice of medicine" doctrine. While this doctrine manifests itself somewhat differently in different states, it has been broadly—if somewhat archaically—summarized by the Supreme Court of Pennsylvania as follows:

> The rule is generally recognized that a licensed practitioner of a profession may not lawfully practise his profession among the public as the servant of an unlicensed person or a corporation; and that, if he does so, the unlicensed person or corporation employing him is guilty of practising that profession without a license. A corporation as such cannot possess the personal qualities required of a practitioner of a profession. Its servants, though professionally trained and duly licensed to practise, owe their primary allegiance and obedience to their employer rather than to the clients or patients of their employer. The rule stated recognizes the necessity of immediate and unbroken relationship between a professional man and those who engage his services.[3]

Though the doctrine most commonly is known as the corporate practice of medicine doctrine, state courts have applied it to other licensed healthcare professions, such as chiropractic, as well.[4]

---

[1] *See*, e.g., 15 PA. CONS. STAT. § 2923; N.J. STAT. § 14A:17-5; N.Y. CLS BUS. CORP. § 1507; MCLS § 450.1283.

[2] *See* N.J.A.C. 13:35-6.16.

[3] Neill v. Gimbel Bros., Inc., 330 Pa. 213, 219 (Pa. 1938).

[4] *See*, e.g., Isles Wellness, Inc. v. Progressive Northern Ins. Co., 703 N.W.2d 513 (Minn. 2005) (holding that the corporate practice of medicine doctrine exists in Minnesota and that the corporate employment of chiropractors is prohibited except as expressly permitted by statute); Liberty Mut. Ins. Co. v. Hyman, 334 N.J. Super. 400 (Law Div. 2000) (corporate practice doctrine applied to chiropractors).

B. The Mechanics of Corporate Structure Fraud Schemes

Many states require healthcare providers to comply with material laws governing healthcare practice in order to be eligible to receive no-fault reimbursement. Conversely, healthcare providers that fail to comply with such laws are ineligible to receive no-fault reimbursement.

For instance, in *State Farm Mut. Auto. Ins. Co. v. Mallela*, 4 N.Y.3d 313 (2005), the New York Court of Appeals deferred to a New York Insurance Department regulation that stated that healthcare providers are not eligible for no-fault reimbursement if they fail to meet "any applicable New York State or local licensing requirement." Although the *Mallela* case involved a medical professional corporation that was not properly licensed in that it was secretly and unlawfully owned by unlicensed persons, subsequent decisions have indicated that failure to meet any pertinent licensing requirement precludes the recovery of no-fault benefits.[5]

Other no-fault states impose similar restrictions. For instance, in New Jersey, a healthcare provider is not eligible to receive no-fault benefits where it has failed to comply with all applicable statutory and regulatory requirements governing healthcare practice, including corporate structure requirements.[6] Michigan has a similar rule.[7] Likewise, in Minnesota, courts have sustained insurers' claims to recover

---

[5] *See*, e.g., Allstate Ins. Co. v. Elzanaty, 916 F. Supp. 2d 273 (2013) (applying the Mallela standard to a medical facility that allegedly failed to meet licensing standards set forth in New York Public Health Law); Gov't Emples. Ins. Co. v. Uptown Health Care Mgmt., 945 F. Supp. 2d 284 (E.D.N.Y. 2013) (same).

[6] *See*, e.g., Liberty Mut. Ins. Co. v. Healthcare Integrated Servs., 2009 N.J. Super. Unpub. LEXIS 2416 (App. Div. 2009) ("This court has held that a provider of such services is not entitled to reimbursement for services covered by PIP unless the provider and the services are in compliance with relevant laws and regulations."); Allstate Ins. Co. v. Orthopedic Evaluations, Inc., 300 N.J. Super. 510, 515–19 (App. Div. 1997) (healthcare service provider's lack of compliance with pertinent regulatory standards rendered it ineligible to collect PIP benefits, whether or not the underlying services were medically necessary).

[7] *See*, e.g., Cherry v. State Farm Mut. Auto. Ins. Co., 195 Mich. App. 316, 320 (Mich. Ct. App. 1992) ("[W]e believe it is clear that the Legislature intended that only treatment lawfully rendered, including being in compliance with licensing requirements, is subject to payment as a no-fault benefit.").

no-fault benefits that were paid to professional entities that were illegally owned by nonprofessionals.[8]

Notwithstanding these restrictions, unlicensed individuals and entities frequently seek to control professional healthcare practices given the compelling financial incentives. Although one occasionally comes across a fraudulently incorporated chiropractic or acupuncture entity, the most common scenario involves a medical practice, because medical practices—by and large—can yield more profit per patient than other types of healthcare practices. These types of illegal arrangements commonly are known as "doc-in-the-box" schemes, for obvious reasons.[9]

For those of us raised to put physicians on a pedestal, it can be difficult to understand why a medical doctor would permit an unlicensed person or entity to control her practice or, indeed, to engage in any type of insurance fraud. Typically, physicians who are amenable to these types of schemes are not at or near the top, or even the middle, of their profession. Instead, they frequently are compromised in some way—by lack of board certification, financial difficulties, addiction, health problems, and so on. Oftentimes, physicians who permit unlicensed people to control their practices are fairly advanced in age, effectively have retired, and appear not to care whether they are putting their licenses at risk. Although the specific circumstances may differ from scheme to scheme, the underlying motive typically is financial.

The mechanics of corporate structure schemes are constantly evolving. Generally, unlicensed individuals and entities cannot openly hold shares in a healthcare practice. Nor—except in limited circumstances—can they openly serve as directors of healthcare practices. With that in mind, unlicensed individuals and entities have to find alternate means of exerting control.

---

[8] *See*, e.g., Liberty Mut. Fire Ins. Co. v. Acute Care Chiropractic Clinic P.A., 2015 U.S. Dist. LEXIS 17933 (D. Minn. 2015) (denying a motion to dismiss insurer's claims to recover no-fault benefits that had been paid to chiropractic clinics that were illegally owned by laypersons).

[9] *See*, e.g., Allstate Ins. Co. v. Bogoraz, 2012 U.S. Dist. LEXIS 68110 (E.D.N.Y. 2012) (citing an insurer anti-fraud complaint alleging an illegal "doc-in-the-box" scheme); Allstate Ins. Co. v. Northfield Med. Ctr., P.C., 2015 N.J. Super. Unpub. LEXIS 1018 (N.J. App. Div. May 4, 2015) (recounting how "doc-in-the-box arrangement[s]" were marketed to chiropractors interested in controlling medical practices).

Though there are many ways for unlicensed individuals and entities to exert control over a healthcare practice, certain methods tend to recur in the cases. For example, in exchange for the promise of regular compensation from unlicensed individuals and entities, a physician will cause a healthcare practice he nominally owns to enter into a series of "management," "billing," "marketing," or "consulting" agreements with the unlicensed individuals and entities. Though ostensibly legitimate service agreements, the contracts require the healthcare practice to pay fees that are far in excess of fair market value, thereby placing virtually all of the practice's profits into the hands of the unlicensed nonprofessionals. At the same time, the agreements vest the unlicensed individuals and entities with near-total control over the day-to-day operations and management of the practice. Oftentimes, as a corollary to these types of management, billing, marketing, or consulting agreements, the physician will provide the unlicensed individuals and entities with a stamp of his or her signature so as to enable them to create and execute billing, treatment records, and corporate checks without the physician's actual involvement.

Another common way in which unlicensed individuals and entities secretly own and control healthcare practices is through exorbitant facility and equipment "lease" agreements. In this type of scheme, the unlicensed nonprofessionals either own or hold a lease for office space in a low-rent neighborhood and stock the office with cheap furniture and outdated medical equipment. Then, they enter into lease agreements with a healthcare practice that require the healthcare practice to pay "rent" that is far out of proportion to the fair market value of the leaseholds. Oftentimes, the underlying real estate and equipment can be purchased for less than a few months' worth of the "rent."

In some cases, unlicensed nonprofessionals are listed as signatories on the healthcare practices' bank accounts so as to consolidate their control over the practices' finances. However, this is becoming less common as insurance fraud rings realize that bank records are discoverable and the presence of an unlicensed person on a healthcare practice's bank signature card is at least some evidence of an illegal corporate structure. More frequently, unlicensed individuals and entities work around this issue by retaining control of the healthcare practice's checkbook and using the physician's signature stamp to execute checks for their own benefit.

In other cases, the physician simply hand-signs multiple blank checks each month and hands them over to the unlicensed individuals and entities to do with as they see fit. Frequently, corporate debit cards also are used to funnel profits from a healthcare practice to its secret lay owners—for instance, by paying the unlicensed owners' personal automobile expenses, restaurant bills, and other lifestyle expenses.

As insurers have grown more sophisticated in detecting corporate structure fraud, no-fault insurance fraud rings have grown commensurately more refined in concealing corporate structure schemes. Where, once, unlicensed individuals and entities would effectuate their illegal control over a healthcare practice through a single corporate entity—typically a "management" company that would oversee the practice, hire the staff, handle the billing, and lease the office location—the more recent approach is to create separate entities to fulfill these discrete functions and to ensure that each such entity is at least nominally under different ownership. Where previously it was common to see a layperson listed as a "vice president" on a healthcare practice's bank signature card and for the layperson to personally sign large numbers of checks for his own benefit, today it is comparably rare. Instead, as discussed above, the common practice is to execute the checks using a stamp of the nominal physician-owner's signature or to have the physician sign large numbers of blank checks to be drawn on the practice's corporate account.

While misrepresentation or concealment regarding the illegal lay ownership of a healthcare practice may be the most prevalent form of corporate structure fraud, there are other varieties. As discussed above, many no-fault states require healthcare providers to comply with all laws and regulations regarding healthcare practice as a condition precedent to no-fault reimbursement. These laws and regulations obviously go far beyond restricting ownership of healthcare practices to licensed professionals.

For example, states may set forth limitations on the permissible scope of a chiropractor's practice to exclude services that should be reserved to licensed physicians.[10] States may require healthcare providers that offer radiology services to obtain separate licenses,

---

[10] *See*, e.g., N.J.A.C. 13:44E-1.1; 64B2-17.002, F.A.C.; 233 CMR 4.01.

certificates, or to meet certain safety or performance standards.[11] States generally impose rather burdensome licensing requirements and standards on ambulatory surgery centers, not least because these types of practices generally are an exception to restrictions on the corporate practice of medicine and may be owned by non-physicians. For instance, ambulatory surgery centers often are required to appoint a licensed physician as a medical director and to implement comprehensive policies and procedures to ensure that patient care is not subordinated to any pecuniary motive.[12] Misrepresentations regarding compliance with these requirements can support an insurer's fraud claim.[13]

C. How to Identify Corporate Structure Fraud

It can be difficult to identify corporate structure fraud, at least at the pleading stage and in advance of substantive discovery. Participants in such schemes generally do not permit the fraud to appear on the face of publicly filed documents. For instance, it is unusual—though not unknown—for an unlicensed non-physician to be listed as an officer or director of a medical practice in the practice's corporate filings.[14] Along similar lines, physicians or other licensed healthcare providers who allow their practices to be unlawfully owned and controlled by unlicensed nonprofessionals typically will not admit as much to SIU investigators or state licensing authorities. On the contrary, such arrangements—being unlawful—are typically concealed.

Even so, there are various ways that insurers can obtain sufficient evidence of corporate structure fraud to be able to plead it in an

---

[11] *See*, e.g., N.Y. CLS Pub. Health § 3502; K.A.R. § 28-35-241.

[12] *See*, e.g., 10 N.Y.C.R.R. § 751.4; N.J.A.C. 8:43A-1.1, *et seq*.; 28 Pa. Code § 553.1, *et seq*.

[13] *See*, e.g., Gov't Emples. Ins. Co. v. Uptown Health Care Mgmt., 945 F. Supp. 2d 284 (E.D.N.Y. 2013) (denying motion to dismiss an insurer's fraud and civil racketeering claims based on misrepresentations regarding compliance with licensing requirements).

[14] *See*, e.g., Gov't Emples. Ins. Co. "GEICO" v. Korn, D.N.J. Case No. 14-5742 (JEI/KMW), at Docket No. 1, ¶¶ 55, 69 (alleging that an unlicensed nonphysician was listed as a director in the corporate filings of one illegally organized professional corporation and as an officer in the corporate filings of another illegally organized professional corporation).

affirmative complaint. The first and most obvious way is to check the corporate filings of the suspect professional practice. While—as noted above—it is unlikely that the corporate filings explicitly will list an unlicensed person as a director, officer, or member of the practice, other information in the corporate filings may provide circumstantial evidence of an illegal ownership structure.

For example, unlicensed individuals who secretly and unlawfully own and control healthcare practices are often concerned with maintaining control over the practices. After all, one of the downsides of unlicensed, illegal ownership of a healthcare practice is that the licensed physician or other healthcare provider who nominally owns the practice can reclaim the practice at any moment and divest the unlicensed party of control.[15] As a result, unlicensed individuals seeking to secretly and illegally own healthcare practices often will list themselves as the registered agent for a practice in the pertinent corporate filings. Concomitantly, they often will list their own homes or offices as the registered office for the practice. While these sorts of tactics help unlicensed parties to retain control over illegally organized healthcare practices, they also can provide a good-faith basis to allege an illegal ownership structure. Attorneys representing insurers in anti-fraud litigation always should look for registered agents or registered offices that have no apparent connection to the billing provider or its principals.[16] In many cases, the registered agent and registered office for one healthcare practice operating within a multidisciplinary clinic will be the same as the registered agent and registered office for the other healthcare practices at the clinic despite the fact that the different practices at the clinic all are ostensibly owned by different licensed practitioners. This, in turn, strongly suggests that all of the licensed practices at the clinic are unlawfully owned by unlicensed individuals or entities.

---

[15] For an interesting discussion of some ways in which unlicensed parties attempt to maintain control over illegally organized medical practices, *see* Allstate Ins. Co. v. Northfield Med. Ctr., P.C., 2015 N.J. Super. Unpub. LEXIS 1018 (N.J. App. Div. 2015).

[16] Of course, there are many legitimate corporate service businesses that exist for the purpose of assisting with corporate filings and providing registered agents and offices to other entities. Before proceeding with allegations of corporate structure fraud based on a questionable registered agent or registered office, attorneys should confirm that the registered agent is something other than a corporate services business.

Oftentimes, the checks issued by insurers to fraudulent practices can also provide evidence of an illegal corporate structure. Most insurers pay no-fault claims the old-fashioned way using paper checks. These no-fault reimbursement checks have to be negotiated somewhere, which means that they have to be endorsed for deposit. Subsequent to their deposit, copies of the cancelled checks are returned by the bank to the insurer, and the endorsements can contain evidence of an illicit corporate structure.

For instance, was the no-fault reimbursement check deposited directly into the account of the billing healthcare provider, or was it endorsed over to some unlicensed individual or entity, such as a "management company"? Was the check negotiated at a check-cashing company for untraceable cash? While perhaps not absolutely dispositive of a healthcare provider's illegal corporate structure, these types of machinations simply are not part of the ordinary course of business in a legitimate healthcare practice. Where they recur on a consistent basis, and especially in the presence of other badges of fraud, they can provide a good-faith basis to allege an illegal corporate structure.

Rapid turnover among licensed healthcare providers at an individual location is also good circumstantial evidence of corporate structure fraud. Of course, businesses of all kinds come and go, and healthcare practices are no exception. But most legitimate neighborhood healthcare providers depend upon a certain amount of word of mouth and goodwill to generate patient referrals. It follows that most legitimate neighborhood healthcare providers will not be especially eager to pull up stakes and relocate after only a few months in a given location.

On the other hand, unlicensed individuals and entities that secretly and illegally own and control healthcare practices often frequently replace the licensed professionals and professional entities under their control at any given multidisciplinary clinic or other location. The likelihood of discovery, which increases over time, simply makes it too risky to run any single doc-in-the-box scheme at any single location in perpetuity. As a result, attorneys representing insurers in anti-fraud cases should try to identify individual locations that play host to a constantly rotating cast of licensed professionals and professional entities and check to see who owns or holds the primary lease at the underlying property.

Relatedly, where an individual licensed healthcare provider is the record owner of a large number of professional entities, it can be a good indication that the entities are not actually owned by the licensee. Participants in corporate structure fraud schemes often seek to serially incorporate multiple professional corporations under a single physician's or chiropractor's license, because they know that large amounts of fraudulent no-fault insurance billing submitted through any one entity will draw the attention of insurer SIUs and, perhaps, state licensing authorities and law enforcement.[17] Considering that a single professional entity can simultaneously operate from multiple locations, there are few legitimate reasons why a licensed physician or other healthcare provider would need to own multiple professional entities at the same time—especially if all of the entities bill for substantially the same types of services.

Still another indication of corporate structure fraud is the ownership of an ostensibly specialized healthcare practice by a nonspecialist in the pertinent field. While, in theory, any licensed physician can own a radiology practice, one would not expect to see a legitimate radiology practice that is owned by a pediatrician or obstetrician. Along similar lines, while any licensed physician could theoretically obtain the training necessary to perform spinal surgeries, one would not expect to see a psychiatrist or anesthesiologist performing such services. If a massive amount of billing for radiology studies is being billed through a professional corporation that is owned on paper by a pediatrician, it will call into question whether the pediatrician truly owns the practice.

Another way to identify corporate structure fraud at the pleading stage, in advance of discovery, is to determine whether there are public filings that indicate that a healthcare practice owes suspicious debt. As noted above, one of the risks attendant to secret and illegal unlicensed ownership of a healthcare practice is that the licensed

---

[17] *See*, e.g., Liberty Mut. Fire Ins. Co. v. Acute Care Chiropractic Clinic P.A., 88 F. Supp. 3d 985 (D. Minn. 2015) (denying a motion to dismiss an insurer's civil RICO and other claims against an alleged no-fault insurance fraud ring, where—among other things—a single chiropractor was alleged to be the nominal or "paper" owner of five separate chiropractic professional corporations that actually were under the control of an unlicensed individual and his management company); Gov't Emples. Ins. Co. v. Gateva, 2014 U.S. Dist. LEXIS 42648 (E.D.N.Y. 2014) (granting a default judgment to an insurer on civil RICO and other claims involving corporate structure fraud, where a single physician was alleged to have simultaneously served as the nominal owner of four separate medical professional corporations that actually were under the control of unlicensed individuals and entities).

practitioner who nominally owns the practice on paper can—at any time—seize control over the practice and "walk away" with it. In such a scenario, there is little that the unlicensed party can do—he cannot generally seek redress in court because the arrangements that vested him with control over the professional practice were illegal in the first instance.

As a result, and as discussed above, unlicensed individuals and entities often exercise control over healthcare practices by entering into exorbitant management, billing, marketing, consulting, or lease agreements with the practices. These types of agreements, which frequently require payments far in excess of the value of any services that are provided and, in many cases, far in excess of the practices' actual revenues, maintain the practices in a constant state of debt to the unlicensed parties and allow the unlicensed parties to effectively control the practices.

Still, however, there is little to stop an individual healthcare provider who nominally owns an illegally organized healthcare practice from causing the practice to default on these agreements, because such healthcare providers typically have enough sense not to personally guarantee the agreements. Consequently, unlicensed individuals and entities who illegally own or control healthcare practices will often file UCC financing statements, listing the practices as the debtors and themselves as the creditors and contending that the practices' debts are collateralized with all of their accounts receivable. Through this approach, they can have some assurance that even if the putative licensed "owner" of the practice causes the practice to default on the agreements, the unlicensed true owner still can retain control over any outstanding receivables and profit. However, a UCC filing—or other, similar public debt records—can be used to allege that the purported "debt" is actually a ruse to conceal the creditor's ownership of the practice, especially if the debt does not comport with what an ordinary healthcare practice might legitimately be expected to owe.

Obviously, the best way to identify corporate structure fraud is through the financial records of a suspect professional entity, such as bank records, tax returns, general ledgers, and the like. While—in most cases—these types of records will be unavailable to a plaintiff-insurer until the discovery phase of an anti-fraud lawsuit, they can occasionally be obtainable when an insurer is defending against a healthcare provider's collections litigation or arbitration. However, judges and arbitrators have considerable discretion in determining whether a healthcare provider's financial records are discoverable, and they ordinarily will not order them disclosed in the context of a small-collections proceeding. The balance shifts when an insurer is a plaintiff in a more substantial anti-fraud lawsuit because the insurer will have a straightforward argument to the effect that the defendant professional entity's financial records are relevant to demonstrate the existence of a long-term corporate structure fraud.

There are many ways in which a healthcare practice's financial records can be used to identify and prove corporate structure fraud. The first and most obvious way is through examination of a practice's bank records. For instance, if a practice routinely issues substantial checks or wire transfers to third parties for no apparent purpose, or in amounts that are out of proportion to the stated purpose, it can be a good indication that an unlicensed individual or entity is siphoning profits from the practice. In some cases, the checks or wire transfers will be structured in amounts of less than $10,000 in an attempt to evade financial reporting requirements. In other cases, the bank records of a healthcare practice with corporate structure issues will reveal regular, contemporaneous payments to two putative management companies or two supposed billing companies. Considering that healthcare practices generally will not require duplicate services from management, billing, or other vendors, duplicate payments for those types of services suggests that one of the "vendors" may have an illegal stake in the practice.

Along similar lines, unlicensed individuals and entities that illegally own healthcare practices often will control a debit or credit card issued in the name of the practice and will use the debit or credit cards to pay their own personal lifestyle expenses. If a healthcare practice is paying for an automobile that is registered to someone other than the owner of the practice or for renovations to the home of someone other than the practice's owner, this can be evidence that the practice is in the hands of someone other than its record owner.

Likewise, where a healthcare practice's debit or credit card is consistently being used in locations where the record owner of the practice is known not to be present, it can be a good indication that the practice's finances—and, by extension, the practice itself—are in the hands of an unlicensed nonprofessional. For example, do the billing records for the practice contend that the owner of the practice was treating patients in New York throughout March, April, and May? But do the bank records for the practice indicate that the practice's debit or credit card was used to pay for international travel throughout March, April, and May? If so, it might not prove that the practice has an illegal corporate structure, but it certainly gets a plaintiff-insurer part of the way there.

The bank records for a healthcare practice will also generally indicate who has signature authority on the pertinent account. While the presence of a signatory other than the record owner of a practice does not necessarily prove that the practice has corporate structure issues, it is at least some indication of corporate structure issues—especially if the practice routinely transfers large sums to or for the benefit of the signatory in question.

More sophisticated no-fault fraud rings generally avoid listing unlicensed parties as signatories on a healthcare practice's bank accounts because this raises questions about the corporate legitimacy of the practice that are difficult to answer. Instead, they may list the record owner of the practice as the sole signatory on the accounts but then take possession of the checkbooks, obtain a stamp of the record owner's signature to issue checks, and arrange for the statements and cancelled checks to be sent to an address that is under their control rather than under the control of the record owner of the practice. Attorneys who litigate no-fault insurance anti-fraud cases should therefore examine the checks to see whether the signatures are applied with a stamp, whether stamped checks are being issued to questionable parties in suspicious amounts, and whether the statements are being sent to an address with no apparent connection to the practice or the licensed professional who supposedly owns it.

In addition to showing large payments to or for the benefit of the unlicensed individuals and entities that illegally own a professional entity, the entity's bank records will oftentimes show that the licensed professional who purports to own the practice receives only a small amount of the practice's revenues. Obviously, where a professional practice generates a great deal of revenue and the record owner of the practice receives only a small amount of the revenue, a plaintiff-insurer will have considerable grounds to allege that someone other than the record owner is the true owner of the practice.

The tax returns for a professional entity can also be used to demonstrate the entity's illegal ownership structure. While courts sometimes are reluctant to order disclosure of corporate tax returns, especially where the evidence they provide is cumulative of other available evidence such as corporate bank records, they generally will be discoverable on a showing of relevance.[18] In this context, and like bank records, the corporate tax returns for a suspect practice will often disclose problematically large payments for leases, management, marketing, billing, or collection services and payments to the record owner of the practice that amount to a pittance in comparison. Similarly, the tax returns for a practice may reveal deductions for purported business expenses that have no colorable connection with the licensed professional who is listed as the owner of the practice. Examples of this include renovations to real property that is not owned or occupied by the record owner of the practice and automobile deductions for a healthcare provider who does not drive. This, in turn, can provide good evidence of corporate structure fraud.

Another way to identify and prove corporate structure fraud is through disclosure of purported vendor contracts. As noted above, one of the more common ways that unlicensed individuals and entities illegally own and control healthcare practices is by entering into exorbitant management, billing, marketing, consulting, or lease agreements with the practices. In the best possible scenario—and as often is the case with a practice's bank records or tax returns—insurers may be able to obtain discovery of these types of agreements as defendants in the context of the healthcare practice's no-fault collections proceedings.

For instance, if an insurer can make a sufficient initial showing that a healthcare practice pursuing collection on its billing has an illegal corporate structure, they may be able to persuade the judge or a no-fault arbitrator hearing the collections matter to order production of the practice's agreements with its purported vendors. More commonly, however, the insurer will have to be the plaintiff in an anti-fraud lawsuit in order to obtain discovery of this type of material given

---

[18] *See*, e.g., State Farm Mut. Auto. Ins. Co. v. CPT Medical Services, P.C., 375 F. Supp. 2d 141, 155-56 (E.D.N.Y. 2005) (finding "financial records, including tax returns of the defendants relating to transactions which generated cash" to be discoverable to demonstrate the extent to which defendants profited from alleged fraudulent billing scheme); MedCity Rehab. Servs., LLC v. State Farm Mut. Auto. Ins. Co., 2013 U.S. Dist. LEXIS 64670 (E.D. Mich. 2013) (ordering production of financial information, including tax returns, where the returns were "relevant to establishing the financial relationships among" the participants in the alleged scheme, as well as "how these participants divvied up the proceeds of their fraud, who they employed in furtherance of their scheme, and how the relationship was structured to further and conceal the fraud.").

the narrow view of discovery usually adopted by courts and arbitrators in the context of small-scale no-fault collections proceedings.

Regardless of the procedural setting in which an insurer obtains a healthcare provider's vendor agreements, the agreements often provide strong indicia of corporate structure fraud. For example, the agreements will often recite purported consideration for leaseholds or services that is far out of proportion to the fair market value of the pertinent property or work. What is more, when the healthcare practice's bank records are cross-referenced with the agreements, it often will appear that the payments by the healthcare practice to a putative vendor or landlord are far in excess of even the exorbitant amounts recited in the underlying agreements. It can be difficult for a healthcare provider and its supposed vendor to contend that these arrangements constitute legitimate, arms-length transactions when they enable the vendor to siphon off virtually every dollar of profit from a professional entity, as often is the case.[19]

As noted above, there are other types of corporate structure fraud in addition to the more common variety involving a healthcare practice (most commonly a medical practice) that is secretly and unlawfully owned or controlled by unlicensed nonprofessionals.

For example, while ambulatory surgery centers usually may be owned or controlled by nonprofessionals, many states impose extensive licensing requirements on such facilities because—among other things—they are an exception to the general rule against the corporate practice of medicine. These licensing requirements typically require ambulatory surgery centers to have a licensed physician on staff as a medical director and to vest the physician–medical director with total or near-total control over on-site patient care.

---

[19] *See*, e.g., Gov't Emples. Ins. Co. v. Zemlyansky, 2015 U.S. Dist. LEXIS 130582 (E.D.N.Y. 2015) (granting a default judgment to the insurer in a corporate structure fraud case, where unlicensed defendants used management, marketing, billing, and collections agreements to "receive all of the profits that were generated by the billings submitted to" insurers through the professional corporation defendants); Gov't Emples. Ins. Co. v. Badia, 2015 U.S. Dist. LEXIS 33667 (E.D.N.Y. 2015) (granting a default judgment to the insurer in a corporate structure fraud case, where unlicensed defendants used management, marketing, billing, and lease agreements to "conceal the fraudulent incorporation of [the professional corporation defendant] and the fact that the Management Defendants owned and controlled [the professional corporation defendant] and took all of its profits. . . .").

Furthermore, while the corporate practice of medicine is generally unlawful in most states, there are exceptions. Florida, for instance, permits ordinary medical practices to be owned and controlled by unlicensed non-physicians as long as they are organized as "clinics" under the Florida Health Care Clinic Act.[20] Much like the rules governing ambulatory surgery centers in many states, Florida law requires clinics that are owned by unlicensed nonprofessionals to engage licensed physicians as medical directors and to vest such medical directors with authority over the provision of healthcare services at the clinics.[21]

In recent years, insurers have successfully predicated fraud-based claims on misrepresentations by ambulatory surgery centers or other healthcare providers to the effect that they were in compliance with these types of medical director requirements, when in fact they were not. For example, in *Allstate Ins. Co. v. Elzanaty*, 916 F. Supp. 2d 273 (E.D.N.Y. 2013), the plaintiff-insurer alleged that a specific type of healthcare facility that could be owned by an unlicensed non-physician under New York law, and therefore was required to have a legitimate medical director, in actuality did not have a legitimate medical director.[22] As a result, the plaintiff-insurer alleged that the facility was out of compliance with New York licensing laws and not entitled to collect no-fault insurance benefits and that its no-fault billing fraudulently misrepresented its compliance with New York licensing laws and eligibility to collect no-fault benefits in the first place. Although the defendants moved for judgment on the pleadings, the court denied the motion in its entirety.[23]

Similarly, in *Allstate Ins. Co. v. Vizcay*, 826 F.3d 1326 (11th Cir. 2015), the plaintiff-insurer alleged that various clinics organized

---

[20] *See* FLA. STAT. § 400.990 et seq.

[21] *See* FLA. STAT. § 400.9935(1) (requiring, among other things, that clinic medical directors assume responsibility for medical record-keeping, ensure that all healthcare services providers at the clinics have the appropriate level of licensure, ensure that all healthcare services providers at the clinics comply with the pertinent professional standards, and ensure that billing is not fraudulent or unlawful).

[22] *Id.*, 916 F. Supp. 2d at 283.

[23] *Id.*, 916 F. Supp. 2d at 304; *see also* Gov't Emples. Ins. Co. v. Uptown Health Care Mgmt., 945 F. Supp. 2d 284 (E.D.N.Y. 2013) (in a substantially similar case by different plaintiff-insurers against many of the same defendants, denying the defendants' motion to dismiss in its entirety).

under Florida law that were required to have legitimate medical directors, did not in fact have medical directors who actually fulfilled their statutory duties. At trial, the insurer obtained a judgment against the clinics, and the 11th Circuit affirmed the judgment on appeal, holding that because claims made by a clinic operating in violation of the Florida Health Care Clinic Act were deemed noncompensable and unenforceable under the statute, an insurer could recover its payments made to a violator-clinic on a theory of unjust enrichment.[24]

Like the general rule against the corporate practice of medicine, the licensing rules for ambulatory surgery centers and clinics make perfect sense, as do the rules prohibiting unlawfully organized ambulatory surgery centers and clinics from recovering no-fault insurance benefits. Without such rules, it would be too easy to subordinate a physician or other licensed healthcare provider's independent medical judgment to the pecuniary interests of unlicensed nonprofessionals.

Practice Points

Identifying Corporate Structure Fraud

- ✓ Do corporate filings suggest lay ownership of a healthcare practice?
- ✓ Are no-fault reimbursement checks deposited suspiciously?
- ✓ Is there rapid turnover at the practice location?
- ✓ Does the practice owner own a large number of practices?
- ✓ Is the specialized practice owned by a nonspecialist?
- ✓ Does the practice owe suspicious debt?
- ✓ Does the practice have suspicious vendor contracts?
- ✓ Do the practice's financial records suggest lay ownership or control?

[24] *Id.*, 826 F.3d at 1330.

3

Identifying Fraud Involving Medically Unnecessary Services and Kickbacks

Every no-fault state, either explicitly or implicitly, limits no-fault insurance reimbursement to medically necessary goods and services.[1] Because automobile insurers are only required to pay no-fault insurance benefits for medically necessary goods and services, misrepresentations as to the medical necessity of a given service or piece of medical equipment can constitute actionable fraud.

This type of misrepresentation can take a large number of forms, limited only by the ingenuity of corrupt healthcare providers in the context of the underlying automobile accidents. However, certain common themes tend to recur in the cases.

A. Predetermined Treatment Protocols Where Patients Are Inventory—Primary Care, Specialists, and the Role of Kickbacks and Runners

In a legitimate clinical setting, patients receive diagnoses and treatment based on their individual circumstances or presentment. By extension, the diagnoses and treatment that each patient receives

[1] *See*, e.g., N.J.S.A. 39:6A-4; Fla. Stat. § 627.736.

at a legitimate healthcare practice should vary considerably from one patient to another. For example, one would not expect to see a legitimate medical office where almost every patient was diagnosed with a cervical sprain and lumbar sprain and subsequently received a substantially similar course of treatment over the course of a substantially similar length of time. Nor would one expect to see a legitimate chiropractic office that referred almost every patient for electrodiagnostic tests like clockwork after two or three months of treatment. By contrast, the typical no-fault insurance fraud scheme is predicated on predetermined fraudulent treatment protocols, in which most patients receive substantially similar treatments over substantially similar periods without regard for their true individual circumstances or presentment. The overall objective is to submit as much billing as possible rather than to treat or otherwise benefit the patients.

With that in mind, and broadly speaking, healthcare providers who bill no-fault can be broken down into two general categories: (i) "primary care" providers, such as chiropractors and physiatrists, who often are the first providers to treat an insured after his or her automobile accident, and (ii) "specialty" or "modality" providers, such as neurologists, pain management physicians, radiologists, dentists, acupuncturists, psychologists, and physical therapists, who purport to provide specialized services pursuant to referrals from primary care providers. Oftentimes, the primary care providers and the specialty providers will all be part of the same no-fault insurance fraud ring, will operate from the same "multidisciplinary" clinic in the same location, and—in cases involving corporate structure fraud—will be under the same common, illegal ownership by unlicensed individuals and entities.[2]

In a no-fault insurance fraud scheme, patients are inventory, and it is important to understand how those patients commonly are obtained and traded between and among the participants in the scheme. Most fraudulent healthcare practices do not purchase any advertising or engage in any genuine efforts to market their services to the general public. To the contrary, the classic no-fault fraud

[2] *See* Gov't Emples. Ins. Co. v. Badia, 2015 U.S. Dist. LEXIS 35224 (E.D.N.Y. 2015) (recommending default judgment for the insurer in connection with one such scheme).

ring operates from an uninviting, dilapidated storefront clinic in a depressed neighborhood, oftentimes demarcated solely by a generic sign announcing "DOCTOR OFFICE" or "CLINIC." In some cases, these storefront clinics will house only primary care chiropractors or physiatrists, although it increasingly is common for such clinics to function on a multidisciplinary basis, with both primary care and specialty providers in regular attendance. The signage at these clinics generally will not specify the identities of the individual physicians or other healthcare providers who operate from the locations, because patients do not arrive at these locations in search of any specific, reputable healers and because there usually is rapid turnover among the healthcare providers at the facility.

These clinics typically obtain their patients through one of two means: Either through referrals from personal injury attorneys or through the use of patient procurers, commonly known as "runners." In the first scenario, where the referral comes from a personal injury attorney, the referral usually is motivated by a desire on the part of the attorney and patient to create a medical record that will enable the patient to exceed the pertinent verbal or monetary statutory threshold and thereby assert a tort claim. Typically, the attorney has a relationship with the healthcare providers who operate from the clinic or with the unlicensed individuals or entities who illegally own and control the clinic behind the scenes. As a result, the attorney can have some assurance that the healthcare providers at the clinic will render ersatz "diagnoses" to support personal injury claims regardless of the patient's true symptomatology or presentment.

The second scenario—wherein no-fault patients are procured by runners—is not necessarily driven by a desire to exceed the statutory threshold and manufacture tort claims. In some cases, runners are paid to bring patients to personal injury attorneys, who in turn refer the patients on to a corrupt clinic. However, it is more common to see runners paid directly by the clinics, by the healthcare providers who operate from the clinics, or by the unlicensed individuals or entities that secretly and unlawfully own and control the clinics. Where runners are involved, the generation of no-fault insurance billing often is an end unto itself.

Many no-fault states have laws and regulations on the books that make it illegal for healthcare providers to obtain patients through the use of runners, and in some states the use of runners actually is a crime.[3] Runners can operate through a variety of means. Some use police scanners to locate and solicit prospective patients at accident scenes. Others, still more entrepreneurial, actually recruit associates to participate in phony, staged accidents: They pack four or five participants in each vehicle and then orchestrate minor collisions between them to provide a phony basis for serious injury claims and long-term, medically unnecessary healthcare services.

Regardless of the manner in which a no-fault insurance patient is recruited to a fraudulent clinic, upon arrival, the patient will first be seen by a primary care provider—again, typically a chiropractor or physiatrist. In some cases, the chiropractor or physiatrist actually controls the clinic, whereas in other cases the clinic is under the control of unlicensed individuals or entities who illegally employ the chiropractors and physiatrists (as well as any specialty providers who operate from the clinic) and control their practices.

Typically, as the first step in any fraudulent treatment and billing protocol, the chiropractor or physiatrist will purport to provide the patient with an initial examination and generate a phony series of "diagnoses." Then, based on these ersatz "diagnoses," the chiropractor or physiatrist will recommend an extended course of chiropractic and/or physical therapy services and will refer the patient for a series of more expensive specialty services such as diagnostic testing and pain management injections.

These types of referrals are not predicated on medical necessity. Rather, they are intended to maximize the amount of no-fault

---

[3] *See*, e.g., N.J.S.A. § 2C:21-22.1 (making the use of a runner a crime and defining a "runner" as "a person who, for a pecuniary benefit, procures or attempts to procure a client, patient or customer at the direction of, request of or in cooperation with a provider whose purpose is to seek to obtain benefits under a contract of insurance or assert a claim against an insured or an insurance carrier for providing services to the client, patient or customer, or to obtain benefits under or assert a claim against a State or federal health care benefits program or prescription drug assistance program."); 18 PA. CONS. STAT. § 4117 (making it a crime to "compensate or give anything of value to a person for providing names, addresses, telephone numbers or other identifying information of individuals seeking or receiving medical or rehabilitative care for accident, sickness or disease, except to the extent a referral and receipt of compensation is permitted under applicable professional rules of conduct. A person may not knowingly transmit such referral information to a lawyer or health care professional for the purpose of receiving compensation or anything of value. Attempts to circumvent this paragraph through use of any other person, including, but not limited to, employees, agents or servants, shall also be prohibited.").

insurance billing that can be submitted for each individual patient. As a result, the specialty or modality providers who obtain the referrals often are required to pay kickbacks to the primary care providers in exchange for the referrals. In the context of a multidisciplinary clinic, the kickbacks frequently are disguised as ostensibly legitimate fees to "rent" space or personnel at the clinics or directly from the primary care providers who make the referrals.[4]

Most no-fault states make it unlawful—or, at a minimum, an act of professional misconduct—for healthcare providers to pay or receive compensation in exchange for a patient referral. Indeed, some states—aware of the fact that corrupt healthcare providers may attempt to disguise their kickbacks as rent, consulting fees, and the like—have drawn their laws and regulations in an attempt to anticipate and prevent such collusion. In New Jersey, for example, physicians "may lease space or medical equipment to or from another licensed health care professional to whom patients are referred, only where rent is a fixed fee set in advance and determined by the fair market value, or less, and is for a regular term and not for sporadic use of the space or equipment."[5] Similarly, Florida makes it unlawful—and indeed criminal—"for any health care provider or any provider of health care services to offer, pay, solicit, or receive a kickback, directly or indirectly, overtly or covertly, in cash or in kind, for referring or soliciting patients."[6]

In this context, and as discussed above, many states require healthcare providers to comply with material laws and regulations governing healthcare practice in order to be eligible to receive no-fault reimbursement. By extension, healthcare providers that pay illegal kickbacks in exchange for patient referrals generally will not be eligible to receive no-fault reimbursement. Where a healthcare

---

[4] The cases contain numerous recent examples of these types of kickback schemes. *See*, e.g., Gov't Emples. Ins. Co. v. Simakovsky, 2015 U.S. Dist. LEXIS 135657 (E.D.N.Y. 2015) (recommending a large default judgment against defendants who paid kickbacks to obtain patients at fraudulent multidisciplinary clinics); Gov't Emples. Ins. Co. v. Badia, 2015 U.S. Dist. LEXIS 35224 (E.D.N.Y. 2015) (same); Gov't Emples. Ins. Co. v. Zuberi, 2015 U.S. Dist. LEXIS 133789 (D.N.J. 2015) (denying the motion to dismiss by the defendants who were alleged to have paid kickbacks in exchange for radiology referrals).

[5] N.J.A.C. 13:35-6.17(h)(3).

[6] Fla. Stat. § 456.054.

provider is engaged in an illegal kickback or referral fee scheme, each of the provider's bills will misrepresent the provider's eligibility to collect no-fault benefits and will provide the basis for a fraud claim.

Aside from the question of legal compliance and its impact on reimbursement eligibility, the payment of kickbacks in exchange for patient referrals calls into question the medical necessity of the resulting services. But for the kickback, would the service have been recommended or provided? As a result, illegal kickback or runner schemes can not only give rise to misrepresentations regarding a healthcare provider's eligibility to collect no-fault insurance benefits, but can also provide an insurer with a strong circumstantial basis to allege that the resulting bills and treatment reports misrepresented the medical necessity of the underlying services.

B. How to Identify Kickback and Runner Schemes

In most cases, insurers interested in commencing no-fault insurance anti-fraud litigation will be unable to obtain concrete evidence of a kickback and runner scheme, at least at the pleading stage, in advance of discovery. While whistleblowers do exist, they are relatively rare, and other types of hard evidence—such as financial records—generally do not emerge in the ordinary insurance claims process. As a result, insurers generally need to develop sufficient circumstantial evidence of kickback and runner schemes to allow them to plausibly allege the scheme and survive a motion to dismiss, at which point discovery can fill in any blanks.

Fortunately, there are many ways in which insurers can identify and present sufficient circumstantial evidence of unlawful kickback and runner arrangements to survive motions to dismiss and get to discovery.

1. Itinerant Specialty Healthcare Services Providers

For example, it seems fair to say that most legitimate healthcare providers operate from a fixed location or, at least, from a handful of fixed locations. For instance, most healthcare providers maintain their own offices or work out of fixed locations such as hospitals or other healthcare facilities. This enables the healthcare providers to build goodwill around their practices and enables patients interested in their healthcare services—or referral sources interested in making referrals—to find the providers when they need them. For these reasons, specialty or modality providers that do not operate from a consistent fixed location, and instead operate on an itinerant basis from the offices of their "primary care" referral sources, are highly suspicious. As discussed above, these providers often pay kickbacks to their referral sources in exchange for patient referrals, which are disguised as ostensibly legitimate fees to rent space or personnel from their referral sources.

These types of schemes usually can be identified through a straightforward process. First, look at the claims that have been filed by the suspect specialty provider. Virtually every no-fault insurance claim will include the location where the underlying service was provided. Does the provider operate from a single, fixed location, or does the provider roam around from office to office? If the specialty provider roams around from office to office, see whether all of its referrals come from other providers at those offices. If the specialty provider operates at multiple offices on an itinerant basis and receives all or most of its referrals from other providers at those offices, it is one indication that the referrals are obtained through kickbacks.

In some cases, specialty providers will attempt to conceal the fact that they are operating on a transient basis from the offices of their referral sources because they know that insurers may find that sort of activity suspicious. These types of providers may, for example, omit the place of service from the billing or from the treatment records that they submit to insurers in support of their bills. These types of machinations, in their own way, raise even more questions than when a specialty provider openly lists the office of his referral source as the location where the specialty service was provided.

2. Long-Distance Patient Travel

Another good way to identify kickback and runner schemes is where a healthcare provider regularly treats patients at locations that are far from the patients' homes or places of employment. Common sense suggests that most patients will seek treatment in the vicinity of where they reside or work. Obviously, there are exceptions to this general rule, inasmuch as patients with serious conditions often will be prepared to travel in order to be seen by a renowned physician. However, soft tissue injuries attendant to automobile accidents are not especially serious conditions, and—for better or worse—healthcare providers who cater exclusively or primarily to a no-fault clientele typically are not especially distinguished in their respective fields. As a result, where a provider regularly treats patients at locations that are far from the patients' homes, it can be another indication that the provider is procuring the patients through some questionable means.

It usually is fairly easy to identify specialty providers who routinely treat patients at locations that are far from the patients' homes. Patient addresses are, by necessity, part of every insurance claims file. As noted above, virtually every insurance claims file also will contain the address at which each individual healthcare service was provided. These data can be entered into spreadsheets that can be sorted to identify patterns in which healthcare providers regularly treat patients at locations that are far from where the patients reside.

3. Data Disparities Among Healthcare Providers

While an insurer may have suspicions about a transient specialty practice, or a practice that routinely treats patients far from their homes, these issues—standing alone—in most cases will not be sufficient to support a colorable kickback allegation. As a result, no-fault insurance anti-fraud litigators should look for other issues to buttress and provide cumulative support for their kickback allegations.

One way to do this is to identify patterns of disparities in the healthcare data generated by referring healthcare providers and specialty providers with respect to individual patients. This is fairly simple to accomplish and often occurs when patients are referred from one provider to another pursuant to a predetermined fraudulent treatment protocol rather than as the result of medical necessity.

First, check and see whether the treatment reports generated by the specialty provider consistently contain data or diagnoses for individual patients that are substantially different from the information in the treatment reports generated by the primary care provider that made the referral, or vice versa. For example, did the referring provider contend that the insured patients had normal range of motion, whereas the specialty provider found serious range-of-motion deficits among the patients? Did the referring provider posit that the patients had sharp and shooting pain, whereas the specialty provider reported that the patients' pain was dull and aching? Did the referring provider diagnose the patient with a lumbar sprain, whereas the specialty provider found the patient to have a cervical sprain? One instance of this sort of thing, or even 10 instances of this sort of thing, typically will not be enough. Rather, anti-fraud litigators should try to identify a consistent pattern of these types of disparities.

Second, check and see whether the disparate data or diagnoses were contemporaneous. Were the incongruent data generated on the same date of service or within a span of only a week or two? This is important, because—while a patient's complaints and symptomatology may change over an extended period of time—it is less plausible that any sort of dramatic change will occur over a relatively short time span.

Third, check whether subsequent treatment notes of the referring provider and the specialty provider comment on these types of data or diagnostic disparities. For instance, does the referring provider make any attempt to explain why her diagnosis of the patient differs from the contemporaneous diagnosis that was provided by the specialist to whom she made the referral, or vice versa? Do their subsequent treatment notes make any attempt to address the disparities? If not, it is a good indication that the specialist's services were not incorporated into the overall treatment of the insured patient and that the referral to the specialist was not based on medical necessity.

These types of unresolved disparities—especially when coupled with evidence that the specialist operates from the referring provider's offices or sees patients far from their homes—can provide a good faith basis to allege a kickback scheme.

Practice Points

Data Disparities and Range of Motion

- ✓ Because range-of-motion testing is a critical component of virtually any examination of a patient with soft tissue injuries, most legitimate healthcare providers will include a patient's range-of-motion data in their examination reports.
- ✓ As a result, when searching for data disparities among healthcare providers, it usually will be a good idea to start by comparing contemporaneous range-of-motion test data generated by the healthcare providers at issue.

4. Regular Referrals for Healthcare Services with No Apparent Purpose

Another issue that can provide cumulative support for a kickback allegation is the presence of regular referrals for services with no apparent purpose. There is, of course, no end to the list of services that might fall within this category. However, as a general rule, anti-fraud litigators should look for services that appear to play no genuine role in the treatment or care of the patient.

For instance, does a provider regularly refer patients to a specialist for diagnostic testing and then take no action based on the putative results of the diagnostic tests? Does the provider routinely refer patients for magnetic resonance imaging studies, ostensibly to diagnose radiculopathies, despite the fact that the patients already have received radiculopathy diagnoses through electrodiagnostic testing? Along similar lines, does a provider routinely refer patients for experimental or unproven forms of testing or treatment? These types of referrals—especially when they consistently involve the same providers and when the recipient of the referrals operates from the referring provider's offices—can provide a good circumstantial basis for a kickback allegation.

C. How to Identify Fraudulent Schemes Involving Billing for Medically Unnecessary or Illusory Treatments

As set forth above, the first step in any fraudulent treatment and billing protocol is—by necessity—an initial examination by a corrupt chiropractor or physiatrist. These putative initial examinations are an essential gateway to subsequent referrals for long-term, medically unnecessary "treatment," all of which is billed to automobile insurance companies pursuant to assignments of benefits that the fraudulent healthcare providers take from the insured patients. For instance, absent some sort of initial examination and resulting diagnosis to the effect that a patient suffered some injury in an automobile accident, there can be no basis to refer the patient for more expensive services such as radiology studies, other forms of diagnostic testing, long-term chiropractic or physical therapy care, or interventional pain management services such as injections or even surgery.

1. Soft Tissue Injuries and the Role of Objectively Unverifiable "Diagnoses"

However, fraudulent healthcare providers involved in no-fault insurance schemes generally cannot legitimately diagnose their patients with serious, objectively verifiable injuries secondary to automobile accidents. There are several reasons why this is the case.

For instance, the underlying automobile accidents usually can be shown through several means to be trivial, low-speed, low-impact fender benders. Automobile insurers often have photographs from the accident scenes and repair bills for the vehicles that reflect only minor collisions. Insurers also virtually always obtain police reports regarding the accidents, which frequently state on their face that no one was injured in the accidents or that the vehicles were all drivable following the accidents. To the extent that an insured seeks treatment at a hospital following an accident, the hospital records often will report only minor injuries, if they report any injuries at all.

Against this type of backdrop, a fraudulent healthcare provider ordinarily cannot plausibly purport to diagnose a patient with a fracture, traumatic brain injury, or other type of serious injury. Such injuries are objectively verifiable—if a patient broke a bone or was injured to a point where she was admitted to a hospital, there will be a record of it.

In any case, no-fault insurance fraud rings almost never will see seriously injured patients in the first instance. Not only are seriously injured patients unlikely to settle on corrupt healthcare practices as their preferred healers, but fraudulent healthcare providers often lack the competency and wherewithal to provide legitimate care in severe cases. As a result, the patients who present at fraudulent healthcare practices ordinarily are not seriously injured, and there is no real opportunity for the healthcare providers to contend—at least initially—that the patients experienced any sort of serious injury.

For this reason, fraudulent healthcare providers often commence their fraudulent treatment and billing protocol by providing an objectively unverifiable, and usually bogus, soft tissue injury diagnosis. A soft tissue injury is the damage of muscles, ligaments, and tendons throughout the body. Common soft tissue injuries include sprains (a stretched or torn ligament), strains (a stretched or torn muscle or tendon), and contusions (a bruised muscle tendon or ligament). Soft tissue injuries can result in pain, swelling, and loss of function, and they often arise in the context of automobile accidents.

No-fault insurance fraud rings begin their billing with a phony soft tissue injury diagnosis because such diagnoses are highly subjective and transient. It is, for example, very difficult for an insurer to prove that a patient did not suffer a sprain or strain as the result of an automobile accident, even a relatively minor accident. As a result, corrupt healthcare providers usually can bill for at least a short period of medically unnecessary treatment on the back of such ersatz diagnoses.

2. Identifying Phony Soft Tissue Injury Diagnoses

Although it can be very difficult to conclusively disprove soft tissue injury diagnoses, it often will be possible to obtain and present evidence to call the diagnoses into serious question. There are several ways to do this.

Initially, it is well established in the medical literature that most soft tissue injuries such as sprains and strains do not cause any long-term, chronic pain in the people who experience them.[7] To the contrary, most soft tissue injuries such as sprains and strains—and any acute pain arising from such injuries—resolve after a few weeks through conservative treatments such as rest, icing, compression, and (if applicable) elevation of the affected body part.[8]

Of course, this is a general rule that is subject to exceptions. Some patients will continue to complain of discomfort or pain long after the underlying accident. These patients may have suffered some sort of nerve or muscle injury beyond an ordinary sprain or strain, or their pain symptoms may be caused by some other type of preexisting condition that was exacerbated by the accident. Nonetheless, most of us have experienced a sprain or strain in our lifetimes, and—in keeping with the general rule—the pain almost always gradually fades and then disappears altogether over the course of a fairly short period of time.

---

[7] *See*, e.g., Roger Chou, et al., *Diagnosis and Treatment of Low Back Pain: A Joint Clinical Practice Guideline from the American College of Physicians and the American Pain Society*. 147 Ann. Intern. Med. 478 (2007); New York State Workers' Compensation Board, New York Mid and Low Back Injury Medical Treatment Guidelines, 2d Ed. (2013); National Collaborating Centre for Primary Care, Low Back Pain. Early Management of Persistent Non-Specific Low Back Pain (2009).

[8] *Id.*

With that in mind, soft tissue injury pain diagnoses that are provided long after the underlying automobile accidents are suspicious. Healthcare providers that routinely purport to diagnose soft tissue injury pain long after the underlying automobile accidents are exponentially more suspicious. This is because the routine diagnosis of soft tissue injury pain long after the underlying automobile accidents tends to contravene the general rule that such injuries typically resolve after a short period of time.

In this context, virtually every insurer's claims and SIU department maintains a record of every claim submitted by a given healthcare provider. These records will show the dates on which the underlying accidents occurred, the dates on which the healthcare provider first treated the insured patients, and the types of diagnoses that were provided during those first patient encounters. In turn, these records can be used to identify healthcare providers that routinely purport to diagnose their patient with soft tissue injuries long after the pertinent accidents. While it can be difficult to conclusively disprove an individual soft tissue injury diagnosis, a consistent pattern of long intervals between accidents and soft tissue injury diagnoses can be compelling evidence that the diagnoses are implausible.

Another way to identify a pattern of phony soft tissue injury diagnoses is by reference to the other information about insured patients or underlying accidents that often is compiled and maintained by insurance companies following automobile accidents.

For example, the police will be called to respond to most automobile accidents that give rise to no-fault insurance claims, and the police virtually always will generate reports about the accidents. In some cases, emergency medical technicians also will be called to an accident scene and also will file a report. These reports will state, among other things, whether the accidents caused any deaths or injuries and whether the vehicles involved in the accidents were left at the scene, towed, or were driven off following the accidents. The reports also will contain information regarding the mechanism of the accident, such as whether the accident was a high-speed, head-on collision or whether it was a low-speed, low-impact, rear-end collision that occurred in a parking lot. Sometimes, the reports will make reference to the severity (or lack thereof) of any reported injuries. Less frequently, the reports will include the responding officer's opinions about any reported injuries—for instance, an officer may include language in her report that contravenes any claims about an accident that the officer finds to be suspicious or unlikely.

Insurers virtually always obtain and maintain copies of police or other first responder reports in their claims files, and anti-fraud investigators and litigators can retrieve and review them in order to identify patterns in which healthcare providers render soft tissue injury diagnoses that are contravened by the reports. Does a healthcare provider routinely supply sprain or strain diagnoses to automobile accident victims where the police or other first responder reports from the underlying accidents stated that no one was injured in the accidents and that the vehicles involved were drivable following the accidents? Is there a pattern of diagnoses that is implausible given the nature of the underlying collisions—for example, cervical sprain or whiplash diagnoses following low-speed, side-swipe accidents? If so, the pattern can be used to allege that the healthcare provider's diagnoses are predetermined and phony.

In this context, it is important to note that a handful of cases in which a provider's diagnoses are contravened by contemporaneous first responder reports usually will not be sufficient to allege that the provider is a fraud. Though most people who experience a soft tissue injury in an accident will manifest symptoms immediately, in some cases it takes time for the symptoms to show themselves. As a result, there may be cases in which a police report states that no one was injured in an accident, but one of the accident victims nonetheless suffered some real injury. For this reason, anti-fraud litigators should look for patterns in which healthcare providers consistently issue diagnoses that are contravened by the police or other first responder reports. While a provider might reasonably contend that a patient's injury took some time to manifest itself after an accident, the provider will have difficulty explaining a pattern of questionable soft tissue injury diagnoses.

Along similar lines, contemporaneous hospital records also can be used to show a pattern of fraudulent soft tissue injury diagnoses. Many automobile accident victims go to a hospital following their accidents. In most cases, this is because they either suffer some actual injury in their accidents or because the accidents leave them shaken up and they want to be examined for prophylactic reasons. In some cases, people visit the hospital because the "conventional wisdom" is that it is a good idea to make a record of an accident, oftentimes in anticipation of litigation.

When a patient visits the hospital following an accident, the resulting hospital records will give a relatively reliable record of the patient's condition in the immediate wake of the collision. For example, the hospital records typically will report, among other things, whether the patient was ambulatory, whether the patient's range of motion was limited in any way, the exact nature of the patient's pain complaints, and—if any radiology studies were taken—whether the radiology work revealed any abnormalities. The hospital records also will contain a diagnosis, or—if the patient has suffered no injury—no diagnosis. Significantly, the hospital records will almost always predate any other medical records relating to a given accident, because the hospital usually will be the first place that a patient seeks treatment after an accident. These records therefore provide a baseline of trustworthiness against which all of a patient's subsequent treatment can be gauged, because hospitals generally will not have any incentive to engage in no-fault insurance fraud schemes.

Like police and other first responder reports, automobile insurers will maintain copies of hospital records in their claims files, because the hospital services—like every other form of post-accident treatment—usually will have been billed to the insurer. As with police and other first responder records, anti-fraud litigators can compare hospital records against a suspicious provider's subsequent treatment notes to identify patterns of disparities between them. For example, does the healthcare provider routinely report that his patients suffer lumbar sprains in their accidents, whereas the hospital records for his patients report no lower back injury? Does the healthcare provider regularly contend that his patients suffer from meaningful range-of-motion deficits as the result of their accidents, when the hospital records for those patients state that they had full range of motion in the immediate aftermath of their accidents? A pattern of this type of dissonance between hospital records and the subsequent treatment notes of a suspect healthcare provider can support allegations to the effect that the provider is providing false diagnoses to his patients in order to support no-fault insurance billing.

The absence of a hospital record also can be used to call a healthcare provider's diagnosis into question. It stands to reason that, where a person is involved in an automobile accident and where that person suffers an injury that warrants weeks or even months of treatment, that person will go to a hospital. Conversely, where an accident victim fails to visit the hospital at all following their accident, it suggests that the person either was not injured in the accident or that the injury was not especially severe. As a result, in addition to identifying patterns of disparities between hospital records and subsequent treatment reports, no-fault insurers and their counsel should look for patterns in which a provider renders soft tissue injury diagnoses and recommends lengthy treatment to patients who never sought hospital treatment immediately after their accidents.

PRACTICE POINTS

Using Post-Accident Hospital Records to Identify Patterns of Medically Unnecessary Treatment

- ✓ Do the hospital records indicate that the patient was briefly observed on an outpatient basis and then quickly discharged?
- ✓ Do the hospital records indicate that the patient was diagnosed with nothing more serious than a sprain or strain?
- ✓ Do the hospital records indicate that the patient had a normal gait and full, normal range of motion throughout her body?
- ✓ Do the hospital records indicate that the hospital did not perform any imaging studies on the patient or that the imaging studies were normal?
- ✓ Do the hospital records indicate that the patient was not prescribed anything more potent than an NSAID like ibuprofen? If so, then why would that patient need many months of subsequent treatment?

While the honesty of hospital records can generally be presumed, records from other healthcare providers who treat insured patients following automobile accidents often can be a closer question. As discussed above, many fraudulent healthcare providers operate in multidisciplinary clinics that essentially operate as no-fault insurance fraud mills. Oftentimes, these clinics not only play host to one or more physicians, but also to chiropractors, acupuncturists, physical therapists, psychologists, and dentists—all of whom are interested in providing the maximum number of ersatz "diagnoses" to the patients so as to support the maximum amount of fraudulent billing. As a result, a phony diagnosis provided to a given patient by one corrupt healthcare provider may be reiterated and amplified in the treatment notes of another corrupt healthcare provider treating that same patient. Indeed, this sometimes is part of the scheme, inasmuch as it is that much more difficult for an insurer to disprove a bogus diagnosis if that diagnosis has been echoed by more than one healthcare provider.

Even so, anti-fraud litigators should scrutinize contemporaneous records from healthcare providers other than the target provider, even if there is reason to believe that all of the providers are working together to enact the same no-fault insurance fraud scheme. Oftentimes, they are careless and will not carefully coordinate their treatment notes. As a result, one provider may claim that the insured patient suffered from a lower back injury, whereas a different provider may contemporaneously report that the patient had no lower back complaints and instead suffered from a neck sprain. Patterns of these types of discrepancies can be used to colorably allege that none of the diagnoses were legitimate.

In addition, boilerplate language in treatment reports can be used to identify fraudulent billing for medically unnecessary services. Of course, it is reasonable to expect some recurring complaints and diagnoses among patients who have been involved in automobile accidents. Many patients will complain of back or neck pain, for instance, and many patients will be diagnosed with some sort of sprain or strain secondary to their automobile accidents. By extension, it is reasonable to expect some degree of similarity among the examination reports generated by a healthcare practice that is dedicated to treating automobile accident victims.

Nonetheless, there should be some meaningful distinctions between and among the examination reports generated by a healthcare practice for different patients, and too much similarity could be evidence of a predetermined, fraudulent treatment protocol. This is the case even if the practice's patients—by and large—all complained of pain arising from automobile accidents. The patients should, for instance, describe their pain in different ways. The patients also are likely to have different symptomatology—they should have different range-of-motion deficits and other functional limitations, and the results of any diagnostic testing that is conducted during the examinations should vary from patient to patient.

More generally, there should be some meaningful disparity among patients who are old versus young, male versus female, heavy versus light, and in good condition as opposed to poor condition. There also should be meaningful differences between patients who were involved in different types of accidents—someone who was in a high-impact, head-on collision reasonably can be expected to have different complaints and symptoms than someone who was in a low-speed side swipe, and so on.

No-fault insurers and their counsel should therefore carefully scrutinize the examination reports generated by a suspicious healthcare practice to determine whether the practice is supporting its soft tissue injury diagnoses with boilerplate or "cut-and-pasted" examination reports.

In one common scenario, a corrupt healthcare provider realizes that by using certain language in an examination report to describe a patient's soft tissue injuries, he can successfully persuade insurers to approve a lengthier course of more expensive treatment. As a result, the healthcare provider begins to use identical language in every patient's examination report regardless of the patients' unique circumstances or presentment. This, in turn, constitutes a misrepresentation of the subsequent patients' individualized conditions. For example, do the examination reports for a given healthcare provider virtually always state that every patient complained of "sharp and shooting" lower back pain; that it "is worse with bending forwards, backwards, lifting, coughing, sneezing, straining, walking, and any prolonged activities" and that is rated as "8 out of 10 in severity"? If so, the provider is likely to be using boilerplate language to falsify his examination results.

In some cases, a corrupt healthcare practice's examination reports will contain identical grammar, style, and formatting idiosyncrasies across multiple patient reports, which is a strong indication that the language at issue predated the patient examinations. For instance, critical language regarding patient symptoms may appear in Courier font in every examination report, whereas the balance of the reports is rendered in Times New Roman. Along similar lines, important language recounting how the patients described their pain may contain identical misspellings in every examination report.

Some especially brazen healthcare providers go even further and do not even attempt to create the illusion that they have generated an individualized examination report for each patient. Instead, they employ preprinted checklist examination forms, which set forth a very limited range of potential symptoms and potential diagnoses next to boxes that are checked off as the purported examinations proceed.

While, of course, some complaints and diagnoses may recur among a large group of patients who have been involved in automobile accidents, the regular use of a preprinted checklist to conduct patient examinations is a good indication that the outcomes of the examinations are foreordained.

In the most extreme cases, a healthcare practice's examination reports will actually contain duplicated diagnostic data. For example, every patient will be reported as having identical range-of-motion or muscle strength deficits. These cases are the most serious because diagnostic data ostensibly is objective—a patient's range of motion is what it is, and it does not depend on how the patient may choose to describe it. As a result, any recurrent duplication among the diagnostic data in a given universe of patients cannot be put down to similarity among the patients' subjective complaints or the style in which the healthcare provider may choose to write them down. The consistent presence of identical diagnostic testing data in examination reports generated by a single healthcare provider for a substantial number of patients strongly suggests that neither the data, the examinations, nor the resulting soft tissue injury diagnoses are legitimate.

3. Diagnostic Testing as a Basis for the Continuation of Medically Unnecessary Treatment

Eventually—usually within a month or two after a patient receives a phony soft tissue injury diagnosis—it becomes difficult to sustain the fiction that continued treatment is warranted by the diagnosis. Most people have, at some point in their life, experienced a soft tissue injury such as a sprain, strain, or contusion. By extension, most people—including the judges, juries, or arbitrators who will ultimately determine the validity of a contested no-fault claim—know that ordinary soft tissue injuries generally resolve after a course of conservative treatment or no treatment at all. If conventional wisdom does not suffice, as discussed above, there is no shortage of reputable medical opinion to support this view.[9]

In order to continue to provide medically unnecessary treatment to a no-fault insurance patient, corrupt healthcare providers therefore

---

[9] *Id.*

must falsely purport to diagnose the patient with something more serious than a soft tissue injury such as a sprain or strain. As indicated above, this generally must be done about a month or two after the patient first begins treatment, because—by that point—it starts to become difficult for the provider to legitimately contend that the patient is continuing to suffer the ill effects of an ordinary sprain or strain.

In this context, fraudulent healthcare providers face a quandary: Although they need to falsely diagnose patients with something more serious than a sprain or strain in order to justify continued and more expensive forms of treatment, they still cannot diagnose the patients with conditions that are easily and objectively verifiable. As a result, many fraudulent providers settle on some form of chronic nerve injury as their preferred, ersatz diagnosis. These types of diagnoses have the benefit of being both difficult to objectively contravene and sufficient to provide a false basis for various types of expensive interventional treatment.

While there is a potentially large number of potential nerve injuries that can arise secondary to an automobile accident, some form of neuropathy, or peripheral nerve damage, is—in the authors' experience—the most common phony diagnosis. Not only will a false neuropathy diagnosis support many months of medically unnecessary pain management treatment, but corrupt practitioners can generate thousands of dollars in billing for medically unnecessary diagnostic tests that supposedly are necessary in order to reach the diagnosis.

There are three primary diagnostic tools that are well established in the medical, neurological, and radiological communities for diagnosing the existence, nature, extent, and specific location of abnormalities (i.e., neuropathies) in the peripheral nerves and nerve roots. These diagnostic tests are nerve conduction velocity (NCV) and electromyography (EMG), which both are forms of electrodiagnostic (EDX) testing, as well as magnetic resonance imaging (MRIs). All of these tests are attractive to no-fault insurance fraud rings because virtually any licensed physician (or, in some cases, chiropractor) can claim to be competent in their performance and interpretation, whether or not they actually are. What is more, the equipment necessary to perform NCVs, EMGs, and MRIs is widely available at a relatively low cost, putting it within the reach of even a small-scale insurance fraud ring, yet the tests themselves generally are reimbursable at high rates.[10]

EDX tests and MRIs are the most commonly abused forms of diagnostic testing in the no-fault insurance context because a phony neuropathy diagnosis can provide a false basis for additional medically unnecessary treatment by a very broad range of healthcare providers. Not only do the healthcare providers who purport to provide EDX tests and MRIs themselves get to profit from their billing for the tests, but the resulting, ersatz diagnoses can support months of chiropractic, pain management, physiatry, and acupuncture billing by other healthcare providers—all for services intended to remediate a phony neuropathy. Where—as often is the case—providers in all of these disciplines share space in a single, corrupt multidisciplinary clinic, a single phony neuropathy diagnosis can result in tens of thousands of dollars of fraudulent billing per insured patient.

In some cases, corrupt healthcare providers will attempt to support bogus neuropathy diagnoses with types of EDX tests other than EMG and NCV tests. The most commonly abused EDX tests other than EMGs and NCVs are somatosensory evoked potential (SSEP) tests and voltage nerve conduction threshold (v-NCT) tests, which are also commonly referred to as "small pain fiber" or "pf-NCS" tests. Neither SSEP tests nor v-NCT tests have much legitimate utility in diagnosing neuropathies, and—to the extent that either of these types of tests appears to any large extent in a healthcare provider's no-fault insurance billing—the provider likely is using them to create a billing opportunity rather than to treat her patients.

SSEP tests are noninvasive tests in which peripheral nerves in the arms and legs are stimulated with electrical currents. The potentials—brain waves—evoked by this electrical stimulation are then recorded by electrodes attached to the scalp. SSEP tests are medically necessary only in limited instances, such as when an individual suffers from severe spinal impairment (spinal stenosis), or as an intra-operative guide during the course of scoliosis surgery upon children. The American Association of Neuromuscular Electrodiagnostic

[10] In New York, for instance, the New York Workers' Compensation Fee Schedule, which is applicable to claims for no-fault insurance benefits, permits charges in excess of $1,500 for a typical round of EMG and NCV testing. The New Jersey PIP Fee Schedule permits a similar level of EMG and NCV reimbursement.

Medicine (AANEM), which consists of thousands of neurologists and physiatrists and is dedicated solely to the scientific advancement of neuromuscular medicine, has adopted a recommended policy regarding the optimal use of electrodiagnostic medicine in the diagnosis of various forms of neuropathies, including the various types of neuropathies that sometimes arise in the context of automobile accidents.[11] In keeping with the fact that SSEP tests are not medically necessary to diagnose neuropathies, the AANEM's recommended policy does not recommend the use of SSEP tests to diagnose neuropathies.[12] Even so, fraudulent healthcare providers will often purport to diagnose neuropathies using SSEP tests because the tests are relatively esoteric, and in the context of a no-fault collections lawsuit or arbitral proceeding, it is difficult for insurers to rebut a claim that the tests were medically warranted.

Unlike SSEP tests, which can be medically necessary for at least some purposes, v-NCT tests are generally not accepted or employed by legitimate physicians or chiropractors. V-NCT tests supposedly can be used to diagnose sensory nerve abnormalities, and many fraudulent no-fault providers will claim that v-NCT tests can be used to diagnose neuropathies earlier than MRIs, EMG, and NCV tests. However, there are no legitimate data to support this proposition. Indeed, the Centers for Medicare & Medicaid Services (CMS) have determined that v-NCT tests are not medically reasonable and necessary for diagnosing sensory neuropathies and are therefore not compensable.[13] Nevertheless, like SSEP tests, fraudulent healthcare providers will often bill for v-NCT testing because the mechanism behind the test is difficult to understand and therefore can confound any attempt to demonstrate that the test is medically useless.

Much like a neuropathy diagnosis generated by MRIs or EDX testing, a patient's inability to carry on the activities of daily life can support months of healthcare services. As a result—and like MRIs and EDX testing—computerized range of motion, muscle strength, and other types of computerized physical performance tests are frequently employed by fraudulent no-fault practices in order to provide

---

[11] *See* American Association of Neuromuscular Electrodiagnostic Medicine, Recommended Policy for Electrodiagnostic Medicine (2004).

[12] *Id.*

[13] *See* Centers for Medicare & Medicaid Services, National Coverage Determination (June 18, 2014).

false "evidence" of ongoing functional deficits and thereby provide a false justification for long-term, medically unnecessary care.

A traditional, or manual, range-of-motion test consists of a nonelectronic measurement of the joint's ability to move in comparison with an unimpaired or "ideal" joint. In a traditional range-of-motion test, the healthcare provider asks the patient to move his or her joints at various angles, or the physician moves the joints. The healthcare provider then evaluates the patient's range of motion either by sight or through the use of a manual inclinometer or a goniometer (i.e., a device used to measure angles).

Along similar lines, a traditional muscle strength test consists of a nonelectronic measurement of muscle strength, which is accomplished by having the patient move his body in a given direction against resistance applied by the healthcare provider. For example, if a provider wanted to measure muscle strength in the muscles surrounding a patient's knee, she would apply resistance against the patient's leg while having him move the leg up and then apply resistance against the patient's leg while having him move the leg down.

In this context, physical examinations performed on patients with soft tissue injuries necessarily require range-of-motion and muscle strength tests, inasmuch as these tests provide a starting point for injury assessment and treatment planning. Unless a healthcare provider knows the extent of a given patient's joint or muscle strength impairment, there is no way to properly diagnose or treat the patient's injuries. Evaluation of range of motion and muscle strength is therefore an essential component of the "hands-on" examination of a trauma patient.

In contrast to ordinary, manual range-of-motion and muscle strength testing, computerized range-of-motion and muscle strength testing is—as the name suggests—conducted using electronic equipment. In a computerized range-of-motion test, a digital inclinometer or goniometer is affixed with straps on various parts of a patient's body while the patient is asked to attempt various motions and movements. The test is, in all practical respects, virtually identical to the manual range-of-motion testing described above, except that a computer generates a printout of the test results rather than the test results being manually recorded by the examining healthcare provider.

Similarly, in a computerized muscle strength test, a measurement apparatus similar to a strain gauge is affixed onto a stationary object, and the patient is asked to push against it using various muscle groups. As with a computerized range-of-motion test, a computerized muscle strength test is virtually identical to manual muscle strength testing except that a computer generates a digital printout of the test results.

Computerized range-of-motion and muscle strength tests play no genuine role in the treatment of soft tissue injuries secondary to automobile accidents. At most, they generate more exact data as to range-of-motion or muscle strength deficits. However, the difference of a few percentage points in a patient's range of motion, or pounds of resistance in a patient's muscle strength, will generally be meaningless considering that any serious deficits will be self-evident from ordinary, manual testing.

Rather, computerized range-of-motion and muscle strength testing is generally employed by no-fault insurance fraud rings for two separate, but related, purposes. First, and most obviously, the testing creates a billing opportunity for fraudulent providers, who can claim—however falsely—that it constitutes an independent service that can be billed separately from the underlying patient examinations. Second, the computerized printouts that result from the tests appear to be more "scientific" and objective than ordinary, handwritten or typewritten notes recording range of motion or muscle strength in a given patient's chart. Judges and arbitrators may give more credence to the computerized printouts despite the fact that they can be falsified as easily as the results of ordinary, manual range of motion and muscle strength testing. As a result, the tests can be used to falsely represent that a patient continues to suffer functional deficits secondary to an automobile accident and therefore requires continued medical treatment that can be billed to automobile insurance companies.

4. Identifying Fraudulent Diagnostic Testing

It is impossible to anticipate and detail all of the potential ways in which a corrupt healthcare practice can fraudulently perform and bill for diagnostic testing—not least because of the sheer number of diagnostic tests that can be provided and billed. Furthermore, diagnostic testing fraud can be difficult to spot, especially where the tests are highly specialized or require professional training to evaluate. As a result, it almost always will be necessary to engage an expert—typically a physician—to review suspected instances of diagnostic testing fraud. Even so, several common types of diagnostic testing fraud tend to recur in the cases, and anti-fraud litigators should be aware of them.

MRIs, some forms of EDX tests, and physical performance tests have at least some colorable connection to the diagnosis and treatment of the soft tissue injuries that commonly are caused by automobile accidents. However, some no-fault insurance fraud rings indulge in diagnostic testing that is far less likely to be necessary in the context of an accident. Although there are any number of tests that might fall into this category, tests such as videonystagmography (VNG); quantitative electroencephalography (EEG), popularly known as "brain-mapping"; brainstem auditory evoked potential tests (BAEP); and visual evoked potential tests (VEP) are among the most commonly abused.

In legitimate medical practice, VNG testing can be used to determine the cause of a patient's dizziness or balance disorder in cases where there are no readily recognizable contributing factors to the patient's condition. In other words, VNG tests are not used to confirm the existence of dizziness or balance disorder, but rather to identify the origin of the condition in the relatively rare cases where it cannot be determined through a routine medical examination. For example, if the origin of the patient's dizziness or imbalance is not readily identifiable, a physician may seek to employ VNG tests to determine whether the condition is attributable to medical disorders such as low blood pressure or from psychological problems such as anxiety. Generally, VNG tests are employed to determine whether or not dizziness or imbalance may be due to inner ear disease.

Brain mapping refers to a comprehensive analysis of brainwave frequencies that make up a patient's raw electroencephalogram. Specifically, brain mapping provides a complex analysis of various brainwave characteristics. Subtle disruptions of cortical electrical activity in the brain may be an early sign, or the only sign, of brain injury or some other brain problem. Brain mapping is thus generally utilized to evaluate for seizures (epilepsy), localized (focal) dysfunction, and generalized dysfunction.

BAEP tests measure the brain wave activity that occurs in response to auditory stimuli and are generally used to diagnose pathological neurological conditions such as multiple sclerosis, acoustic neuromas, and brainstem tumors. Along similar lines, VEP tests—which measure the brain's electrical response to a visual stimulus—generally are used to diagnose pathological neurological conditions.

Specialized training is required to properly perform and interpret all of these types of tests, and—in most cases—the physiatrists and pain management physicians who ordinarily treat no-fault insurance patients will lack the requisite expertise. Furthermore, the types of symptomatology that might warrant these tests generally will not actually be present in a large number of patients being treated at a single, multidisciplinary no-fault clinic.[14] As a result, healthcare providers that consistently submit no-fault insurance billing for these types of tests warrant careful scrutiny, because the tests likely are being performed to create billing opportunities or to create a false basis for a tort claim rather than to treat or otherwise benefit the insured patients.

In determining whether a given form of diagnostic testing is or is not medically necessary, it is important to understand the distinction between tests that can be medically necessary outside of the ordinary no-fault context and tests that generally will be unnecessary in any context. For instance, many tests will be medically useful in some circumstances but simply have no colorable connection to the diagnosis of conditions that commonly arise in the context of an automobile accident. VNG, brain mapping, BAEP, VEP, and SSEP tests fall within this category. Other types of diagnostic tests seem to exist primarily to facilitate various forms of insurance fraud, in that there are limited legitimate peer-reviewed data to support their use, they are not commonly accepted as useful by physicians, and they appear to be marketed for questionable purposes. These tests include v-NCT tests and computerized range-of-motion and muscle tests. Anti-fraud litigators should ensure that their complaints explain why a given test was unnecessary in the context in which it was performed.

One of the most common ways in which healthcare providers defraud insurers through medically unnecessary diagnostic testing is through the provision of duplicative or redundant tests. For example, and as discussed above, computerized range-of-motion and muscle testing almost always will add nothing to the ordinary, manual range-of-motion and muscle testing that is part of virtually every soft tissue

---

[14] For instance, the American Academy of Neurology (AAN)—the country's leading professional society of neurologists—has stated that the clinical usefulness of brain mapping is quite limited. In particular, the AAN does not support the use of brain mapping in the diagnosis of patients with postconcussion syndrome or minor or moderate head injury—the types of head injuries one might expect to commonly see among patients injured in automobile accidents. *See* Marc Nuwer, *Assessment of Digital EEG, Quantitative EEG, and EEG Brain Mapping: Report of the American Academy of Neurology and the American Clinical Neurophysiology Society*, 49 NEUROLOGY 277 (1997).

injury patient's routine examination. NCV and EMG testing can be duplicative of MRIs, which—standing alone or together with a clinical examination—can be sufficient to render a neuropathy diagnosis.

What is more, corrupt healthcare providers will often purport to provide more of a given type of test than is necessary to provide the pertinent diagnosis. For instance, the AANEM's recommended policy states that NCV tests of only a few nerves, together with a two-limb EMG, are all that are required to diagnose most neuropathies.[15] Nonetheless, many fraudulent healthcare providers will bill for four-limb EMG tests and NCV tests of 20 or more nerves because they can submit a separate charge for each limb and each nerve.

In order to detect duplicative, redundant, or otherwise unnecessary diagnostic tests, anti-fraud litigators should review the pertinent insured patient's entire course of treatment. Was the testing at issue performed to provide a diagnosis that the patient already had received through some other form of testing? Was any action taken as a consequence of the test results, or did the patient continue to receive the same treatment in the same manner after the test as before the test? If so, then there probably was no reason for the test to be conducted in the first instance.

Another way to identify medically unnecessary diagnostic testing is to determine whether a given healthcare provider always performs the same tests in the same manner for all, or most, of her patients. This type of automatic or "protocol" testing is suspect because every patient is unique, at least to some extent.[16] It therefore is unlikely that a critical mass of no-fault patients treated by a single diagnostic testing provider—some of whom will be old and some young, some in good condition and some in bad, and some in serious accidents and some not—will all require identical forms of testing. Providers who, for instance, always test the same nerves with NCVs, or the same

[15] *See* American Association of Neuromuscular Electrodiagnostic Medicine, Recommended Policy for Electrodiagnostic Medicine (2004).

[16] For instance, the AANEM's recommended policy makes clear that "EDX studies are individually designed by the electrodiagnostic consultant for each patient. The examination design is dynamic and often changes during the course of the study in response to new information obtained." *See* American Association of Neuromuscular Electrodiagnostic Medicine, Recommended Policy for Electrodiagnostic Medicine (2004). Along similar lines, the American Medical Association's CPT Assistant states that "pre-set protocols automatically testing a large number of nerves are not appropriate." *See* CPT Assistant, September 2006.

limbs and muscles with EMGs, are most likely predicating their tests on their own self-interest rather than on their patients' individual circumstances.

In some cases, fraudulent healthcare practices bill insurers for diagnostic tests that were never actually conducted in the first place. Some such practices carefully create counterfeit test reports that appear on their face to be legitimate. However, many fraudulent providers—in their haste to submit the maximum amount of billing in the shortest possible time—carelessly submit test reports in support of their billing that contain impossible or improbable data. While a handful of instances of medically impossible or improbable test data might be excusable due to ordinary human error, a pattern of such data is harder to explain.

It may be difficult for non-physicians to identify medically impossible or improbable diagnostic testing data. Generally, it will be necessary to hire an expert in the appropriate healthcare discipline to determine whether test data are impossible or improbable. Even so, there are some common settings in which even an attorney should be able to spot questionable data. One such setting is where the data generated by a particular diagnostic test conflicts with other contemporaneous medical information in the patient's file. For instance, computerized range-of-motion test results generated by one provider may state that the patient has severe range-of-motion deficits to the point where the patient would be unable to ambulate normally. However, contemporaneous notes from another healthcare provider treating the patient may state that the patient has normal range of motion or less limited range of motion. Along similar lines, NCV or EMG test results may posit that the patient's neck pain is caused by a cervical radiculopathy, whereas all of the other treatment notes for that patient indicate that the patient complained of lower back pain, not neck pain.

Similarly, diagnostic test results can be shown to be improbable or impossible where they conflict with the details of the underlying accident. For example, if the accident in question was a trivial, low-speed, low-impact fender bender but the physician submits diagnostic test results contending that the minor accident caused serious injury, the diagnostic test results may be fabricated.

In other cases, fraudulent healthcare providers will take data from diagnostic tests conducted on previous patients and use them to create phony test reports for new patients. These cut-and-pasted data often will be medically impossible or improbable. For instance, many commercially available EMG machines, which also are used to conduct NCV tests, have a data storage capacity. In other words, the machines can save the data from each EMG and NCV test that is performed. The EMG and NCV data stored on the machines with respect to one patient can then be used to create phony EMG and NCV test reports for new patients to give the false appearance that the tests were conducted in the first instance. However, NCV test data are specific to each individual patient—it is medically impossible for one patient's NCV test results to be identical to another patient's NCV test results. Accordingly, where a provider submits NCV test results for one patient that are identical to the results for another patient, the results for the second patient are medically impossible and fabricated.

Likewise, fraudulent healthcare providers often fabricate range-of-motion data for their patients to falsely contend that the patients suffer from functional deficits and require continued treatment. In contrast to NCV test results, it is possible for two patients to have identical range-of-motion deficits. However, some providers are careless and routinely contend in their range-of-motion test reports that large numbers of their patients suffer from identical deficits. The larger the number of patients with identical deficits, the more improbable the deficits become, and the likelihood that the provider is simply fabricating the test results increases.

PRACTICE POINTS

Identifying Patterns of Fraudulent Diagnostic Testing

- ✓ Most ordinary soft tissue injuries such as sprains or strains should resolve within, at most, two to three months of treatment.
- ✓ Because fraudulent diagnostic testing can be used as a false basis for the continuation of medically unnecessary treatment, corrupt healthcare providers often will purport to perform the tests at or around the two- to three-month mark.
- ✓ Healthcare providers who order the same kind of diagnostic tests for all or most of their patients after providing two to three months of treatment to the patients may be using the tests as a false basis to provide continued, medically unnecessary treatment.

5. Medically Unnecessary Pain Management Services

The ultimate goal of most no-fault insurance fraud rings is to provide as many pain management services as possible and—preferably—for the services to be as expensive as possible. This, in turn, typically requires either that the patient be diagnosed with something more serious than a garden-variety soft tissue injury such as a sprain or strain or that the patient continues to suffer from the lingering effects of a sprain or strain beyond the time in which such injuries ordinarily would resolve. These diagnostic hurdles usually will not be too difficult to surmount considering that a corrupt pain management provider either can generate false diagnoses himself or collude with other healthcare providers to supply the requisite diagnoses. Indeed, and as discussed above, it increasingly is common for several corrupt healthcare providers to operate together under the auspices of a single multidisciplinary clinic, often under the control of unlicensed individuals and entities.

Broadly speaking, there are two main categories of pain management services that recur in the no-fault insurance context: "Conservative" pain management treatments, such as chiropractic, physical therapy, or acupuncture treatments, and "interventional" pain management treatments, which can run the gamut from various types of office-based injections to surgeries performed under general anesthesia. We will discuss them in turn.

Conservative treatment fraud is a volume business because conservative treatments such as chiropractic, physical therapy, and acupuncture services are usually not reimbursable at high rates. As a result, the goal of any conservative treatment fraud scheme is generally to treat as many patients as possible each day and for each patient's course of treatment to last as long as possible. Through this approach, a fraudulent chiropractor, acupuncturist, or physical therapist can, over time, submit a large number of charges for a large number of patients and thereby bill a considerable amount even if the individual charges are relatively small.

In order for this type of approach to work, however, the chiropractor, acupuncturist, or physical therapist must have some arrangement with a physician who is prepared to falsely contend that the pertinent patients suffer from something more serious than a sprain or strain. Absent some more serious diagnosis, insurers will usually stop paying for conservative soft tissue injury treatment after a certain point, and judges and arbitrators tend to support those decisions. It is this dynamic that has fueled the growth of corrupt multidisciplinary clinics, because it is easier for a chiropractor, acupuncturist, or physical therapist to get a phony diagnosis to support continued conservative treatments if the physician rendering the diagnosis works across the hall. The physician likewise benefits, because she not only obtains the opportunity to bill for diagnostic tests, but also eventually can provide and bill for more expensive interventional treatments.

It can be notoriously difficult to prove a conservative treatment fraud scheme. As the term suggests, conservative treatments such as chiropractic, physical therapy, and acupuncture often do not look unnecessary on their face. Chiropractors, physical therapists, acupuncturists, and other conservative treatment providers can therefore generally contend that their services are relevant and necessary in the context of soft tissue injuries arising from automobile accidents. What is more, anti-fraud litigators usually will be hard-pressed to show otherwise—absent evidence of some other type of fraud such as an illegal kickback or corporate structure scheme.

Although it is very difficult to prove a conservative treatment fraud scheme, it is fairly easy to identify such schemes. Specifically, anti-fraud litigators should identify healthcare providers who routinely purport to provide more than three months of conservative treatment, such as chiropractic manipulation, acupuncture, and physical therapy, to patients based on garden-variety soft tissue injuries such as sprains or strains. The key is to identify a pattern of such treatments because while long-term conservative treatment may occasionally be warranted in the relatively rare cases in which a soft tissue injury causes chronic pain, most patients who suffer from soft tissue injuries such as sprains or strains will not experience chronic pain and will not require any type of long-term care, conservative or otherwise.

Because it is difficult to prove a conservative treatment fraud scheme, anti-fraud litigators confronted with such a scheme should try to enlarge the scope of their case. For instance, after identifying healthcare practices that anomalously provide long-term conservative treatment to most of their patients, anti-fraud litigators can dig deeper to see whether the practices exhibit other badges of fraud and whether other potential defendants are involved in the schemes. As discussed above, it is generally difficult to justify continued conservative treatment of an ordinary soft tissue injury once a month or two has elapsed after the underlying accident. As a result, corrupt conservative treatment providers are often engaged in kickback relationships with diagnostic testing providers, such as neurologists. In exchange for medically unnecessary referrals or other compensation from the conservative treatment providers, these diagnostic testing providers will falsely diagnose patients with neuropathies or other chronic conditions in order to provide a phony rationale for longer-term treatment.

Anti-fraud litigators should therefore inspect the relationships between suspicious conservative treatment providers and the diagnostic testing providers that enable them. For instance, does a chiropractor always refer patients to the same neurologist for EDX testing? Does the neurologist operate from the chiropractor's offices? At the conclusion of the diagnostic testing, does the neurologist always report that every patient suffers from a neuropathy or some other condition that would warrant continued, long-term conservative treatment? Subsequent to the diagnosis, does either the chiropractor or the neurologist refer the patient for some different type of treatment, or is the diagnosis simply used as a basis to continue the conservative treatment that hitherto failed to remediate the patient's symptoms? If the answer to any of these questions is "yes," then it may be worthwhile to proceed on the basis of an illegal kickback relationship rather than solely on the basis of medically unnecessary conservative treatment.

In contrast to conservative treatment, interventional treatment such as injections and surgeries is typically not a volume business with respect to any individual insured patient. Interventional treatments generally entail a degree of risk to the patient that makes it difficult for providers to justify their repetitive use in treating a single patient. Such treatments also tend to be substantially more expensive than conservative treatments such as chiropractic or acupuncture, which means that insurers are more likely to scrutinize and deny the resulting claims. What is more, interventional treatments are intended to remediate a patient's pain for an extended period of time or to eliminate it altogether at one fell swoop. Consequently, it is difficult to justify providing interventional treatments to an individual patient over and over again within a short period of time.

With that in mind, the goal of an interventional treatment fraud scheme usually is to create the false impression that less-expensive, more-conservative treatments have failed to resolve the patient's pain complaints and that something more drastic and expensive is required. As a result, interventional treatment fraud usually occurs after the patient has been receiving conservative treatment for a period of at least several months.

In some cases, the conservative treatment provider is also the interventional treatment provider. For instance, a physiatrist may provide more conservative physical therapy treatments to an insured patient for several months and then provide epidural injections to the patient based on a contention that the physical therapy did not fully resolve the patient's pain complaints. More commonly, however, the interventional treatment provider purports to maintain a separate practice from the conservative treatment provider to foster the illusion that the decision to move from conservative to interventional treatment is based on an independent, arm's-length medical judgment. In such cases, there often will be some sort of kickback or referral-fee arrangement between the conservative treatment provider and the interventional treatment provider.

Many of the means of identifying interventional treatment fraud will require the services of an expert consultant. As a practical matter, most anti-fraud litigators and insurance company SIU investigators lack the specialized medical knowledge necessary to determine whether a particular type of interventional treatment was medically necessary and performed in an appropriate manner. Even so, there are several means by which even the lay observer can recognize suspicious patterns of interventional treatment. Once such a pattern is identified, anti-fraud litigators often will have sufficient facts at their disposal to allege a fraudulent scheme and to shift the burden to the treatment provider to explain how her treatments were legitimate.

One of the best ways to spot interventional treatment fraud is by identifying a pattern in which interventional treatments are provided before the patients have failed any legitimate course of conservative treatment. As set forth above, the majority of garden-variety soft tissue injuries such as sprains or strains resolve on their own after a period of conservative treatment or even no treatment at all. What is more, interventional treatment will typically involve a degree of risk for the patient that is absent with more conservative forms of treatment.

As a result, the standard of care for soft tissue injury patients generally requires that conservative treatments be tried first and that more invasive and risky interventional treatments be deferred unless and until the patient's symptoms fail to respond to the conservative treatment modalities.[17] In the authors' experience, different medical experts will provide somewhat different opinions as to how long conservative treatments should be attempted before moving on interventional forms of treatment. However, as a general rule, patients with soft tissue injuries should receive at least two or three months of conservative treatment in advance of any determination that the conservative treatment is not working and more interventional forms of treatment are required.

With that in mind, insurer SIU investigators and anti-fraud litigators should examine the universe of claims that have been submitted by a suspect provider. The claims submissions should, among other things, contain the dates on which each of the insured patients were involved in their respective accidents, the dates on which the patients received any conservative treatments, the dates on which the patients were first referred to interventional treatment providers, and the dates on which the patients first received some form of interventional treatment.

In some cases, these records will show that the patients did not receive any real conservative treatment prior to the interventional treatment, which—as noted above—is not the standard of care. In other cases, the records will disclose a pattern of referrals for interventional treatment within two or three months after the patients' underlying accidents. This, in turn, would call into question whether the patients were actually given the opportunity to benefit from the conservative treatment prior to the commencement of riskier interventional treatments.

In still other instances, the records will show that the patients were steadily improving through the conservative treatment but nonetheless were referred for interventional treatment for unclear or inchoate reasons. Obviously, if conservative treatment is working, a sudden and poorly explained referral for more expensive and invasive interventional treatment will be subject to challenge—and a pattern of such sudden and poorly explained referrals is subject to an even more pointed challenge.

Anti-fraud investigators and litigators also should look at the relationships between and among the conservative treatment providers—who typically make the referrals resulting in interventional

---

[17] Chou, *supra* note 7; New York State Workers' Compensation Board, *supra* note 7; National Collaborating Centre for Primary Care, *supra* note 7.

treatment—and the interventional treatment providers who receive the referrals. If they are the same person, or are within the same multidisciplinary practice, then there may be an illegal self-referral issue.[18] If they work from the same office, then there may be an unlawful kickback or referral-fee arrangement. The likelihood of a kickback or referral-fee arrangement increases if the interventional treatment provider maintains his own offices elsewhere but nonetheless makes occasional "house calls" to the referring provider's offices to receive the referrals.

Even assuming that a group of patients require some form of interventional treatment, both the treatments and the manner in which they are provided should vary from patient to patient. It is highly improbable that all, or even most, patients that are treated by a single provider will require the same types of interventional treatments, let alone the same types of interventional treatments provided in the same or a substantially similar sequence.

For example, it would be highly suspicious if a large number of patients treated by an individual provider received identical lumbar epidural injections three months after their accidents, identical trigger point injections four months after their accidents, and so forth. Anti-fraud litigators and insurer SIU investigators can identify this type of fraud fairly quickly by cross-referencing a pattern of identical interventional treatments among a group of patients with the types of complaints that the patients purportedly had and the circumstances of the patients' underlying accidents. If there was significant diversity among the circumstances of the patients' accidents and their resulting complaints yet the patients received substantially identical interventional treatments, it is a good indication that the treatments were provided on a protocol basis without regard for medical necessity.

---

[18] For example, some no-fault states make it illegal in many circumstances for a healthcare provider to refer a patient for interventional or other forms of services to a practice in which the provider has a financial interest. *See*, e.g., N.J.S.A. 45:9-22.5 (generally making it unlawful for a practitioner to "refer a patient or direct an employee of the practitioner to refer a patient to a health care service in which the practitioner, or the practitioner's immediate family, or the practitioner in combination with the practitioner's immediate family has a significant beneficial interest. . . ."); N.Y. PUB. HEALTH LAW § 238-d (generally making it unlawful for a practitioner to make a referral to a healthcare provider in which the referring practitioner has an ownership interest, except upon disclosure of the ownership interest to the patient); FLA. STAT. § 456.052 (same).

Furthermore, pain management injections and similar types of interventional treatments should generally not be provided to an individual patient in close temporal proximity to one another. Rather, to the extent that interventional treatments such as pain management injections are warranted in the first instance, they should not be administered more than once every two months or more than six times in any given year.[19] This is because (i) properly administered interventional treatments should provide pain relief lasting for at least two months and (ii) if a patient's pain is not relieved through the interventional treatment, the pain may be caused by something other than what the interventional treatment was intended to remediate, and the perpetuating factors of the pain must be identified and managed.

As a result, where an interventional treatment provider administers a large number of pain management injections within a short period of time, it begs the questions, Why did the previous rounds of injections fail to work, and why—if the previous rounds of injections failed to work—is the provider administering the same failed treatment over and over again? Indeed, not only does the repeated administration of failed treatments call into question the medical necessity of the treatment, it also increases the risks attendant to interventional treatment because it suggests that the patient's pain is caused by some perpetuating factor that is not being properly identified or addressed.

Practice Points

Another Way to Identify Suspicious Pain Management Injections

✓ In most cases, it will be inappropriate to provide multiple varieties of pain management injections to a patient in a single sitting—for example, epidural injections provided at the same time as facet injections or trigger point injections at the same time as transforaminal injections.

[19] *See*, e.g., Laxmaiah Manchikanti, et al. *Interventional Techniques in the Management of Chronic Pain: Part 2.0.* 4 Pain Physician. 24 (2001).

- ✓ This is because, if the patient reports some pain relief following the injections, the physician will not know which of the different types of injections was responsible for the improvement.
- ✓ Even so, corrupt healthcare providers often will purport to provide multiple varieties of pain management injections to a patient in a single sitting in order to maximize their fraudulent billing.
- ✓ Therefore, in addition to looking for *similar* types of pain management injections provided in close temporal proximity to one another, anti-fraud litigators should look for *different* types of pain management injections that are provided to single patients on the same dates of service.

6. Other Common Types of Medically Unnecessary Goods and Services—Durable Medical Equipment, Dentistry, and Psychology

Most no-fault insurance fraud rings stick to billing for the tried and true services, such as "conservative" chiropractic, physical therapy, acupuncture treatments, diagnostic testing like EMG and NCV tests, and—eventually—more expensive interventional pain management treatments such as pain management injections. They do so because these types of services, however medically unnecessary and fraudulent they may be in practice, arguably "make sense" in the context of automobile accidents.

Judges and arbitrators, for example, may accept the premise that a patient who was injured in a minor automobile accident would benefit from chiropractic treatment or an epidural injection. By contrast, it often will be more difficult to justify expensive dental services or long-term psychological treatment for the victim of an automobile accident that can be shown to be minor or trivial in nature. Similarly, it can be difficult to demonstrate that expensive durable medical equipment is medically necessary for the victim of a minor accident, especially if the durable medical equipment is—as often is the case—prescribed before the patient has tried or failed any course of conservative treatment. Nonetheless, these types of goods and services do occasionally feature in no-fault insurance anti-fraud litigation, so it is worthwhile to discuss the manner in which they commonly are used to perpetrate fraud.

(i) Durable Medical Equipment

As the term suggests, "durable medical equipment" generally consists of medical items that can withstand repeated use and which are intended to be used for medical purposes by patients outside of their doctors' offices. This type of material includes such things as cervical collars or pillows, infrared heat lamps, lumbar cushions, transcutaneous electrical nerve stimulators, heating pads, and wrist braces. Durable medical equipment schemes are attractive to no-fault insurance fraud rings because—unlike most other healthcare services providers—durable medical equipment suppliers typically do not have to be licensed.

While some forms of durable medical equipment can be quite expensive, most legitimate durable medical equipment is both inexpensive and—arguably—medically warranted for the treatment of basic soft tissue injuries such as sprains and sprains. Because durable medical equipment is often medically necessary and inexpensive, the most common type of no-fault insurance fraud related to durable medical equipment involves misrepresentations about the wholesale cost of the durable medical equipment or the reasonable and customary charges for the durable medical equipment in the geographical location in question. This is because states that permit no-fault billing for durable medical equipment commonly impose limits on the amount that may be charged for individual items of such equipment.

In New York, for example, the maximum permissible charge for durable medical equipment is the fee payable for such equipment under the New York State Medicaid program.[20] If the New York State Medicaid program has not established a fee payable for the specific item, then the fee payable has to be the lesser of either the acquisition cost (i.e., the line item cost from a manufacturer or wholesaler net of any rebates; discounts or other valuable considerations; mailing, shipping, handling, and insurance costs; and any sales tax) to the provider plus 50 percent or the usual and customary price charged to the general public.[21] Similarly, New Jersey has promulgated a fee schedule that governs no-fault reimbursement for many common varieties of durable medical equipment. To the extent that a given

[20] *See* 11 N.Y.C.R.R. (Appendix 17-C, Part F(a), effective Oct. 6, 2004).

[21] *Id.*

type of equipment is not covered under the fee schedule, then reimbursement is limited to a reasonable amount, as determined by reference to various factors tied to geographic location and national fee databases.[22]

Thus, in the context of durable medical equipment, no-fault insurance fraud usually involves misrepresentations regarding the durable medical equipment supplier's wholesale acquisition cost for the equipment in question. If a corrupt durable medical equipment can falsely contend that it paid a high wholesale price for durable medical equipment that it supplied to an insured, that supplier will be in a good position to falsely contend that its subsequent, exorbitant retail charges to the insurer are legitimate.

As a result, one of the most common types of durable medical equipment fraud involves a durable medical equipment retailer that is in league with a corrupt wholesaler. The corrupt wholesaler provides phony, inflated wholesale "invoices" to the retailer, who then uses them to provide a subsequent, false justification for its inflated downstream charges to the insurer. In the more sophisticated schemes, the retailer actually will issue a check to the wholesaler in payment of the inflated wholesale invoice, and the wholesaler then will cash the check and rebate a substantial portion of the "payment" to the retailer. Then, the cancelled check can be produced in subsequent no-fault collections proceedings as "evidence" that the retailer actually paid the inflated wholesale invoice despite the fact that a large portion of the putative wholesale "cost" of the durable medical equipment was rebated to the retailer.

In other cases, the durable medical equipment retailer may not use a wholesaler at all. Rather, the retailer itself will procure cheap durable medical equipment from factories in countries with inexpensive manufacturing and will then make false statements regarding its acquisition costs on the assumption that they will be difficult for the insurer to disprove.

Oftentimes, corrupt durable medical equipment suppliers are in league with the physicians or chiropractors who prescribe the durable medical equipment, and they kick back a portion of the proceeds of the durable medical equipment to the prescribing physicians or chiropractors.

---

[22] *See* N.J.A.C. 11:3-29.4.

The most common way to identify no-fault insurance fraud schemes involving durable medical equipment is by examining the charges being submitted for the equipment and contrasting those charges with publicly available information regarding charges for the same or similar items. Is a supplier billing $150 for an ordinary foam cervical collar that is available online for $10? If so, that supplier is likely to be misrepresenting either its acquisition cost for the collar or the actual usual and customary charge for such collars within the pertinent geographic area. Another way to identify durable medical equipment fraud is by examining links between the prescribing physician or chiropractor and the durable medical equipment supplier. Do the patients who are treated by the prescribing physician always seem to fill their prescriptions with a single durable medical equipment supplier, and are that supplier's rates far higher than what is being charged by other suppliers within the same area? If so, it is at least some indication that a kickback scheme is afoot and that a portion of the inflated charges are being routed to the physician as consideration for his prescriptions.

(ii) Dentistry

No-fault insurance fraud schemes involving billing for medically unnecessary or illusory dental services are comparatively rare. The main reason for this is that common sense suggests that a seat-belted passenger who is in a minor accident where the airbags in the vehicle do not deploy is unlikely to suffer any legitimate dental injuries. By extension, a corrupt dentist may have difficulty persuading a court or arbitrator in a no-fault collections proceeding that the insured actually could have suffered injuries requiring dental treatment.

Moreover, most legitimate dental injuries will be objectively verifiable. If an insured patient fractures her jaw in an accident, there probably will be an x-ray showing the fracture. Even in the unlikely event that a patient suffers a sprained or strained jaw in an accident, there is likely to be some documentation that legitimately will show the sprain or strain. For instance, when a patient visits the hospital complaining of a sprained back, the attending physician will usually have to rely on the patient's say-so regarding the pain and its attendant consequences. By contrast, a patient with a sprained jaw is more likely to manifest visible signs of the injury, such as an inability to speak, prominent swelling, and so on.

As a result, most no-fault fraud schemes involving dentistry seem to rely on objectively unverifiable—and phony—"diagnoses" of temporomandibular joint (or TMJ) disorder. TMJ disorders are a group of conditions that affect the temporomandibular joint and the muscles that control chewing. Typically, a corrupt dentist will contend that his patient's head was shaken around in an accident, and that—as a result—she suffered some injury to her TMJ that took a while to manifest itself and then caused worsening symptoms over time. This, in turn, provides a false explanation as to (i) how a patient who did not actually strike her head on the vehicle or airbag could have suffered any injury to her mouth or jaw and (ii) why the contemporaneous police report and hospital records make no reference to any injury to the patient's mouth or jaw.

While fraudulent dentists can be quite ingenious in explaining how minor accidents caused their patients to suffer from delayed-onset TMJ disorder requiring months of expensive dental treatment, such contentions are contravened by the legitimate literature.

For example, the National Institute of Dental and Craniofacial Research at the National Institutes of Health has stated that "[F]or most people, pain in the area of the jaw joint or muscles is not a signal that a serious problem is developing. Generally, discomfort from [TMJ disorder] is occasional and temporary, often occurring in cycles. The pain eventually goes away with little or no treatment."[23] The American Association for Dental Research, a not-for-profit professional organization with more than 3,700 members with a mission to advance research and increase knowledge for the improvement of oral health, likewise strongly recommends that treatment of TMD initially should be based on the use of conservative, reversible, and evidence-based therapeutic modalities, because many of the conservative modalities have proven to be at least as effective in providing symptomatic relief as most forms of invasive treatment. Because those modalities do not produce irreversible changes, they present much less risk of producing harm.[24]

---

[23] *See* National Institute of Dental and Craniofacial Research, TMJ Disorders, (March 6, 2017), https://www.nidcr.nih.gov/oralhealth/topics/tmj/tmjdisorders.htm.

[24] *See* American Association for Dental Research, Science Policy, Temporomandibular Disorders (TMD) (March 6, 2017), http://www.iadr.org/i4a/pages/index.cfm?pageid=3465#TMD.

Against this backdrop, TMJ disorder "treatment" fraud—the most common type of dental no-fault fraud—may be easy to spot. First, insurers should identify any dentists who routinely submit no-fault insurance billing. Second, insurers should determine whether these dentists are diagnosing and treating objectively verifiable injuries—such as fractures—or whether these dentists are purporting to diagnose and treat more inchoate conditions such as TMJ disorders. Third, if the dentists are purporting to treat difficult-to-verify conditions such as TMJ disorders, it is worthwhile to look at the circumstances of the underlying accidents. Were the accidents generally minor fender benders, in which the patients wore their seatbelts and the airbags in their vehicles did not deploy? If so, it is some indication that the patients did not actually suffer any injuries to their faces, mouths, or jaws—especially if, as often is the case, the patients did not report any such injuries to the police at the scenes of the accidents. Fourth, look at the contemporaneous hospital records and records of other healthcare providers who treated the patients. Did they generally fail to make any reference to the fact that the patients injured their mouths or jaws in the underlying accidents? If so, it is a good indication that any resulting TMJ disorder "diagnoses" are phony and that any resulting TMJ disorder "treatment" is medically unnecessary and fraudulent.

(iii) Psychology and Psychiatry

Like dentistry, ordinarily one would not expect to see much billing for psychology or psychiatry services in the context of automobile accidents. While, of course, a serious accident can cause a patient to suffer from mental health issues, it is unlikely that more minor accidents actually will cause patients to incur any genuine psychological harm. By extension, psychologists or psychiatrists who routinely purport to diagnose patients with mental health problems arising from relatively minor automobile accidents are inherently suspicious.

Nonetheless, some corrupt psychologists or psychiatrists will routinely purport to diagnose patients with adjustment disorders or—in the more egregious cases—posttraumatic stress disorder as the result of minor accidents. Then, they will use these phony "diagnoses" as a false basis to bill insurers for months of psychotherapy and psychological testing.

As with billing for medically unnecessary dental services, the best way to identify fraudulent billing for medically unnecessary psychological services is to start by identifying psychologists or psychiatrists who routinely submit no-fault insurance billing. Then, insurers and anti-fraud litigators should look at the circumstances of the underlying accidents. If the accidents were, for the most part, trivial fender benders, common sense suggests that the accidents did not and could not have caused the patients to actually experience any legitimate mental health issues, much less any adjustment disorders or posttraumatic stress disorders. Similarly, it is important to review any hospital records or records from other healthcare providers who treated the patients contemporaneously with the psychologists or psychiatrists. Do these records indicate that the patients presented without any apparent psychological issues? If so, it is a good indication that any adjustment disorder or posttraumatic stress disorder "diagnoses" are phony and that any subsequent psychological or psychiatric "treatment" is medically unnecessary.

In this respect, insurers and anti-fraud litigators should be aware of the fact that corrupt psychologists and psychiatrists are often in league with other fraudulent healthcare providers. As a result, insurers and anti-fraud litigators may find it best to discount treatment reports from the healthcare providers who may have referred patients to the psychologists and psychiatrists as well as any healthcare providers who work with the psychologists and psychiatrists in the same multidisciplinary practice. In some cases, treatment reports from healthcare providers that are in the same practice as the psychologists and psychiatrists, or which have longstanding referral relationships with them, may themselves contain fraudulent and inaccurate information regarding the patients' psychiatric conditions. As always, records of hospital treatment and treatment from independent healthcare providers will provide the most disinterested, and therefore reliable, account of the patients' true mental state.

7. Staged Accidents and Medical Necessity

As previously discussed, some of the more entrepreneurial no-fault insurance fraud rings go beyond merely paying kickbacks or other consideration in exchange for patient referrals and actually stage phony accidents in order to bill for the resulting healthcare services. Indeed, the reported cases disclose many such schemes—though they generally are criminal cases.[25] These types of "staged loss" frauds can be difficult to plead and prove given their conspiratorial nature and the limited discovery tools available to civil litigants as opposed to law enforcement.

Nonetheless, in the relatively rare cases in which it is possible to colorably allege a staged loss ring, the existence of such a scheme will be powerful evidence that any healthcare services provided to the participants in the scheme were medically unnecessary. Therefore, it is worthwhile to briefly discuss the most common indications that a staged loss scheme is afoot.

If patients are inventory in a no-fault insurance fraud scheme, then every seat in a vehicle involved in a staged loss is like a shelf in a warehouse. By extension, every empty seat means a missed billing opportunity. Therefore, the ringleaders of staged accident schemes typically will ensure that every seat in every vehicle involved in an "accident" is full. While, of course, two or more fully occupied vehicles is not inherently suspicious, SIU investigators and anti-fraud litigators should consider whether the occupants of any one of the vehicles have any relationship to each other that would explain why they all were in the vehicle together at the same time. Are they related? Is there any record of them knowing one another prior to the accident? Where were they going together? If the vehicle's occupants have any difficulty answering these types of questions in a consistent and plausible manner, it is some evidence that they were packed into the car in order to stage a loss and generate fraudulent no-fault insurance claims.

Similarly, if the occupants of one of the vehicles involved in a suspicious accident have some connection to the occupants of another of the vehicles involved in the accident, it could be evidence of a staged accident. For example, is an occupant of one vehicle related to the occupant of another? Do the occupants of one vehicle live in the

---

[25] *See*, e.g., United States v. Delgado, 285 Fed. Appx. 725 (11th Cir. 2008) (affirming the conviction and sentence with respect to the criminal defendant who participated in a staged loss no-fault insurance fraud scheme); United States v. Lucien, 347 F.3d 45 (2d Cir. 2003) (same); Commonwealth v. Shuman, 391 Mass. 345 (Mass. 1984) (affirming a conviction with respect to a criminal defendant who participated in a staged loss no-fault insurance fraud scheme); Allstate Ins. Co. v. Lopez, 325 N.J. Super. 268 (N.J. Law Div. 1999) (granting a partial summary judgment to a plaintiff-insurer in a case involving an automobile accident fraud ring where the defendants staged accidents and filed false claims).

same apartment building as the occupants of another? If so, how did they happen to be involved in the same collision? While, certainly, a rear-end collision between two cars containing family members is explainable—for instance, the occupants of one car may have been following the other car to church—an inadequate explanation will raise questions as to whether the accident was genuine.

Another way to identify staged loss rings is to see where those involved in an accident seek treatment. If two automobiles are involved in an accident, each of the automobiles contains five passengers, and all 10 of the passengers thereafter seek treatment from the same multidisciplinary clinic, it is a good indication that there is something unsavory about the accident. Why, for instance, would 10 ostensibly distinct passengers in two supposedly unrelated vehicles wind up seeking treatment from the same healthcare provider? Chances are, the participants in the accident will not have an especially good explanation for this sort of "coincidence."

In addition, staged accidents necessarily cause damage to the involved vehicles. Because no-fault insurance fraud rings are concerned with making a profit, they will rarely use new or well-maintained older vehicles when orchestrating a staged accident. What is more, in many cases they will obtain a used or decrepit vehicle specifically for the purpose of staging an accident and will purchase automobile insurance immediately prior to the accident. Consequently, in addition to examining the relationships between those involved in the accident, SIU investigators and anti-fraud litigators should look at the vehicles and policies involved to see whether there is any indication that they were purchased specifically to stage a loss.[26]

Staged loss fraud is a broad and multifaceted topic that could fill an entire—albeit small—book. While it is important to note the role that staged losses play in the overall no-fault insurance fraud problem, a full discussion of staged loss fraud is, by necessity, beyond the scope of this book.

---

[26] Most commonly, this will involve policies purchased immediately, or almost immediately, prior to the putative "accident," especially where the policies on all of the involved vehicles were purchased just prior to the "accident." Notably, many states with staged loss problems appear to have those problems, at least in part, because they do not permit insurers to retroactively cancel insurance policies, even where it appears that the policies were purchased specifically for the purpose of staging an accident.

4

Identifying Fraud Involving Illusory Services

Some fraudulent healthcare providers go beyond merely billing for medically unnecessary services and instead simply bill for illusory services that never were provided in the first instance. This type of billing takes two main forms: In some cases, no service was provided at all to support the charges, whereas in other cases some less expensive form of service actually was provided, yet the practitioner falsely claims that she provided a more expensive service.

The most obvious way to identify treatments that never were provided in the first instance is to speak with the pertinent patients. In a perfect world, the patients' memories will be flawless, their hearts will be in the right place, and their communications skills will be outstanding. In the real world, however, the types of people who receive treatment from no-fault insurance fraud rings often lack these exemplary qualities. To the contrary, they tend to be motivated by self-interest and represented by personal injury attorneys who may have referred them to the fraudulent healthcare providers in the first instance to build support for a tort claim.

As a result, while SIU investigators and anti-fraud litigators occasionally may hit upon an exceptionally forthright patient-witness, more commonly they will have to identify illusory treatments through other means.

A. Impossible or Improbable Day Scenarios

Perhaps the best way to identify completely illusory treatments is by identifying patterns in which an individual healthcare practitioner purports to provide an impossible or improbable number of treatments on individual dates of service. In this context, and as the term suggests, an impossible day scenario occurs when a practitioner bills for more than 24 hours' worth of services on a single day. By contrast, an improbable day scenario occurs where a practitioner, in a single day, bills for an amount of services that could in theory have been performed but is unlikely to have actually been performed. There is room for debate as to how many hours of services in a single day constitutes an improbable day. However, it seems fair to say that an individual healthcare practitioner who consistently bills for more than 15 hours of services per day is billing an improbable number of services and that at least some of the services are likely to be illusory.

Insurer SIU investigators and anti-fraud litigators can identify impossible and improbable day scenarios through a straightforward process. First, review the claims data for the suspect practitioner to determine whether the practitioner regularly bills for what appears to be a high volume of services each day. Then, determine whether the types of services that are being billed have any time component attached to them. Healthcare providers, including those who treat no-fault insurance patients, generally must bill for their services using the current procedural terminology (CPT) codes promulgated by the American Medical Association, with each type of service correlating to an individual CPT code. Some CPT codes, such as the CPT codes attendant to patient examinations, some forms of physical therapy, and some forms of diagnostic testing, have a time component attached to them.[1] In other words, the use of these CPT codes represents that the healthcare provider spent a specific amount of time performing the service.

[1] For example, pursuant to the American Medical Association, the use of CPT code 99204 to bill for an initial patient examination typically requires that a physician spend 45 minutes of face-to-face time with the patient or the patient's family in the context of the examination. Along similar lines, pursuant to the American Medical Association, the use of CPT code 97750 to bill for a physical performance test usually requires that the test took at least 15 minutes to perform.

If a healthcare practitioner primarily bills for CPT codes that have a time component attached to them, it will be fairly easy to determine whether the provider is billing for impossible or improbable days—all that needs to be done is to add up the number of individual CPT codes the practitioner bills in a single day and multiply it by the time components applicable to those codes.

However, most CPT codes and, by extension, some services do not have any particular time component attached to them. As a result, it will be necessary to get an expert opinion as to how long a given type of service should take to perform. This is a fairly simple type of opinion to obtain and usually should not require anything more than a telephone call to a practitioner who is experienced in the pertinent field.

For example, most neurologists will be able to quickly state how long various types of EDX testing should take to perform. Along similar lines, most physiatrists or pain management specialists will be in a position to say how long different sorts of interventional pain management injections should take to perform and so forth. Once an SIU investigator or anti-fraud litigator has this information in hand, she can quickly tally up how long it should have taken the practitioner in question to perform the pertinent services. If the time it would have taken to perform the services billed in a single day appears to exceed the amount of time in which the practitioner reasonably could have been expected to work in a single day, the practitioner is likely to be billing for fictitious services.

Another important factor to consider in identifying impossible or improbable day scenarios is the locations at which the practitioners purport to provide the services. If the practitioner is operating from multiple locations in a single day, then the travel time between these locations must be factored into the equation. Since most no-fault insurance billing lists the location at which the underlying treatment was provided, it should be easy to determine whether a practitioner is operating on an itinerant basis on any given day and easy to calculate how long it would have taken the practitioner to move from one location to the next in the context of any given day. In some cases, the practitioner may appear to be working a plausible number of hours each day—for example, if all of the services provided in an individual day, taken together, would not require more than 12 hours to perform. However, if the services were provided at three separate locations and if the locations were an hour apart from one another, then the workday starts to look improbable.

PRACTICE POINTS

Impossible or Improbable Days

- ✓ In determining whether an individual healthcare provider is billing for an improbable or impossible number of services on a single date, it is important to look at every practice or entity through which the provider submits his billing—not just the entity that is the subject of the investigation.
- ✓ Many fraudulent healthcare providers—especially electrodiagnostic testing providers—work for multiple practices or entities at the same time.
- ✓ As a result, an individual healthcare provider's billing through any one practice or entity may not give the complete picture of the total amount of billing that the provider is submitting on individual dates of service.

Finally, in considering whether a provider is billing for an impossible or improbable number of hours per day, it is important to take into account the market share of the insurer receiving the suspicious billing. Consider the example discussed above, in which an insurer has only 25 percent of the market in a given state, yet routinely receives billing for five or six hours of healthcare services per day from a single chiropractor in that state. In light of the insurer's market share, it is reasonable to expect that whatever billing that insurer receives from the chiropractor will constitute about 25 percent of the chiropractor's overall billing. As a result, a chiropractor who bills five or six hours of services per day to an insurer with a 25 percent market share is likely to be simultaneously billing a substantial amount of services to the insurers who cover the other 75 percent of the market. In that context, the five or six hours per day that the chiropractor is billing to the insurer with the 25 percent market share starts to look suspiciously improbable, if not impossible.

B. DUPLICATED OR CLONED TREATMENT REPORTS

Another excellent way to identify illusory treatment is to identify duplicated or cloned treatment reports. Every patient is, to some extent, unique, and therefore the treatment notes with respect to any individual patient should, to some material extent, also be unique.

As a result, treatment notes that use identical language to describe disparate patients' complaints, contain identical diagnostic testing "results," or prescribe an identical course of treatment for differently situated patients are an indication that the underlying examinations or diagnostic testing may never have been performed in the first instance.

In this context, it is important to emphasize that even the most brazenly fraudulent providers will likely include at least some distinct language in their treatment reports. For example, most examination notes will have to describe the patient's physical appearance and provide at least some detail as to the circumstances of the underlying accident. These types of descriptors are unlikely to be cut-and-pasted from one patient's treatment notes to another's because that level of duplication would make the fraud too apparent. Rather, where duplicated or cloned treatment reports are used in furtherance of a no-fault insurance fraud scheme, the duplication usually occurs in the sections of the treatment notes that identify the patients' purported complaints, set forth the results of the patients' examinations (including any diagnostic testing results), and prescribe some sort of course of continued treatment for the patients. This is because the purpose of any no-fault insurance fraud scheme is usually to provide either substantially identical, long-term, medically unnecessary conservative treatment; to provide substantially identical, medically unnecessary, and highly expensive interventional treatment; or both.

As a result, the sections of the treatment notes dealing with patient complaints, symptoms, diagnoses, and recommendations must be substantially identical, because any significant disparities among them would make it difficult to justify an identical, and identically expensive, course of treatment for each patient.

C. Upcoding, Unbundling, and Misrepresentations as to the Nature or Extent of Healthcare Services

The second type of illusory service fraud involves billing for some form of more expensive service, when in actuality a less expensive service was provided. This type of fraud commonly is referred to as "upcoding." As noted above, healthcare providers generally bill for their services using CPT codes promulgated by the American Medical Association, with each type of service corresponding to a given CPT code. When a healthcare provider upcodes a service, he bills for a less expensive type of service using a CPT code that is applicable to a more expensive type of service and therefore misrepresents the type of service that actually was provided.

One variation on upcoding is a practice known as "unbundling," or fragmented billing. Unbundling involves artificially separating or partitioning what inherently is a single service covered by a single CPT code into several services, which then are billed separately using more than one CPT code in order to increase the amount of the billing.

In addition to promulgating the CPT codes themselves, the AMA also publishes the CPT Assistant, which contains guidelines as to the proper use of the various CPT codes. Along similar lines, CMS has developed the National Correct Coding Initiative (NCCI), which promotes national correct coding methodologies to prevent improper coding from leading to inappropriate payment. In some states, such as New Jersey and New York, the AMA's CPT Assistant and/or the CMS NCCI are incorporated by reference into the no-fault reimbursement regimes.[2] However, even in states that have not explicitly incorporated the CPT Assistant or the NCCI into their no-fault reimbursement regimes, the CPT Assistant and NCCI still set the standard for the interpretation and proper use of the various CPT codes. In this context, the NCCI generally prohibits upcoding and unbundling, inasmuch as they misrepresent the type of service that actually was provided.[3] The CPT Assistant likewise generally prohibits upcoding and unbundling.

Although upcoding and unbundling can occur in various forms, there are several prevalent types of upcoding and unbundling fraud that occur in the no-fault context. One of the most common types of upcoding involves upcoded patient examinations.[4] In order to under-

---

[2] *See*, e.g., N.J.A.C. 11:3-29.4; 11 NYCRR § 68.1; Official New York Workers' Compensation Medical Fee Schedule.

[3] *See* NCCI Policy Manual for Medicare Services, Chapter I, pp. 7–8 ("Physicians must not unbundle the services described by a HCPCS/CPT code. . . . Physicians must avoid upcoding. A HCPCS/CPT code may be reported only if all services described by that code have been performed.").

[4] *See*, e.g., Allstate Ins. Co. v. Tapper, 2015 U.S. Dist. LEXIS 151803 (E.D.N.Y. 2015) (granting the default judgment to the plaintiff-insurer based, among other things, on fraud allegations involving upcoded patient examinations); State Farm

stand how patient examinations can be upcoded, it is necessary to discuss the requirements for the use of the CPT codes that are commonly used to bill for patient examinations in the no-fault context.

The CPT includes five codes that may generally be used to bill for initial patient examinations—that is, the initial evaluative encounter between a healthcare provider and her patient. They are CPT codes 99201, 99202, 99203, 99204, and 99205. Along similar lines, the CPT includes five codes that generally may be used to bill for follow-up examinations or subsequent encounters between a healthcare provider and her patient. Those CPT codes are 99211, 99212, 99213, 99214, and 99215.

The use of any particular code represents that the examination met the requirements of the code. For example, the use of CPT codes ending in "5," such as 99205 (for initial examinations) or 99215 (for follow-up examinations) represents that the healthcare provider conducted the lengthiest, most comprehensive, and most complex type of examination for patients with the most serious types of complaints. The use of CPT codes ending in "4" (i.e., 99204 or 99214, depending on whether the examination was an initial examination or a follow-up examination) represents that the provider conducted relatively shorter and less complex examinations, but that still were rather extended and thorough and still involved fairly serious medical complaints. The use of CPT codes ending in "3" (such as 99203 or 99213) represents shorter, but still detailed, consultations or examinations, and so forth, down to the "1" codes, which represent perfunctory consultations or examinations for minor issues. As a general rule, the higher the number at the end of the CPT code used to bill for a given examination, the higher the rate of reimbursement will be.[5]

Mut. Auto. Ins. Co. v. Healthcare Chiropractic Clinic, Inc., 2015 U.S. Dist. LEXIS 144573 (D. Minn. 2015) (denying a motion to dismiss the plaintiff-insurer's fraud and related claims that were based, in part, on allegations that patient examinations were upcoded).

[5] The CPT also includes various other codes that may be used to report and bill for the evaluation and management of a patient, including CPT codes 99241, 99242, 99243, 99244, and 99245, which are usually used when a healthcare provider is called upon to consult with another healthcare provider regarding a particular patient. Like the CPT codes for examinations, the consultation codes and most of the other evaluation and management codes operate on a scale of "1" to "5," with codes ending in "5" representing the most extensive level of service.

There are various standards that must be met in order to bill a patient examination at each particular CPT code level. By extension, the use of a particular CPT code to bill for a patient examination represents that the examination met the pertinent requirements for that code. Though there are a large number of individual rules governing the use of the various CPT codes applicable to patient examinations, there are several points—in particular—that insurer SIU investigators and anti-fraud litigators should bear in mind when reviewing suspicious billing for examinations.

Initially, it is important to emphasize that the AMA has not set any hard and fast rules as to how long it should take to perform patient examinations that are billable using any particular CPT code. Instead, the CPT codes simply state that examinations billable under one or another of the examination CPT codes "typically" should involve a certain amount of face-to-face time between the healthcare provider conducting the examination and either the patient or the patient's family. In particular, with respect to initial patient examinations, the AMA has specified that (i) the use of CPT code 99205 typically involves 60 minutes of face-to-face time, (ii) the use of CPT code 99204 typically involves 45 minutes of face-to-face time, (iii) the use of CPT code 99203 typically involves 30 minutes of face-to-face time, (iv) the use of CPT code 99202 typically involves 20 minutes of face-to-face time, and (v) the use of CPT code 99201 typically involves 10 minutes of face-to-face time.

Along similar lines, with respect to follow-up patient examinations, the AMA has specified that (i) the use of CPT code 99215 typically involves 40 minutes of face-to-face time, (ii) the use of CPT code 99214 typically involves 25 minutes of face-to-face time, (iii) the use of CPT code 99213 typically involves 15 minutes of face-to-face time, (iv) the use of CPT code 99212 typically involves 10 minutes of face-to-face time, and (v) the use of CPT code 99211 typically involves 5 minutes of face-to-face time.

Because these temporal guidelines refer only to the "typical" amount of time that a healthcare provider should spend face-to-face with a patient or her family during the various types of examinations, anti-fraud litigators should be wary about predicating an entire case on a provider's periodic or intermittent failure to meet the guidelines with respect to individual examinations. Even so, where a provider exhibits a pattern of billing for examinations using codes ending in "4" or "5," yet the provider's examination notes suggest that he could not possibly have spent a substantial amount of time with the patients, it will suggest that the provider is deliberately misrepresenting the time spent on the examinations.

The AMA has also announced certain guidelines as to the types of patient presenting problems that will support the use of the various CPT codes applicable to patient examinations. As with the temporal guidelines, the presenting problem guidelines do not set strict rules. However, they do provide that when a given CPT code is used to bill for a patient examination, the patient's presenting problems "usually" will rise to a certain level. In particular, the AMA has specified that (i) where CPT code 99205 or 99204 is used to bill for an initial examination, the patient usually will have presenting problems of moderate to high severity; (ii) where CPT code 99203 is used to bill for an initial examination, the patient will usually have presenting problems of moderate severity; (iii) where CPT code 99202 is used to bill for an initial examination, the patient will usually have presenting problems of low to moderate severity; and (iv) where CPT code 99201 is used to bill for an initial examination, the patient will usually have presenting problems that are self-limited or minor in nature.

Similarly, the AMA has specified that (i) where CPT code 99215 or 99214 is used to bill for a follow-up examination, the patient will usually have presenting problems of moderate to high severity; (ii) where CPT code 99213 is used to bill for a follow-up examination, the patient will usually have presenting problems of low to moderate severity; (iii) where CPT code 99212 is used to bill for a follow-up examination, the patient will usually have presenting problems that are self-limited or minor in nature; and (iv) where CPT code 99211 is used to bill for a follow-up examination, the patient will usually have presenting problems that are minimal in nature.

Obviously, a presenting problem that might be only "moderately" severe to one observer can be "highly" severe to another. However, the CPT Assistant provides various helpful examples of presenting problems at various severity levels, so as to lend some objectivity to the analysis.[6] For instance, the CPT Assistant includes—as examples of moderately to highly severe presenting problems that might warrant a 99205-level initial examination—such things as "a 65-year-old

[6] *See* CPT Assistant, *Clinical Examples of New CPT Codes for Evaluation and Management (E/M) Services* (1992).

female with exertional chest pain, Intermittent claudication, syncope and a murmur of aortic stenosis"; "a 69-year-old male with severe chronic obstructive pulmonary disease, congestive heart failure, anti-hypertension"; and "a 73-year-old male with an unexplained 20-pound weight loss."[7] Note the frightening and even life-threatening nature of these problems.

By contrast, the CPT Assistant includes "a 48-year-old man with recurrent low back pain radiating to the leg" as an example of a moderately severe presenting problem that might warrant only a 99203-level initial examination.[8] What is more, the CPT Assistant lists "[o]ffice visit with 65-year-old female, established patient, returns for 3-week follow-up for resolving ankle sprain" as an example of a "self-limited or minor" presenting problem that would warrant only a 99212-level follow-up examination.[9]

In other words, it should be a rare occasion indeed when an initial examination of a patient with a soft tissue injury such as a sprain or strain secondary to an automobile accident is billed using any CPT code higher than 99203 or when a follow-up examination for such a patient is billed using any CPT code higher than 99212. As a result, where a healthcare provider routinely uses CPT codes 99205 or 99204 to bill for initial examinations of such patients or CPT codes 99215, 99214, or 99213 to bill for follow-up examinations, the provider is likely to be misrepresenting the nature and extent of the examinations.

Furthermore, CMS, in coordination with the AMA, has promulgated certain documentation guidelines that healthcare providers are generally expected to follow when billing for patient examinations using one CPT code or another.[10] These guidelines generally require healthcare providers to document in their examination reports that they took the requisite level of history from the patient, conducted the requisite level of examination of the patient, and engaged in the requisite level of medical decision making in the context of

---

[7] *Id.*

[8] *Id.*

[9] *Id.*

[10] *See* CMS, Documentation Guidelines for Evaluation and Management Services (1995); CMS Documentation Guidelines for Evaluation and Management Services (1997).

the examination.[11] Failure to adhere to these guidelines might not, in and of itself, be sufficient to prove that a healthcare provider has upcoded its patient examinations.[12] However, a pattern of billing for high-level examination CPT codes, coupled with consistent deviation from the guidelines applicable to those codes, can provide a strong basis to allege that the provider is misrepresenting the extent of the underlying examinations. It therefore is worthwhile to discuss some of the more important documentation guidelines applicable to the CPT codes that most commonly are abused in billing for patient examinations.

As the term suggests, a patient history is the background information that a healthcare provider should take from a patient in the context of a patient examination. For example, is the patient a smoker, is there any history of chronic illness in the patient's family, or has the patient previously had any complaints similar to the complaints that she is currently experiencing? Most of the CPT codes used for billing patient examinations do not impose particularly stringent documentation requirements with respect to patient histories. However, the use of CPT codes 99205 and 99204 requires healthcare providers to document a "comprehensive" patient history.[13] This requires, among other things, (i) fairly exhaustive documentation of the history of the patient's current illness; (ii) documentation to show a review of at least 10 of the patient's organ systems, in addition to the organ system giving rise to the patient's current complaint; and (iii) documentation to show that the healthcare provider took a complete past, family, and social history of the patient, which should include the patient's medical history, a review of medical events in the patient's family, and a review of the patient's past and current activities that could bear on the patient's treatment.[14] If a healthcare provider bills for his patient examinations using CPT codes 99205 or 99204, but the underlying

---

[11] *Id.*

[12] Although some states, including New York and New Jersey, have incorporated these guidelines by reference into their no-fault reimbursement regimes. *See*, e.g., N.J.A.C. 11:3-29.4; 11 N.Y.C.R.R. § 68.1; Official New York Workers' Compensation Medical Fee Schedule.

[13] *See* CMS, Documentation Guidelines for Evaluation and Management Services (1995); CMS, Documentation Guidelines for Evaluation and Management Services (1997).

[14] *Id.*

examination notes do not document comprehensive patient histories, then the examinations likely were upcoded.

As with patient histories, most of the CPT codes used for billing patient examinations do not impose especially onerous documentation requirements with respect to the performance of the physical examinations themselves. Again, however, the most commonly abused examination CPT codes—namely CPT codes 99205 and 99204—do require rather extensive documentation of the actual patient examinations. In particular, for an examination to be billable under CPT codes 99205 or 99204, the healthcare provider must document a "comprehensive" patient examination.[15] This, in turn, requires that the healthcare provider, among other things, either (i) documents a very extensive examination of one organ system or (ii) documents at least some examination of at least eight organ systems or nine body areas.[16] If a healthcare provider bills for his patient examinations using CPT codes 99205 or 99204 but the underlying examination notes do not document comprehensive patient examinations, then the examinations likely were upcoded.

In addition, the use of CPT code 99205 requires that the healthcare provider document some sort of "highly complex" medical decision making, and the use of CPT code 99204 requires that the healthcare provider document some sort of "moderately complex" medical decision making. Pursuant to the CMS documentation guidelines, the relative complexity of medical decision making is measured by (i) the number of diagnoses and/or the number of management options to be considered; (ii) the amount and/or complexity of medical records, diagnostic tests, and other information that must be retrieved, reviewed, and analyzed; and (iii) the risk of significant complications, morbidity, mortality, as well as comorbidities associated with the patient's presenting problems, the diagnostic procedures, and/or the possible management options.[17]

Obviously, these factors are somewhat subjective, and it can be difficult to make an objective determination as to whether the number of potential diagnoses, diagnostic tests, risks, or possible management options is sufficiently high to make medical decision making

---

[15] *Id.*

[16] *Id.*

[17] *Id.*

moderately or highly complex in a given case. Even so, examination reports generated by no-fault insurance fraud rings will generally not document consideration of a large number of potential diagnoses or management options because the diagnoses and management options typically are predetermined, with most patients receiving a substantially similar set of diagnoses and treatment recommendations.

Likewise, the examination reports will usually not document the retrieval, review, or analysis of any significant amount of complex diagnostic tests. To the contrary, diagnostic tests typically are unwarranted where, as often is the case with no-fault insurance fraud, the "diagnoses" are predetermined.

Finally, the examination reports generated by fraudulent practitioners will almost never document the existence of any risk attendant to the patients' conditions or whatever predetermined treatment plans are prescribed. This is because no-fault patients typically present with ordinary soft tissue injuries to the extent that they have any actual complaints at all, and neither soft tissue injuries nor the treatments commonly prescribed for soft tissue injuries pose any meaningful risk to the patients. Moreover, in the event that a fraudulent healthcare provider actually did document any serious problems in a patient, the healthcare provider would be exposed to liability unless he took steps to either treat the problems or to refer the patient to another healthcare provider for treatment. This, in turn, would tend to inhibit the fraudulent provider's ability to provide his own, predetermined course of medically unnecessary treatment to the patient.

As a result, it is rare to see documentation regarding any sort of serious medical problems in the examination reports generated by no-fault insurance fraud rings. Much more commonly, such examination reports recount ordinary soft tissue injury complaints, requiring medical decision making of low complexity at best. If the examinations are billed using CPT codes 99205 or 99204, they likely are upcoded.

Because every CPT code that is commonly used to bill for patient examinations requires—at least to some extent—that the treating provider take a patient history and conduct a physical examination, the charges that a healthcare provider submits for patient examinations should include the cost of the underlying patient histories and examinations. Even so, many fraudulent healthcare providers attempt to increase their billing by artificially unbundling portions of the history and physical examination components of the examinations into separate charges, as if they were separately compensable services.

As discussed above, physical examinations performed on patients with soft tissue injuries necessarily require range-of-motion and muscle strength tests, inasmuch as these tests provide a starting point for injury assessment and treatment planning. As a result, any charges for range-of-motion and muscle strength tests should be part and parcel of an initial examination charge under CPT codes 99201 to 99205 or a follow-up examination charge under CPT codes 99211 to 99215. Even so, and as described above, many fraudulent healthcare providers seek to increase their billing by purporting to conduct computerized range-of-motion and muscle strength testing contemporaneously with their patient examinations. Then, these providers will submit separate charges for the testing, as if the testing was reimbursable separately from the CPT codes used for the underlying patient examinations. These types of charges falsely represent that the range-of-motion and muscle strength tests are entitled to be reimbursed separately from the underlying examinations.[18]

In some cases, fraudulent healthcare providers not only will unbundle charges for computerized range-of-motion and muscle strength testing from the charges for the underlying patient examinations, but also will further unbundle the charges for the range-of-motion and muscle strength tests, themselves. Specifically, the CPT Assistant makes clear that the proper CPT code to bill for contemporaneously provided computerized range-of-motion and muscle testing is CPT code 97750.[19] CPT code 97750 is a time-based code, inasmuch as it permits a single, fixed charge for every 15 minutes of testing that is performed. In other words, if a healthcare provider performed 15 minutes of combined computerized range-of-motion and muscle strength testing, that provider would be entitled to submit a single charge under CPT code 97750. If the provider performed 30 minutes

---

[18] *See*, e.g., CPT Assistant, *Coding Communication*, *Physical Medicine and Rehabilitation Services*, *Part I* (December 2003).

[19] *Id.*; *see also* CPT Assistant (February 2004) (when "range of motion testing . . . [is] performed as part of a physical performance test or measurement, only CPT code 97750 should be reported."); CPT Assistant (May 2008) ("computerized muscle testing should be reported using code 97750. A separate written report is required. Only direct patient contact time is reported.").

of testing, the provider would be entitled to submit two charges under CPT code 97750, and so on.[20]

These restrictions pose problems for fraudulent healthcare providers, because it is generally difficult to show that range-of-motion and muscle strength testing takes more than 15 minutes to perform on any individual patient. This is especially true where the testing is computerized and therefore takes even less time to provide.

Therefore, even if the testing was medically necessary and separately reimbursable in the first instance, the provider will generally be limited to a single, relatively low charge under CPT code 97750 for each date of service when the testing was performed. As a result, many fraudulent healthcare providers will attempt to unbundle what should at best be a single charge under CPT code 97750 for combined range-of-motion and muscle strength testing into multiple charges under CPT codes 95831 and 95832 (which are applicable to independently provided muscle strength testing), and CPT codes 95851 and 95852 (which are applicable to independently provided range-of-motion testing). In contrast to CPT code 97750, CPT codes 95831, 95832, 95851, and 95852 are not time based. Rather, CPT codes 95831, 95832, 95851, and 95852 permit a separate charge to be submitted for each extremity or trunk section of a patient on whom range-of-motion or muscle strength testing is performed.

By unbundling what should be a single, time-based charge under CPT code 97750 into multiple charges under CPT codes 95831, 95832, 95851, and 95852, a fraudulent healthcare provider can not only unbundle his billing for range-of-motion and muscle testing from the underlying patient examinations, but then can increase the amount of that billing by an order of magnitude.

In this context, it is important to note that the use of not only CPT code 97750 but also CPT codes 95831, 95832, 95851, and 95852 requires that the healthcare provider prepare a written report interpreting the underlying test results.[21] In many cases, the reports

---

[20] Of course, this assumes that the computerized range-of-motion and muscle strength testing was entitled to be reimbursed separately from the underlying charge for the patient examination. As discussed above, where the provider purports to perform computerized range-of-motion and muscle strength testing contemporaneously with a patient examination, the testing will not be separately reimbursable.

[21] *See*, e.g., CPT Assistant (May 2008) (noting that, for CPT code 97750, documentation should include "a description of the test and measure protocol, the data

generated by the machines used to conduct computerized range-of-motion and muscle strength tests simply will contain raw data that purport to show the patients' range of motion and muscle strength. These data do not constitute any sort of interpretation of the data, and most healthcare providers involved in fraudulent billing for computerized range-of-motion and muscle strength tests will not bother to engage in any interpretation of the data, much less create any separate written report setting forth their interpretation. Rather, such providers will more commonly simply submit the computer-generated raw data from the test results and contend that the raw data, on its alone, is sufficient to support their charges for the tests.

This tends to compound the fraud, inasmuch as the providers not only unbundle the tests from the underlying patient examinations and unbundle what, at best, should be a single charge under CPT code 97750 into multiple charges under CPT codes 95831, 95832, 95851, and 95852, but also falsely represent that the tests were provided in the first instance. Simply put, a range-of-motion and muscle strength test with results that are not interpreted in any manner is not really a test at all.

In addition to unbundling charges for range-of-motion and muscle strength testing from the charges for contemporaneous examinations, some of the more blatantly fraudulent healthcare providers will attempt to unbundle a separate charge for taking their patients' histories from the underlying examination charges. In particular, when a patient arrives at one of these healthcare provider's offices for an examination, the patient will be given a questionnaire, which often is denominated as an "outcome assessment test."[22] The questionnaire will invite the patient to fill out various details about the symptoms he purportedly is experiencing and the supposed impact of those putative symptoms on his life. The completed questionnaire will then be

---

collected, and the impact of the outcome of the test and measure on the patient's plan for care (i.e., need for continuing treatment, discharge from treatment, or referral to other provider[s])," for CPT codes 95851 and 95852 "[i]nterpretation of the results with preparation of a separate, distinctly identifiable, signed written report is required," and for CPT codes 95831 and 95832, "preparation of a separate, written report of the findings [is] a necessary component of the procedure.").

[22] *See*, e.g., Allstate Ins. Co. v. Williams, 2014 U.S. Dist. LEXIS 170191 (E.D.N.Y. 2014) (recommending default judgment for the plaintiff-insurer in a case that involved, among other things, fraudulently unbundled charges for medically unnecessary "outcome assessment tests.").

fed into a computer, which will "score" the patient's entries on the questionnaire using various preset criteria. Thereafter, the healthcare provider will purport to examine the patient, will submit a charge for the examination under CPT codes 99201 to 99205 or 99211 to 99215, and will submit a separate charge for the "outcome assessment test" under some other CPT code.

However, patient history is a required component of virtually every type of patient examination. What is more, if a healthcare provider is using a high-level CPT code to bill for her patient examinations—such as CPT codes 99204 or 99205—the provider must generally have taken a fairly in-depth history from the patient at issue. As a result, healthcare providers cannot submit a charge for a patient examination and then submit a separate charge for "outcome assessment tests," which at most simply provide pertinent information regarding a patient's ongoing healthcare issues.

When confronted with a suspected example of unbundled billing for outcome assessment or similar types of questionnaires/tests, insurer SIU investigators and anti-fraud litigators should check what kind of information is derived from the tests. Is it any different from the information that would be generated by an ordinary, verbal patient interview? Does it in any way impact the patients' treatment plans? Is there anything to suggest that the healthcare provider who administers the test actually reviews or interprets the test results? If the answer to any of these questions is no, then the provider is misrepresenting that the tests are medically necessary and reimbursable separate from the underlying patient examinations.

5

Confirming a Good-Faith Basis to Initiate Anti-Fraud Litigation

In most cases, attorneys will not be involved in an insurer's initial investigation of suspected fraud. Rather, the initial investigation will typically be handled by the insurer's SIU department, either alone or in coordination with the claims handling personnel who likely brought the suspected fraud to the attention of SIU investigators.

To the extent that outside counsel is involved in the early stages of an insurer's anti-fraud investigation, the involvement will usually be based on the attorney's representation of the insurer in some prior, related case. Although this certainly does occur, it is relatively uncommon. As a result, anti-fraud litigators—at least at first—will usually receive all of the information regarding a suspected fraud from their insurer-clients on a second-hand basis. It is therefore incumbent upon any diligent anti-fraud litigator to ensure, at least to the extent possible, that their clients' fraud contentions have sufficient color. Indeed, the Federal Rules of Civil Procedure and the civil procedure rules of every state require litigants and their attorneys to have a good-faith basis for their claims on pain of sanctions.[1]

[1] *See*, e.g., Fed. R. Civ. P. 11; 22 NYCRR § 130-1.1; N.J. Stat. § 2A:15-59.1; MCR 2.114; 42 Pa. Cons. Stat. § 8355; Mass. R. Civ. P. 11; K.S.A. § 60-211.

In this context, it is essential to emphasize that insurer investigative files will generally be discoverable in the context of anti-fraud litigation. For example, the details of an SIU investigation will likely be relevant to an insurer's contention that it reasonably relied on a fraudulent claim or series of fraudulent claims. If the insurer's investigative files disclose knowledge of a healthcare provider's fraud in June, the insurer will have some difficulty proving that it reasonably relied on a fraudulent claim submitted by that provider in July. Along similar lines, insurer investigative files also can be relevant to the adjudication of any limitations defenses that might be raised by a defendant in an anti-fraud case. For instance, the files will usually disclose when the insurer first suspected or discovered a fraudulent scheme, which in turn will bear upon application of discovery accrual rules. Although, in some cases SIU investigative files have been held to be subject to work product protection or protected from disclosure as material prepared in anticipation of litigation, the conservative approach is to assume that they will be disclosed over the course of an anti-fraud case.[2]

It therefore is important to ensure that the insurer's internal files disclose a good-faith basis for the initiation of anti-fraud litigation. Otherwise, the insurer—and the insurer's attorneys—could be subject to claims of bad faith, especially if the litigation is ultimately resolved against the insurer. Of course, the contents of an insurer's internal investigative files do not have to be completely dispositive of the alleged fraudulent scheme. They should, however, be adequate to allege a scheme that is sufficiently plausible and particularized to survive a motion to dismiss and to demonstrate a good-faith basis to commence the litigation in the first place.

A. Review of Claims Data and Claims Files

With that in mind, anti-fraud litigators should confirm that their insurer-clients' fraud investigations are thorough, well documented, and based on facts rather than speculation or conjecture. In most cases, any investigation of suspected no-fault insurance fraud will

[2] *See*, e.g., State Farm Mut. Auto. Ins. Co. v. Eastern Med., P.C., 2008 U.S. Dist. LEXIS 59891 (E.D.N.Y. 2008) (generally requiring disclosure of SIU investigation files in context of anti-fraud litigation).

begin with the receipt of a questionable claim or series of claims. Typically, the insurer's claims handling personnel will make note of some issue that appears on the face of a claim or series of claims and then refer the healthcare provider that submitted the claims to the SIU department for further investigation. As a result, the first step in most anti-fraud investigations should be a review of the totality of a suspect provider's claims to determine whether the questionable claim is an isolated outlier or whether it is part of a larger pattern of suspicious submissions.

There are two related ways in which to conduct a review of the totality of a suspect provider's claims—via the actual claims files themselves and via the claims data that are derived from the claims files. Broadly speaking, claims files are the paper or electronic records relating to an individual no-fault claim. Typically, they will contain—among other things—the police report of the underlying accident; photographs of the accident scene; hospital records and bills (if the insured patient sought treatment at a hospital); treatment notes and bills from other healthcare providers who treated the insured patient; records of any peer reviews or independent medical examinations that may have been conducted at the behest of the insurer to confirm the validity of any claimed injuries arising from the accident; and correspondence between and among the insurer, the insured patient, the healthcare providers who purported to treat the insured patient, and any attorneys who became involved in the claims process along the way.

In addition to the claims files themselves, many insurers will compile data derived from the claims files. These data often are distilled into spreadsheets, which can set forth—among other things—the accident dates for each insured patient treated by a given healthcare provider, the dates on which the provider first began to treat each patient, the individual diagnoses that the provider rendered to the patients, the individual CPT codes and treatments that were billed by the provider, the dates of service on which each of the individual treatments were provided, the amounts that were billed for each individual service, the payments made by the insurer for each service, the patients' addresses, and the addresses at which the provider rendered the treatments.

A great deal of information can be gleaned from the claims files and claims data relative to any individual healthcare provider. For example, a spreadsheet containing all of the claims data for a suspect healthcare provider can be sorted by date of service to identify each individual service that the provider billed to an insurer on an individual date. As discussed above, it then is possible to tally up the amount of hours that should have been required for the healthcare provider to perform all of the services that were billed on a given date. If the claims data disclose a pattern in which the healthcare provider routinely is purporting to work an improbable or impossible number of hours per day, some of the services are probably illusory.

Along similar lines, claims files and spreadsheets containing claims data can be used to identify patterns in which healthcare providers routinely submit statistically incongruous claims for unusual or expensive services. As discussed above, some types of diagnostic tests have little legitimate application in diagnosing the types of conditions that may arise secondary to an automobile accident. Moreover, the most common injuries that arise in the context of an automobile accident—namely, garden-variety soft tissue injuries such as sprains or strains—will usually resolve on their own after a short course of conservative treatment.

As a result, most patients will not require more than two or three months of conservative treatment, let alone invasive interventional treatments such as pain management injections or surgeries. If the claims data for a healthcare provider indicate that the provider provides long-term conservative treatments or invasive interventional treatments to the substantial majority of his patients, chances are that the provider is misrepresenting the medical necessity of the treatments.

Similarly, claims files can be used to identify providers who routinely include medically impossible or improbable data in their treatment reports. This often will require the services of an expert consultant in the pertinent discipline, considering that SIU investigators and anti-fraud litigators will typically lack the knowledge necessary to spot medically questionable data. However, even a layperson can identify wide discrepancies between contemporaneous data and diagnoses generated by two healthcare providers that simultaneously treated an individual patient. Likewise, even a layperson can identify instances in which a healthcare provider renders a substantially identical, boilerplate "diagnosis" to every patient she treats or who cuts-and-pastes language from one patient's treatment notes into the treatment notes for many other patients regardless of the patients' individual circumstances or presentment.

Claims data and files also can be used to quickly identify providers who upcode or unbundle their billing. For instance, a spreadsheet containing claims data for a given provider can be sorted by patient name and date of service to determine whether the provider routinely unbundles separate charges for computerized range-of-motion and muscle strength tests from contemporaneous charges for patient examinations. Likewise, claims data and files can be examined to determine whether a provider routinely bills for comprehensive and expensive patient examinations when the examination notes indicate that the examinations were perfunctory and reimbursable at a lower rate.

Furthermore, no-fault insurers generally have the right to require their insureds to submit to independent examinations by third-party professionals in the pertinent discipline or to submit claims for peer review by such professionals.[3] The results of these peer reviews and independent examinations will typically be included in insurer claims files and can be used to identify patterns where the medical necessity or competence of a provider's treatments are routinely questioned by other professionals in the provider's field. Once identified, these patterns can provide a strong basis for affirmative litigation.

PRACTICE POINTS

Reviewing Claims Files and SIU Files

- ✓ In reviewing claims and SIU files, it not only is important to look for information that can *support* an affirmative anti-fraud lawsuit, but also to be aware that *potentially problematic* information or commentary may be included in the files.
- ✓ As discussed above, no-fault states generally require insurers to process claims in good faith.
- ✓ If a claims examiner or SIU investigator has included any inappropriate remarks or commentary in a file, it can create problems if and when the statements are disclosed in discovery.
- ✓ Should an anti-fraud litigator identify any inappropriate remarks or commentary in a claims or SIU file, it may be worthwhile to counsel the insurer-client regarding the potential consequences.

[3] *See*, e.g., FLA. STAT. § 627.736; HRS § 431:10C-308.5; ALM GL ch. 90, § 34M.

B. Requests for Additional Verification

Claims handling must be expedited in order for a no-fault insurance system to function. As a result, automobile insurers will generally have limited means at their disposal to confirm the validity of healthcare claims before paying the claims. Even so, some no-fault states provide insurers with certain limited means to seek additional verification of claims and to toll their obligation to pay such claims until and unless the requested verification is received.

For instance, and as discussed above, no-fault insurers can generally require their insureds to submit to independent examinations or can submit a suspect claim for a peer review. What is more, many states permit insurers to take limited discovery with respect to a claim before paying the claim. Depending on the state, this discovery can include an examination under oath of the healthcare provider, an examination under oath of the insured patient, or documents relevant to the treatments that were provided and the licensure and corporate legitimacy of the provider.[4]

The responses to insurer requests for additional verification will usually be contained within the insurer's claims files and often can provide a good-faith basis for affirmative litigation. For example, if peer reviewers or physicians conducting independent examinations consistently determine that a healthcare provider's services are medically unnecessary, it will be at least some indication that the provider is billing for medically unnecessary services. Of course, it is important that the results of the peer reviews or independent examinations are consistent—a single instance or a handful of instances in which a provider's treatments are questioned by a peer reviewer or independent examiner usually will be insufficient to support an anti-fraud lawsuit.

Furthermore, insurers and anti-fraud litigators should consider the quality of the peer reviews and independent examinations. As discussed above, many fraudulent healthcare providers do not actually treat their patients and instead simply create boilerplate treatment notes for each patient containing identical diagnostic "findings" and prescribing identical treatment plans. Understandably, when

---

[4] *See*, e.g., 11 N.Y.C.R.R. § 65-3.5 (generally permitting insurers to seek additional verification of claims, including through independent medical examinations and examinations under oath); N.J. Stat. § 39:6A-13 (setting forth mechanisms for limited discovery in the context of no-fault claims); Fla. Stat. § 627.736 (same).

confronted with this sort of cookie-cutter "treatment," peer reviewers or physicians conducting independent examinations themselves may be tempted to use boilerplate language in their peer review or initial examination reports. This may be appropriate in some cases—for instance, if a healthcare provider purports to diagnose every patient with the same conditions and prescribes an identical treatment plan for each patient, it follows that the peer reviewers and independent examiners assessing the treatment might reasonably use similar language in their reports. However, before relying on such reports as a basis for anti-fraud litigation, it is important to ensure that the peer review and independent examination reports contain some substance and meaningfully address the necessity of the specific services under review.

If either a healthcare provider or an insured patient has appeared for an examination under oath, the resulting transcript—like the results of a peer review or independent examination—will typically be contained either in the insurer's claims file or in the files maintained by the insurer's SIU department. Transcripts of examinations under oath often are not especially revealing, considering that the patients and healthcare providers who appear for the examinations typically will be represented by counsel and will have little interest in assisting an insurer's anti-fraud investigation. To the contrary, they will generally want to derail the insurer's anti-fraud investigation out of concern for their own self-interest. As a result, they will usually come prepared to be as vague and dissembling as possible. From time to time, however, a witness will slip and disclose some worthwhile piece of information—a treatment never received, a questionable referral relationship, a suggestion of illegal corporate structure, or the like. A complete review of any examination under oath transcripts is therefore an essential component of a prelitigation investigation.

In some cases, an insurer's files will indicate that a healthcare provider consistently has failed or refused to provide additional verification of its claims. For instance, the provider may regularly disregard requests for examinations under oath or may consistently refuse to provide information sufficient to demonstrate the legality of its corporate structure. While, of course, there may be some legitimate reason for a healthcare provider to ignore additional verification requests—the provider may have suffered an incapacitating illness, or the requests may have been lost in the mail—more commonly it will be a badge of fraud. Not only will healthcare providers who fail to provide statutorily authorized additional verification be unable to collect on their no-fault claims, but insurers will be able to allege the failure to provide additional verification as a form of fraudulent concealment.

C. Site Visits and Inspections

Insurer SIU files also may contain reports of site visits or inspections, such as visits by SIU investigators to the offices of a questionable healthcare practice or clinic. While these types of reports can be useful to determine whether a healthcare provider has something to hide, as a general rule they will not be useful to show what, exactly, the provider is hiding. For example, site visit or inspection reports will often recount that the SIU investigators were barred from entering a clinic by clinic personnel, that the clinic personnel provided evasive or dissimulating responses to the investigators' inquiries, or that they simply referred the SIU investigators directly to the clinic's attorneys. While this type of conduct might tend to suggest something untoward about the clinic and certainly provides a basis for further investigation, it does not really prove that the clinic is fraudulent.

Occasionally, however, a site visit or inspection will turn up harder evidence of fraud. For instance, a clinic receptionist might profess not to know a certain doctor despite the fact that the insurer has received hundreds of thousands of dollars in billing for services allegedly provided by that doctor at that clinic. Or, to take another example, the clinic might not possess an EMG machine despite the fact that the insurer receives large amounts of EMG billing from that clinic. While these sorts of discoveries do occur during site visits, SIU investigators are more commonly confronted by tight-lipped and unhelpful clinic personnel who have been coached not to volunteer any information.

D. Corporate Record and Associated Person Reviews

As an element of any prelitigation investigation, it also is important to review the corporate filings of a suspicious healthcare practice and to analyze available information regarding the persons and entities associated with the practice. Not only can this type of review and analysis help to identify corporate structure fraud—for instance, a medical professional corporation that secretly and illegally is owned and controlled by nonprofessionals—but it will also help to ensure that any subsequent complaint names the proper defendants.

As an initial step, insurer SIU investigators and anti-fraud litigators should obtain the corporate filings regarding the healthcare practice at issue. Depending on the state and the manner in which the practice is organized, these filings may contain the names of the registered agent for the healthcare practice, the location of the registered office for the healthcare practice, and the names of the corporate officers and shareholders (if the practice is organized as a professional corporation) or limited liability company members (if the practice is organized as an LLC). These filings also often will contain the name of the person or entity that performed the ministerial task of filing the corporate paperwork. In the best-case scenario, these corporate filings will confirm the existence of an illegal corporate structure. For example, an unlicensed individual may be listed as a director of a medical professional corporation or as a member of a chiropractic professional limited liability company.

In other cases, the corporate filings may not conclusively prove the existence of an illegal corporate structure, but—in context—will strongly suggest a corporate structure problem. For instance, the corporate filings for a medical professional corporation may list a licensed physician as the sole officer and director of the corporation. At the same time, however, the corporate filings may list an unlicensed person as the registered agent for the corporation and a property owned by that unlicensed person as the registered office for the corporation. In such circumstances, anti-fraud litigators and SIU investigators will be justified in taking additional steps to ascertain the identity of the unlicensed person and the legitimacy of his connection to the professional practice at issue.[5]

In this context, it is worthwhile not only to examine the corporate filings for the suspicious practice, but to see what other individuals or entities operate from the same space as the practice and to check their corporate filings as well. Databases such as Lexis or Westlaw will

[5] As noted above, the exception is where the unlicensed person listed as a registered agent for a professional practice is associated with a legitimate corporate services business that exists for the purpose of assisting with corporate filings and providing registered agents and offices to other entities.

often contain information as to the identity of each person or entity associated with a specific address during a discrete time period. This information can be revealing.

For example, and as discussed above, one way in which unlicensed individuals secretly and illegally own professional healthcare practices is by causing the professional practices to enter into exorbitant "management," "billing," "marketing," or "consulting" agreements with themselves or with entities they own or control. With that in mind, it is worthwhile to see whether any putative management or billing companies are sharing space or telephone numbers with an ostensibly independent healthcare practice. Along similar lines, it is important to check who owns the property from which the healthcare practice operates, considering that unlicensed individuals and entities frequently exert control over professional healthcare practices through extortionate "lease" agreements. In some cases, these people will not only be the landlord for the practice and maintain putative "management" or "billing" entities on the premises, but also will list themselves as the registered agent for the practice—the better to maintain their unlawful control over it.

Obviously, there is nothing intrinsically suspicious or illegal about a healthcare practice that utilizes the services of a management company or that pays rent to a landlord. The critical question is whether—given the totality of the circumstances—the arrangements seem to suggest illegal control over a healthcare practice by an unlicensed person or entity.

For instance, if a management company operates from a given multidisciplinary clinic over an extended period of time but the healthcare practices that operate from that clinic are constantly changing, it can be a good indication that the clinic and the rotating cast of healthcare practices operating from the clinic are in the hands of the management company and its principals rather than in the hands of licensed professionals.

Likewise, if a management company or landlord has filed UCC financing statements contending that they are creditors of a healthcare practice, it can be an indication that they have some unlawful interest in the practice. This is especially so if the collateral reported in the UCC statement seems out of proportion to any debt that a healthcare practice might legitimately owe to a services vendor or landlord—for instance, if the putative debt is collateralized by all of the healthcare provider's accounts receivable.

E. Review of Court Dockets and Records

Standing alone, the mere fact that a healthcare provider has been accused of fraud in a prior lawsuit generally will be insufficient to provide a good-faith basis for a different plaintiff's anti-fraud litigation.[6] Nonetheless, court dockets and records can provide important leads for further investigation, and—in some cases—can themselves contain sufficient support for a separate, affirmative suit.

For example, if a healthcare practice has been sued by one insurer in the past, the court records may contain evidence that could support a fresh suit by a second insurer—especially if the first case proceeded through discovery or involved substantial dispositive motion practice. The same is true if a healthcare provider has been the subject of a criminal prosecution predicated on insurance or healthcare fraud.

Assume, for instance, that an insurer sued a healthcare practice and alleged that the healthcare practice had an illegal corporate structure. While every single document exchanged in that case during discovery might not be on file with the court, certain material that might demonstrate the healthcare provider's illegal corporate structure—such as bank records, tax filings, or deposition transcripts—might well have been filed as exhibits to motions, especially dispositive or discovery motions.

Similarly, in cases where a healthcare provider was alleged to have billed for medically unnecessary or illusory treatments, the plaintiff may have filed an expert report as part of a summary judgment motion that spelled out, chapter and verse, exactly why the underlying services were medically unnecessary or illusory. Anti-fraud litigators and insurer SIU investigators should therefore always conduct a search to determine whether a suspect healthcare provider has been sued in the past and to what extent the records from that lawsuit provide support for a subsequent suit by a different insurer against the same provider.

---

[6] *See*, e.g., Pace v. Quintanilla, 2015 U.S. Dist. LEXIS 20515 (C.D. Cal. 2015) (noting that, pursuant to Rule 11, "An attorney cannot rely solely on another complaint as the sole basis for his or her allegations. However, sources such as newspaper articles and other complaints combined with an attorney's own investigative efforts can be a reasonable source of allegations based on information and belief."); Homeward Residential, Inc. v. Sand Canyon Corp., 2014 U.S. Dist. LEXIS 77068 (S.D.N.Y. 2014) (noting that Rule 11 "seems to allow incorporation of allegations from other complaints if they are combined with material the plaintiff has investigated personally that lends credence to the borrowed allegations.").

In this context, the federal courts' Public Access to Court Electronic Records ("PACER") system provides, for reasonable fees, quick and easy access to court records in most federal cases that have been filed in the past 5 to 10 years.[7] The PACER system is searchable across a number of categories, including by party name, attorney name, filing date, and case number. However, there is no way to quickly search across the entire federal courts system for cases involving an individual party, and PACER searches therefore must be conducted on a district-by-district basis. This typically does not pose much of a problem considering that anti-fraud litigators and insurer SIU departments will usually know the state in which a prospective defendant was operating and can therefore simply search PACER for that defendant in the district courts within that state.

On the other hand, many state courts systems do not provide easy online access to their court dockets and records, and even those that do generally offer a more cumbersome, less user-friendly interface. As a result, in some states, it remains necessary to do things the old-fashioned way and actually retrieve and photocopy records at the courthouse.

F. Review of Professional Disciplinary and Regulatory Records

As with previous lawsuits, the mere fact that a healthcare practitioner has been subjected to professional discipline in the past will generally be insufficient—on its own—to support an anti-fraud lawsuit. Nonetheless, and much like court records, professional disciplinary records can be combined with other information to obtain a good-faith basis for anti-fraud litigation.

Where a healthcare practitioner has been subjected to professional sanctions for conduct tantamount to fraud and the insurer's investigation of that practitioner is predicated on the same type of fraud, the professional disciplinary records will obviously go a long way toward building the insurer's case.

For example, the professional disciplinary records might contain admissions by the healthcare provider regarding the submission of

[7] *See* www.pacer.gov.

fraudulent billing or admissions regarding the existence of an illegal corporate structure, kickback payments, and the like. While these types of admissions might not necessarily prove that a given bill submitted to an insurer was or was not fraudulent, they certainly would be useful for pleading purposes, inasmuch as they could help the insurer allege the practitioner's motive, the pattern of racketeering activity necessary to plead a claim under the Racketeer Influenced and Corrupt Organizations (RICO) Act, the identities of the potential defendants involved in the underlying scheme, and so forth.

Even professional sanctions that do not involve fraud can provide support for a subsequent anti-fraud case against the practitioner. For example, professional disciplinary records typically are available to the public, and—indeed—often are published online. As a result, a practitioner who is disciplined for engaging in activities such as sexual misconduct or substance abuse is likely to find it difficult to obtain legitimate professional employment and may be more likely to turn to fraud in order to make a living. By extension, a plaintiff-insurer can use the practitioner's professional disciplinary history as a basis to allege the scienter element that is required of fraud and fraud-based claims.[8]

G. Use of Consulting Experts

In some cases, a defendant's fraudulent conduct will be so self-evident that no consulting experts will be required to determine whether there is a good-faith basis for affirmative litigation. For example, if an unlicensed non-physician is listed as an officer or director of a medical practice in the medical practice's corporate filings, a plaintiff-insurer typically will not need an expert to tell it that the practice has an illegal corporate structure. Along similar lines, if a healthcare provider reports that all of her patients suffer from completely identical range-of-motion deficits, then—arguably—there will be no need to retain

[8] *See*, e.g., Gov't Emples. Ins. Co. v. Eastern Neurodiagnostic Associates, P.C., D.N.J. Case No. 1:12-cv-07074-NLH-JS, at Docket No. 55 (denying defendant healthcare practitioner's motion to strike allegations in plaintiff-insurer's complaint regarding to the practitioner's professional disciplinary history for substance abuse, where the plaintiff-insurer had argued that the allegations were relevant to demonstrate the practitioner's motive to engage in the alleged fraudulent scheme).

a consulting expert to say that such identical deficits are medically impossible.

However, where a plaintiff-insurer suspects that a healthcare provider routinely bills for medically unnecessary or illusory services, it is usually best practice to retain a consulting expert in the pertinent discipline to confirm the suspicions. Not only will this help insulate against any claim that the insurer did not adequately conduct a pre-litigation investigation, but it also can lend specificity and heft to any resulting complaint.

Fed. R. Civ. P. 26 generally shields consulting expert opinions from disclosure, provided that there is no expectation that the consulting expert will be called to testify at trial.[9] Furthermore, while state civil procedure laws on the subject vary to some extent, they, too, usually protect the consulting expert's opinions from disclosure unless there is some expectation that he or she will testify at trial.[10] Even so, when retaining and using the services of a consulting expert, it is important to know—at the outset—whether and to what extent the civil procedure rules and attendant case law in the venue may require disclosure of consulting experts' opinions.

[9] *See* Fed. R. Civ. P. 26(b)(4)(D).

[10] *See, e.g.*, Fla. R. Civ. P. 1.280(a)(5); Minn. R. Civ. P. 26.02(e)(2); Pa. R. Civ. P. 4003.5(a)(3); N.Y. C.P.L.R. § 3101(d).

6

Selecting the Defendants, Selecting the Venue, and Preparing the Anti-Fraud Complaint

Once a good-faith basis to institute affirmative litigation is clear, the next steps are to identify the proper defendants, select a venue, and prepare the anti-fraud complaint.

A. Identifying the Proper Defendants

While it is usually simple enough to determine who can be held liable for participation in an insurance fraud scheme, anti-fraud litigators should pause and consider the tactical and strategic impact of each prospective defendant's inclusion in—or exclusion from—the case. Initially, however, it is necessary to identify every potential defendant. Typically, the pool of potential defendants will include—at a minimum—the individual healthcare provider or providers in whose names the fraudulent billing was submitted. To the extent that the fraudulent billing was submitted through an entity, such as a professional corporation or professional limited liability company, then not only the entity but also the shareholders or members of the entity should be considered as prospective defendants even if they did not personally submit the fraudulent charges at issue.

In cases involving fraudulent billing for medically unnecessary or illusory services, the potential defendants will usually include the individual professionals who purported to perform the services in question, even if they did not own or control the practice through which the resulting billing was submitted and even if they did not play any larger role in the overall scheme. If a fraudulent provider required a referral in order to bill for medically unnecessary or illusory services, anti-fraud litigators also should consider naming the provider's referral sources as defendants, especially if there is evidence of illegal referral-fee or kickback arrangements between the provider and its referral sources.

It will generally be fairly easy to identify potential defendants who fall into the categories outlined above, because the identities of these defendants usually will be discernable from the face of the fraudulent billing and underlying treatment records—all of which will be available to the plaintiff-insurer. Nevertheless, other categories of defendants might not be so readily identifiable at the pleading stage in advance of discovery.

For example, if the case involves claims that unlicensed individuals or entities secretly and unlawfully owned and controlled a professional practice and used it as a vehicle to submit fraudulent no-fault billing, then of course the unlicensed individuals or entities should be considered as potential defendants based on their control over the practice through which the billing was submitted. However, unlicensed individuals and entities that engage in corporate practice of medicine or doc-in-the-box schemes generally do not advertise their illegal interests in professional practices. Along similar lines, if a fraudulent practice depends on runners or patient procurers, their role in the scheme, and their identities, will often not be apparent at the pleading stage. As a result, in some cases it will be necessary to await discovery and name these types of defendants in an amended complaint.

Nonetheless, as part of the process of identifying potential defendants, scrupulous anti-fraud litigators will at least want to conduct the corporate record and associated person review described above. This will ensure that the initial pleading sets forth the scheme and the parties to the scheme as fully as possible and will help stave off arguments to the effect that the plaintiff-insurer failed to conduct a sufficient prefiling investigation. Inevitably, however, there will be some cases in which it will be necessary to include "John Doe" defendants in the initial pleading and await discovery to amend the complaint as necessary to identify the John Doe defendants by name. Most courts find this acceptable provided that the allegations against the other, named defendants are sufficiently robust.[1]

Once every potential defendant is identified, anti-fraud litigators should consider which of those potential defendants should actually be sued. While there are many considerations that might affect that decision, it almost always will be best practice to look at the economic considerations first. For example, anti-fraud litigators should determine whether a prospective defendant has any assets with which to satisfy a judgment or whether the prospective defendant is judgment-proof. This can be an inexact science considering that the kind of people who engage in insurance fraud oftentimes are the kind of people who secrete their assets. Nonetheless, databases such as those maintained by Lexis and WestLaw, as well as public property records, will typically give at least some idea of a potential defendant's personal wealth. If a potential defendant appears to be living well but database searches are insufficient to show the identity of the individual's assets, then it may be worthwhile to engage a private investigator to dig a bit deeper.

Other economic considerations also may bear upon the decision whether to include a potential defendant in a case. For instance, a potential defendant's wealth can cut both ways—she may easily be able to satisfy a judgment but also could use that wealth to defend against an insurer's claims, raising the specter of protracted litigation. If the potential damages available to a plaintiff-insurer are low relative to the potential cost of litigation against a given defendant, the insurer may want to consider whether the cost of the litigation could outweigh the benefit. In any case, good anti-fraud litigators should take these issues into account when counseling their clients to avoid

---

[1] *See*, e.g., Gov't Emples. Ins. Co. v. Hollis Med. Care, P.C., 2011 U.S. Dist. LEXIS 130721 (E.D.N.Y. 2011) (on reconsideration, reinstating plaintiff-insurers' fraud claims against unlicensed John Doe defendants alleged to illegally own and control a professional corporation based on a determination that the insurers should have the opportunity to pursue discovery to learn the identities of the John Doe defendants); 5A Charles Alan Wright and Arthur R. Miller. *Federal Practice & Procedure* § 1321 (3d ed. 2005) (internal citations omitted) ("[M]ost federal courts typically will allow the use of a fictitious name in the caption so long as it appears that the plaintiff will be able to obtain that information through the discovery process; should that not prove to be true, the action will be dismissed.").

frustration if what was recommended as a quick case turns into an extended and draining war of attrition.

On the other hand, there are scenarios in which it can worthwhile to sue a defendant even if she does not have any assets with which to satisfy a judgment. Many no-fault insurance fraud schemes depend upon the participation of numerous wrongdoers. For example, a non-physician may illegally own a diagnostic testing practice, illegally employ licensed physicians to perform the diagnostic tests, and pay illegal kickbacks to chiropractors in exchange for patient referrals. The chiropractors, in turn, may unlawfully use runners or patient procurers to obtain their patients. In this scenario, it will usually be worthwhile to name every participant in the scheme—the non-physician, the licensed physicians, the chiropractors, and the runners—as defendants, even if only the non-physician appears to have assets with which to satisfy a judgment. Even assuming, for argument's sake, that only one of the potential defendants appears to have any money, the other potential defendants may well be prepared to trade information and cooperation in exchange for being released from the case.

One particular consideration that often arises in the defendant identification context is whether or not to name as defendants attorneys or other "outside" service providers who, in some way, gave some assistance to the underlying scheme. For example, no-fault insurance fraud rings will typically engage outside counsel to pursue collection on their billing through litigation or arbitration, and these outside counsel can get quite abrasive in their dunning efforts. These collections attorneys can wind up being the "face" of the fraudulent scheme, and—as a result—insurers often want them named as defendants in any resulting anti-fraud litigation. Similarly, a fraud ring may engage the services of an outside billing company, which will send strident and insistent correspondence to the insurer until and unless a claim is paid in full. These communiqués can likewise lead insurers to want to name the billing companies as defendants in anti-fraud cases.

While naming a fraud ring's collection attorney or billing company as a defendant certainly has plenty of surface appeal and while insurer-clients may push for it, anti-fraud litigators should be wary of overreaching. For example, unless there is some real indication that a collections attorney has gone beyond the attorney role to have personally engaged in some fraudulent misrepresentation, it will be quite difficult to hold him liable.[2] What is more, courts may look askance at an insurer that seeks to hold outside service providers liable without some showing that the service providers actually knew or should have known that their services were being used in furtherance of a fraudulent scheme.

B. Identifying the Most Advantageous Venue

In most cases, after identifying the proper defendants, the next step will be to identify and recommend the most advantageous venue. To some extent, this decision will be dictated by the venue in which one or more of the defendants reside or the venue in which the events giving rise to the lawsuit occurred.[3] However, plaintiff-insurers typically will have a claim to federal jurisdiction because the parties will meet the requirements for diversity jurisdiction, because the case will permit the insurer to assert a RICO claim that provides federal question jurisdiction, or both.[4]

As a result, when determining the most advantageous venue for an anti-fraud case, the main choice faced by plaintiff-insurers will be whether to bring the case in state or federal court. This, in turn, requires the consideration of a number of factors, all of which are, to some extent, subjective and will depend on individual experience and preferences.

For example, one critical consideration in determining the most advantageous venue is the quality of the bench. Some anti-fraud litigators prefer to have their cases heard by federal judges. These litigators may note the number of federal judges that are alumni of elite law schools or point to the number of former federal prosecutors serving as federal judges as an indication that a judge's prosecutorial background

---

[2] *See*, e.g., Progressive N. Ins. Co. v. Alivio Chiropractic Clinic, Inc., 2005 U.S. Dist. LEXIS 27538 (D. Minn. Oct. 22, 2005) (dismissing RICO claim against an attorney alleged to have been involved in a no-fault insurance fraud scheme, despite the fact that the attorney was alleged to have falsely notarized documents and submitted misleading documents in no-fault collections arbitration, where there was no indication that the attorney participated in the operation and management of the enterprise through which the fraudulent scheme allegedly was conducted).

[3] *See*, e.g., 28 U.S.C. § 1391; N.Y. C.P.L.R. § 503; FLA. STAT. § 47.011.

[4] *See*, e.g., 28 U.S.C. § 1331; 1332(a)(1).

may result in a more sympathetic hearing. Lawyers with such preferences often will argue, as a corollary, that state court judges somehow are less well educated, less likely to have an elite prosecutorial background, and more likely to be the product of local political machinery with ties to the personal injury industry and, by extension, healthcare providers that focus on no-fault patients.

On the other hand, some anti-fraud litigators swear by their state courts. They will argue that state court judges better understand their state's no-fault insurance regime and are more familiar with state-specific no-fault insurance fraud problems. These lawyers may also know their state court judges personally from long experience and feel that their state court judges will treat their insurer-clients fairly. More generally, some anti-fraud litigators feel that federal judges see no-fault fraud as a relatively petty social malaise when set against the massive Wall Street fraud and international terrorism cases on the federal docket and that—as a result—federal judges do not pay sufficient attention to their cases.

Another important consideration in determining the most advantageous venue is the difference between the discovery procedures that are available in the venues under consideration. There almost always will be considerable differences between federal court discovery procedures and state court discovery procedures, and these differences may not always be apparent upon a cursory review. For example, both federal and state courts typically allow for interrogatories, document requests, requests for admission, motions to compel, protective orders, discovery sanctions, and the like. The scope of relevance is substantially similar in federal and state courts.

Even considering these general similarities, however, there are real disparities at the more granular level. For instance, many federal courts permit discovery motions to be brought on via a brief letter and set abbreviated briefing schedules for such discovery motions. Federal courts also employ magistrate judges to supervise discovery. In contrast, many state courts require formal motion practice for discovery motions, permit extended briefing of discovery motions, and lack magistrate judges (or other court staff playing the role of a magistrate judge) to supervise discovery. The overall result is that discovery disputes tend to be resolved more quickly in federal court than in state court.

Along similar lines, while both federal courts and most state courts permit motions to be brought on via order to show cause, the reception for emergency or expedited motions can vary widely. In some state courts, orders to show cause are an acceptable part of the prevailing culture, and local judges will not look askance at a proposed order to show cause even if the proffered justification is relatively flimsy. Federal judges with lifetime appointments and a docket full of more "serious" matters may take a dim view of any type of emergency application that is not supported by an actual or imminent emergency.

It also is important to review the extent to which either the state or federal court has developed a body of precedent in analogous insurance fraud cases. Where a given court has played host to a large number of no-fault insurance fraud cases over a period of years, the resulting decisions can provide a road-map for virtually every aspect of similar, subsequent anti-fraud cases.

For example, a court's existing precedent in analogous cases can help an anti-fraud litigator know the level of detail that the court is likely to require in a fraud-based complaint, the extent to which the court is likely to permit discovery regarding the anti-fraud claims, and whether or not the court is likely to grant provisional remedies such as a prejudgment attachment. As a result, when choosing between a federal or state venue, anti-fraud litigators should check the extent to which other no-fault fraud cases have been filed in the respective courts and how the courts handled those cases as they proceeded.

Another critical consideration in choosing between a federal and state venue is the extent to which the plaintiff-insurer may want to seek a stay of the defendants' no-fault collections proceedings during the pendency of the anti-fraud lawsuit. In many cases, the defendant healthcare providers will respond to an anti-fraud lawsuit by aggressively redoubling their efforts to collect on their pending, fraudulent billing. Plaintiff-insurers that are disinclined to fund their adversaries' defense may therefore wish to seek a stay of the defendant healthcare providers' collections proceedings during the pendency of the anti-fraud litigation.

In this context, it is important to emphasize that—pursuant to the federal Anti-Injunction Act—federal courts will generally lack the ability to stay or enjoin state court proceedings.[5] As a result, if

---

[5] *See* 28 U.S.C. § 2283 ("A court of the United States may not grant an injunction to stay proceedings in a State court except as expressly authorized by Act of Congress, or where necessary in aid of its jurisdiction, or to protect or effectuate its judgments.").

a healthcare provider seeks to collect on its no-fault insurance billing through state court litigation, a plaintiff-insurer generally will be unable to seek a stay of those collections in the context of a federal anti-fraud lawsuit. This, in turn, may militate for filing the anti-fraud case in state court, considering that a state court judge will be able to order a stay of collections actions that are likewise pending in state court.

On the other hand, if a healthcare provider seeks to collect on its no-fault insurance billing through arbitration—either pursuant to state no-fault arbitration statutes or an arbitration provision in the underlying insurance contracts—the Anti-Injunction Act will not apply and federal courts will have the power to issue a stay.[6]

Finally, in selecting a venue, anti-fraud litigators should consider whether, and to what extent, they may want to take an interlocutory appeal during the pendency of their case. It often is difficult to take an interlocutory appeal in federal court, inasmuch as litigators must make a motion in the District Court pursuant to Fed. R. App. P. 5(a)(3) and 28 U.S.C. § 1292(b) for an order permitting an application to the Circuit Court of Appeals for an interlocutory appeal. Typically, the litigant will have to meet a burdensome standard to take the requested interlocutory appeal by demonstrating that the underlying issue involves a controlling question of law, that there is a substantial ground for difference of opinion as to the issue, and that an immediate appeal actually would materially advance the ultimate termination of the litigation.

While it is hard to know at the outset of a case whether an interlocutory appeal will be desirable down the road, they can be important to a case. For example, an early decision dismissing some of an insurer's claims in a case—for example, civil RICO claims—can have a material impact on the scope of discovery, damages, and other aspects of the case. If the insurer has to wait until the end of the case to appeal from the partial dismissal and then prevails on the appeal, the insurer can find itself having to litigate key aspects of its case almost from the beginning. For this reason, and especially where the case involves novel legal questions that might not be clear to the

---

[6] *See*, e.g., Allstate Ins. Co. v. Hisham Elzanaty, 929 F. Supp. 2d 199 (E.D.N.Y. 2013) (staying the defendant healthcare providers' no-fault collections arbitration during the pendency of plaintiff-insurer's anti-fraud lawsuit).

court at the outset, it may be preferable to file the case in state court, where interlocutory appeals often are more easily available.

C. Preparing the Anti-Fraud Complaint

After identifying good-faith bases for anti-fraud litigation, deciding on the proper defendants, and choosing a venue, it will be time to begin drafting the complaint.

1. The Importance of Narrative and Style

When considering how to approach the drafting process, the critical, overarching issue is the importance of narrative and style. In this context, Fed. R. Civ. P. 8—which requires that a complaint contain a "short and plain statement of the claim showing that the pleader is entitled to relief"—provides some general guidance in federal cases. So does Fed. R. Civ. P. 12(f), which enables the court to strike "any redundant, immaterial, impertinent, or scandalous matter" from a complaint. State civil procedure rules contain analogous provisions.[7] While these rules may help attorneys to paint within the lines, they will not necessarily result in an aesthetically compelling narrative—and, for at least two reasons, anti-fraud complaints should have an aesthetically compelling narrative.

First, the defendant is reasonably likely to read the complaint himself and to review the allegations without having them "filtered" through his or her attorney. As a result, a well-written complaint with a strong narrative can have an in terrorem effect on a defendant and, by extension, can facilitate an early settlement. Even if the defendant does not personally read the complaint himself and relies on his attorney to translate its contents, a powerfully written complaint can influence the advice that a defense attorney provides to her client. Second, the court is reasonably likely to read the complaint, especially in the context of any pre-answer dispositive motion practice or discovery motion practice aimed at showing that certain discovery is or is not relevant. A strong narrative can add weight to a plaintiff's allegations and help persuade the court to deny a dispositive motion or allow certain discovery to proceed.

[7] *See, e.g.*, Fla. R. Civ. P. 1.110; ALM R. Civ. P. Rule 8; Minn. R. Civ. P. 8.01.

With that in mind, it is essential for anti-fraud litigators to ensure that their complaints tell a cohesive story. The characters—such as the plaintiffs, defendants, and any supporting cast—should be properly introduced, with all of the relevant background provided. As a starting point, this requires that a complaint have a framework or narrative structure.

While pleading customs inevitably will vary from state to state, and even from court to court within a state, most anti-fraud complaints will contain the following sections: (i) a preliminary statement, or introduction, that introduces the plaintiffs and defendants and provides a general overview of the events giving rise to the litigation; (ii) a section that provides greater detail regarding the plaintiffs, defendants, and any nonparties who will go on to play some role in the complaint's narrative, including their citizenship, ownership structure, and their roles in relation to one another and to the underlying fraudulent scheme; (iii) a section setting forth the basis for the court's jurisdiction and why the chosen venue is appropriate under the governing federal or state law; (iv) an overview of the law that is pertinent to the claims that are asserted in the complaint; (v) a detailed description of the defendants' fraudulent conduct, including the "who, what, when, where, and why" of as many discrete misrepresentations or fraudulent omissions as possible; (v) an explanation of why the plaintiff-insurer was entitled to rely upon the defendants' misrepresentations or omissions; (vi) an exposition of the various causes of action or claims that are asserted that sufficiently explains why the alleged facts set forth all of the requisite elements of the various causes of action or claims; and (vii) the ad damnum clauses.

This general framework can provide a starting point for drafting an anti-fraud complaint, but it will not ensure that the content contained within the framework is well written and cogent. While there are any number of writing and style guides on the market, some of which focus specifically on legal writing, the best advice tends to recur throughout all of them. First, try to use the active voice (i.e., "the dog bit the man") rather than the passive voice (i.e., "the man was bitten by the dog"). The active voice identifies actions and who is performing the actions more clearly. Second, omit any unnecessary words. There is no need to allege that a defendant "is a man who did something" when you simply can allege that a defendant "did something." Third, never use a long word when a short one will suffice. It may sound fancier to allege that a defendant "prevaricated," but the point is that he "lied." Fourth, and relatedly, avoid florid language, and especially florid adjectives. A well-written complaint should show, rather than tell. Fifth, avoid foreign words and legalese when plain English is sufficient to convey the desired idea. Sixth, avoid overused metaphors, similes, and figures of speech. Seventh, and as recommended by George Orwell, "Break any of these rules sooner than say anything outright barbarous."[8] Eighth, and most important, always remember you are telling a story.

2. Selecting and Pleading the Claims

While there are any number of causes of action that a plaintiff-insurer might potentially be able to assert in a no-fault insurance anti-fraud complaint, the causes of action are typically either aimed at recovering money that the insurer already has paid in reliance on fraudulent misrepresentations or are intended to prevent the defendants from obtaining any additional money from the insurer. The most prevalent causes of action aimed at recovering money that already has been paid by an insurer are claims for common law fraud, aiding and abetting fraud, unjust enrichment, civil claims under the RICO Act, and claims under state law anti-fraud statutes. In addition, to prevent a defendant from continuing to enact his scheme in the future, insurers often will assert a declaratory judgment claim, seeking a declaration to the effect that the defendant is ineligible to collect on any of its pending billing. We will discuss each category of claims in turn.

(i) Common Law Fraud Claims

While it may be remedial for some readers, it is worthwhile to briefly recollect the elements of common law fraud. While the elements may be phrased differently from jurisdiction-to-jurisdiction, a plaintiff alleging common law fraud generally must plead: (i) that a defendant made a misrepresentation or omission of material fact; (ii) that the defendant made the misrepresentation or omission with the intent

---

[8] George Orwell, *Politics and the English Language in* A Collection of Essays (1954).

to deceive the plaintiff; (iii) that the plaintiff justifiably relied on the misrepresentation or omission; and (iv) that, as a result, the plaintiff suffered damages.[9]

In the context of no-fault insurance anti-fraud litigation, and as discussed in detail above, the most common misrepresentations involve contentions by a healthcare provider (i) that its services were medically necessary, when in fact they were not; (ii) that its services actually were provided, when in fact they were not; (iii) that the CPT codes used to bill for its services accurately reflected the underlying services, when in fact they did not; (iv) that the professional entity through which the services were billed was owned and controlled by a licensed professional, when in fact it was not; and (v) that the healthcare provider otherwise was in compliance with pertinent laws and regulations and therefore was eligible to collect no-fault benefits, when in fact it was not.

Along similar lines, the most common material omissions or acts of fraudulent concealment that arise in the no-fault context are (i) concealment of illegal kickback or referral-fee arrangements; (ii) relatedly, concealment of unlawful runner schemes; and (iii) concealment of a professional entity's illegal corporate structure, which most commonly arises when an unlicensed individual or entity unlawfully owns or controls a professional practice.

The case law continues to develop, and some federal and state courts have generated a larger body of precedent on these issues than others. However, courts in no-fault states around the country generally have found these types of misrepresentations and omissions sufficient "material" to state fraud claims.

---

[9] *See*, e.g., Gov't Emples. Ins. Co. v. Spectrum Neurology Group, LLC, 2016 U.S. Dist. LEXIS 19960 (E.D.N.Y. 2016) (noting that a "plaintiff asserting a claim of common law fraud under New York law must allege: (1) a material representation or omission of fact; (2) made with knowledge of its falsity; (3) with scienter or an intent to defraud; (4) upon which the plaintiff reasonably relied; and (5) [that] such reliance caused damage to the plaintiff.") (Internal quotations and citation omitted); State Farm Mut. Auto. Ins. Co. v. Altamonte Springs Diagnostic Imaging, Inc., 2011 U.S. Dist. LEXIS 146926 (M.D. Fla. 2011) (observing that the elements of common law fraud under Florida law are "(1) a false statement of fact; (2) known by the person making the statement to be false at the time it was made; (3) made for the purpose of inducing another to act in reliance thereon; (4) action by the other person in reliance on the correctness of the statement; and (5) resulting damage to the other person.").

For instance, in *Gov't Emples. Ins. Co. "GEICO" v. Korn*, 310 F.R.D. 125 (D.N.J. 2015), the plaintiff-insurer asserted common law fraud (and other) claims against several physicians and medical practices as well as various unlicensed non-physicians. The fraud claims were based on allegations that the unlicensed non-physicians secretly and unlawfully owned and controlled the medical practices, while paying the physicians to falsely pose as the nominal owners of the practices. The fraud claims also were based on allegations that the non-physicians used the unlawfully organized medical practices as vehicles to submit large-scale no-fault billing for medically unnecessary and illusory services. As a result, the plaintiff-insurer alleged that all of the billing submitted through the practices misrepresented the practices' compliance with New Jersey law and eligibility to collect no-fault benefits, as well as the medical necessity of the underlying services. Although the defendants filed several motions to dismiss, the district court held that the allegations stated claims for fraud.

Similarly, in *State Farm Mut. Auto. Ins. Co. v. Radden*, 2015 U.S. Dist. LEXIS 17788 (E.D. Mich. 2015), the plaintiff-insurer asserted common law fraud (and other) claims against a physician and medical practice based on allegations that the defendants billed for medically unnecessary and illusory services, while falsely representing that the services were medically necessary and actually performed. As in Korn, the district court held the allegations sufficient to state the fraud claims.

Other cases are broadly in accord. See, for example, *Liberty Mut. Fire Ins. Co. v. Acute Care Chiropractic Clinic P.A.*, 88 F. Supp. 3d 985 (D. Minn. 2015), which denied a motion to dismiss plaintiff-insurer's fraud and other claims that were predicated on allegations that the defendants falsely represented that several chiropractic clinics were lawfully owned by a chiropractor when in fact they were unlawfully owned by a layperson; State *Farm Mut. Auto. Ins. Co. v. Comprehensive Physician Servs.*, 2014 U.S. Dist. LEXIS 172824 (M.D. Fla. 2014), which denied a motion to dismiss the plaintiff-insurer's fraud and other claims that were based on allegations that the defendants' no-fault billing falsely represented that the underlying services were medically necessary and provided in compliance with Florida law; and *State Farm Mut. Auto. Ins. Co. v. James M. Liguori, M.D.*, P.C., 589 F. Supp.2d 221 (E.D.N.Y. 2008), which recognized the plaintiff-insurer's right to seek recovery for medically unnecessary electrodiagnostic tests based on a fraud theory.

As every litigator knows, fraud must be pleaded with specificity. For instance, Fed. R. Civ. P. 9(b) provides that "[i]n alleging fraud or mistake, a party must state with particularity the circumstances constituting fraud or mistake. Malice, intent, knowledge, and other conditions of a person's mind may be alleged generally." To the extent that a plaintiff-insurer elects to file in state court, state law fraud pleading requirements are substantially similar.[10]

Generally, to plead fraud with the requisite particularity, a plaintiff should try to plead the who, what, when, where, and why of each fraudulent misrepresentation or act of fraudulent concealment.[11] However, courts recognize that it is not always necessary, or possible, for a plaintiff to set forth such a high level of detail in a complaint. For instance, courts have relaxed the fraud pleading standards in cases where the information necessary to plead with specificity is concealed by a defendant or where the alleged fraud scheme was carried out in the context of a corporate setting and where it might not immediately be clear which party within the corporation did what or when.[12] What is more, in complaints alleging prolonged, multi-act schemes, courts typically do not require each and every discrete misrepresenta-

[10] *See*, e.g., N.Y. C.P.L.R. 3016(b) ("Where a cause of action or defense is based upon misrepresentation, fraud, mistake, willful default, breach of trust or undue influence, the circumstances constituting the wrong shall be stated in detail."); Fla. R. Civ. P. 1.120(b) ("In all averments of fraud or mistake, the circumstances constituting fraud or mistake shall be stated with such particularity as the circumstances may permit. Malice, intent, knowledge, mental attitude, and other condition of mind of a person may be averred generally."); Mass. R. Civ. P. 9(b) ("In all averments of fraud, mistake, duress or undue influence, the circumstances constituting fraud, mistake, duress or undue influence shall be stated with particularity. Malice, intent, knowledge, and other condition of mind of a person may be averred generally.").

[11] *See*, e.g., Shandong Yinguang Chemical Industries Joint Stock Co., Ltd. v. Potter, 607 F.3d 1029 (5th Cir. 2010); AnchorBank, FSB v. Hofer, 649 F.3d 610, 80 Fed. R. Serv. 3d 385 (7th Cir. 2011); E-Shops Corp. v. U.S. Bank Nat. Ass'n, 678 F.3d 659 (8th Cir. 2012); Jones v. AIG Risk Management, Inc., 726 F. Supp. 2d 1049 (N.D. Cal. 2010).

[12] *See*, e.g., E&E Co. v. Kam Hing Enters., 429 Fed. Appx. 632, 633 (9th Cir. 2011) (noting that the fraud pleading standards may be relaxed as to matters within the opposing party's knowledge or in cases of corporate fraud); Weiner v. Quaker Oats Co., 129 F.3d 310, 319 (3d Cir. 1997) (same).

tion to be pleaded with granular detail. Instead, a plaintiff can plead a representative sample of the discrete fraudulent acts with particularity, together with an overview of the mechanics of the fraudulent scheme.[13]

In a no-fault anti-fraud case, it will often be difficult for a plaintiff-insurer to specify exactly which one of several defendants who were involved in the scheme created a specific fraudulent bill or dropped the bill into the mailbox. For example, several defendants may be collectively operating a scheme to submit fraudulent billing to an insurer, and—while the plaintiff-insurer knows who they are—he may not be in a position to say which one of them individually was responsible for a discrete fraudulent bill. In the context of a no-fault anti-fraud case, it also may be difficult to plead the who, what, when, where, and why of every individual fraudulent act, considering that such cases typically involve hundreds or thousands of individual fraudulent claims submitted over a span of months or years.

However, anti-fraud litigators will typically be able to satisfy Rule 9(b) by (i) detailing the overall mechanics of the fraudulent scheme—in other words, explaining why the defendants' claims were fraudulent; (ii) pleading a representative sample of the individual fraudulent claims in detail; and (iii) attaching, as an exhibit to the complaint, a chart identifying all of the claims that were submitted pursuant to the scheme, by claim number, CPT code, amount charged, and the dates on which each claim was sent or received.

---

[13] *See*, e.g., Hill v. Morehouse Med. Assocs., 2003 U.S. App. LEXIS 27956 at *11 (11th Cir. 2003) (noting that Rule 9(b) may be relaxed "in appropriate circumstances to aid those alleging prolonged multi-act schemes," and that in such an instance, the plaintiff "is not required to provide a detailed allegation of all facts supporting each and every instance of submission of a false claim . . . , but the complaint must set forth a representative sample detail[ing] . . . the defendants' allegedly fraudulent acts, when they occurred, and who engaged in them. . . .") (Internal quotations and citation omitted); United States ex rel. Bilotta v. Novartis Pharms. Corp., 50 F. Supp. 3d 497, 517–18 (S.D.N.Y. 2014) ("[I]n cases where the alleged fraudulent scheme is extensive and involves numerous transactions that occurred over a long period of time, . . . it [is] impractical to require the plaintiff to plead the specifics with respect to each and every instance of fraudulent conduct [to comply with Rule 9(b)]. Pleading the specifics of thousands of claims would be cumbersome, unwieldy, and would accomplish no purpose.") (Internal quotations and citations omitted).

Numerous courts in no-fault anti-fraud cases have held this level of detail sufficient to satisfy Rule 9(b).[14]

Though different courts may formulate the requirement in different ways, plaintiff-insurers will generally be able to sufficiently allege scienter, or the intent to deceive, either by alleging facts that show that the defendants had a motive and opportunity to engage in the fraud or by pleading facts that constitute strong circumstantial evidence of conscious misbehavior or recklessness.[15] The Federal Rules of Civil Procedure and many state rules of civil procedure permit scienter to be alleged generally, and there do not appear to be any reported decisions dismissing no-fault insurance anti-fraud cases for failure to sufficiently allege scienter. As a practical matter, where a plaintiff-insurer alleges that a healthcare provider submitted billing

---

[14] *See*, e.g., Gov't Emples. Ins. Co. v. Korn, 310 F.R.D. 125, 131 (D.N.J. 2015) (rejecting argument for dismissal pursuant to Rule 9(b) where "the Complaint gives numerous specific examples of Defendants' allegedly fraudulent conduct--complete with dates, patient identifiers, diagnoses, and the type of treatment involved" and "attached as exhibits to the Complaint are voluminous spreadsheets, itemizing specific bills by provider, claim number, and date."); State Farm Mut. Auto. Ins. Co. v. Warren Chiropractic & Rehab Clinic P.C., 2015 U.S. Dist. LEXIS 104332 at *20 to *21 (E.D. Mich. 2015) (collecting cases in which an explanation of the mechanics of a no-fault insurance fraud scheme, together with spreadsheets identifying individual fraudulent claims submitted pursuant to the scheme, were held sufficient under Rule 9(b)); State Farm Mut. Auto. Ins. Co. v. Comprehensive Physician Servs., 2014 U.S. Dist. LEXIS 172824 at *5 (M.D. Fla. 2014) (rejecting argument that automobile insurer's anti-fraud complaint was insufficiently particularized under Rule 9(b), where the complaint alleged "that the Defendants submitted claims and charges to State Farm as services lawfully rendered, knowing that the claims or charges were not lawfully rendered," and where the complaint contained a chart identifying "over 400 claims in which Defendants made these false statements, along with the State Farm claim number and amount paid on each claim," and "further explain[ed] why the services are not lawfully rendered because they violate Florida law, are not in compliance with generally accepted standards of medical practice, and are not related or medically necessary.").

[15] *See*, e.g., Allstate Ins. Co. v. Williams, 2015 U.S. Dist. LEXIS 126020 (E.D.N.Y. 2015) (in no-fault anti-fraud case, observing that scienter may be established either "by alleging facts to show that defendants had both motive and opportunity to commit fraud; or by alleging facts that constitute strong circumstantial evidence of conscious misbehavior or recklessness.") (Internal quotations and citation omitted); State Farm Mut. Auto. Ins. Co. v. Pointe Physical Therapy, LLC, 107 F. Supp. 3d 772 (E.D. Mich. 2015) (in a no-fault anti-fraud case, observing that the scienter element could be satisfied by alleging facts to show that the defendants either acted with a specific intent to defraud or with recklessness).

that misrepresented the medical necessity or reimbursability of the underlying services in order to obtain payment, the defendant will be hard-pressed to mount a scienter challenge.

On the other hand, defendants in no-fault anti-fraud cases frequently contend that plaintiff-insurers have failed to sufficiently allege the justifiable reliance element of their fraud claims. There are many potential factual scenarios that can give rise to an argument that a plaintiff-insurer has not justifiably relied on a healthcare provider's misrepresentation or omission. However, the most common argument is that the insurer has sophisticated investigative tools at its disposal, had reason to suspect the provider's claims, and—as a result—any reliance by the insurer could not possibly have been justifiable. While insurers may face a more powerful version of this argument in the post-discovery context of a summary judgment motion, courts typically have rejected it at the pleading stage.

For example, in *Allstate Ins. Co. v. Lyons*, 843 F. Supp. 2d 358 (E.D.N.Y. 2012), the plaintiff-insurer asserted common law fraud and other claims against a number of healthcare providers and related defendants based on allegations that the healthcare providers misrepresented their corporate structure and legitimacy as well as the medical necessity of the underlying services. The defendants moved to dismiss, contending—among other things—that the plaintiff-insurer could not justifiably have relied on their misrepresentations because it was a "sophisticated insurer" with the "ability to detect" the defendants' alleged fraud. However, the court "emphatically" rejected that argument, based not only on the defendants' efforts to conceal the alleged fraud, but also on the fact that an insurer is entitled to rely on facially valid claims submitted through apparently legitimate professional entities.[16]

Nonetheless, anti-fraud litigators should take care to allege not only that their clients reasonably relied on a defendant's misrepresentations or acts of concealment, but also to set forth facts in the body of the complaint that support the reasonableness of the reliance. For example, if the fraud involves a professional entity with an illegal corporate structure, it is best to allege that the professional entity's corporate structure was facially valid and that the insurer was entitled

---

[16] *See also* Allstate Ins. Co. v. Valley Physical Med. & Rehab., P.C., 2009 U.S. Dist. LEXIS 91291 (E.D.N.Y. 2009) (rejecting a similar reliance argument).

to rely on its apparent legitimacy. Along similar lines, if the fraud involves billing that misrepresents the medical necessity of the underlying services, it is a good idea to allege that the services appeared to be provided by a properly licensed professional and that the treatment reports generated in support of the services were created in order to give the services a false appearance of validity. In any event, it is a good idea to allege—in the body of the complaint—the expedited claims handling requirements that exist in no-fault states. This, in turn, can help to set up a later argument that the reasonableness of the insurer's reliance should be judged in the context of these expedited claims handling requirements.

With respect to damages, pleading the requisite fraud injury should be a fairly straightforward process. All that must be done is to allege sufficient facts to demonstrate that the plaintiff-insurer paid no-fault benefits and, but for the misrepresentations or concealment, it either would not have paid the claims or would not have been obligated to pay the claims.

In some cases, a plaintiff-insurer may be able to assert claims for aiding and abetting fraud in addition to the underlying fraud claims. To state a claim for aiding and abetting a fraud, a plaintiff-insurer usually will have to allege facts showing (i) the existence of the underlying fraud, (ii) the defendant's knowledge of the fraud, and (iii) that the defendant provided substantial assistance to the fraud. Although a plaintiff is not required to allege that an aider and abettor had the intent to defraud, they must allege that the liable party had actual knowledge of the underlying fraud.[17] As a result, in no-fault anti-fraud cases, aiders and abettors usually will be individuals or entities that facilitated the submission of the fraudulent billing in some way.

For example, physicians or other healthcare services providers who purported to treat patients while working on behalf of a

[17] *See*, e.g., Gov't Emples. Ins. Co. v. Alrof, Inc., 2013 U.S. Dist. LEXIS 135880 (E.D.N.Y. 2013) (observing that these are the requirements for an aiding and abetting claim under New York law); Wiand v. Wells Fargo Bank, N.A., 938 F. Supp. 2d 1238 (M.D. Fla. 2013) (noting identical requirements under Florida law). However, not every state recognizes claims for aiding and abetting fraud. *See*, e.g., Schwartzman v. Morningstar, Inc., 2014 U.S. Dist. LEXIS 107054 (E.D. Pa. 2014) (noting uncertainty as to whether Pennsylvania law recognizes a cause of action for aiding and abetting common law fraud).

fraudulent practice—but did not own the practice, control the practice, or directly submit the fraudulent billing themselves—often are alleged to have aided and abetted the underlying fraud. Similarly, healthcare providers who referred patients to a fraudulent practice with the knowledge that their referrals would be used as an opportunity to submit fraudulent billing can be made defendants on aiding and abetting counts. Billing companies that create and submit billing for fraudulent practices can often be alleged as aiders and abettors provided that there is some indication that the billing company knew the underlying services to be fraudulent.

(ii) Unjust Enrichment Claims

The elements of a claim for unjust enrichment should be well known to any litigator. To state a claim for unjust enrichment, a plaintiff must allege facts to show that (i) a defendant was enriched (ii) at the plaintiff's expense and (iii) the circumstances were such that equity requires restitution.[18]

Unlike common law fraud, civil RICO, or claims under many state law anti-fraud statutes, unjust enrichment claims do not permit recovery of punitive or treble damages. However, it is commensurately easier to plead and prove the elements of an unjust enrichment claim. For example, there usually will be no need to allege (much less demonstrate) fraudulent intent, justifiable reliance, or any of the multitudinous elements necessary to state civil RICO claims. As a result, it almost always will be worthwhile to include unjust enrichment claims in an anti-fraud complaint, as a backstop against complete dismissal in the event that one or more of the elements necessary to a fraud or statutory claim is missing.

---

[18] *See*, e.g., Gov't Emples. Ins. Co. v. Tri-County Neurology & Rehab., LLC, 2015 U.S. Dist. LEXIS 162630 (D.N.J. 2015) (observing that under New Jersey law, a cause of action for unjust enrichment "requires proof that defendant[s] received a benefit and that retention of that benefit without payment would be unjust.") (Internal quotations and citation omitted); Liberty Mut. Fire Ins. Co. v. Acute Care Chiropractic Clinic P.A., 88 F. Supp. 3d 985 (D. Minn. 2015) (noting that, under Minnesota law, unjust enrichment requires "(1) a benefit conferred; (2) the defendant's appreciation and knowing acceptance of the benefit; and (3) the defendant's acceptance and retention of the benefit under such circumstances that it would be inequitable for him to retain it without paying for it.") (Internal quotations and citation omitted).

(iii) Civil RICO Claims

The federal RICO Act—and specifically its provisions permitting treble-damages civil lawsuits—has become a potent tool in the automobile insurance industry's efforts to combat no-fault insurance fraud. The pertinent provisions can be found at 18 U.S.C. § 1962, which sets forth the conduct that is proscribed under RICO, and 18 U.S.C. § 1964, which provides a civil remedy including the aforesaid treble damages, as well as costs and attorneys' fees, to anyone injured "by reason of a violation" of Section 1962.[19]

Broadly speaking, Section 1962 of the RICO Act prohibits "persons" from engaging in four kinds of actions that relate to "enterprises" involved in interstate commerce. Specifically, 18 U.S.C. § 1962(a) makes it illegal "to use or invest . . . any part" of "any income derived . . . from a pattern of racketeering activity" in the "acquisition of any interest in, or the establishment or operation of, any enterprise." Section 1962(b) prohibits "acquir[ing] or maintain[ing] . . . any interest in or control of any enterprise" "through a pattern of racketeering activity."

However, Sections 1962(a) and (b) will not usually apply in the context of no-fault insurance anti-fraud litigation because it can be difficult to show injuries that are proximately caused "by reason of" the "use or investment" of income or the "acquisition or maintenance" of an interest in an enterprise. More commonly, insurers will find it easiest to proceed on the basis of Sections 1962(c) and (d).

With that in mind, Section 1962(c) provides that:

> It shall be unlawful for any person employed by or associated with any enterprise engaged in, or the activities of which affect, interstate or foreign commerce, to conduct or participate, directly or indirectly, in the conduct of such enterprise's affairs through a pattern of racketeering activity or collection of unlawful debt.

Section 1962(d) provides, in pertinent part, that:

> It shall be unlawful for any person to conspire to violate any of the provisions of subsection . . . (c) of this section.

---

[19] In particular, 18 U.S.C. § 1964(c) states that "Any person injured in his business or property by reason of a violation of section 1962 of this chapter may sue therefore in any appropriate United States district court and shall recover threefold the damages he sustains and the cost of the suit, including a reasonable attorney's fee. . . ."

Thus, to state a viable claim for violation of Section 1962(c), a plaintiff must sufficiently allege (i) that the defendants (ii) through the commission of two or more acts (iii) constituting a pattern (iv) of racketeering activity (v) directly or indirectly conduct or participate in (vi) an enterprise, (vii) the activities of which affect interstate or foreign commerce.[20] To state a claim for violation of Section 1962(d), a plaintiff must sufficiently allege a conspiracy to violate Section 1962(c), or—though such claims are less common in the context of no-fault insurance anti-fraud litigation—Sections 1962(a) or (b).

Furthermore, to invoke the RICO civil remedies pursuant to Section 1964, a RICO plaintiff must also allege that it was "injured in [its] business or property by reason of" the Section 1962(c) or (d) violation. This essentially is a proximate causation requirement inasmuch as it requires that there be some direct relation between the injury asserted and the injurious conduct alleged.[21]

Each element of a civil RICO claim under Sections 1962(c) and (d) contains its own internal complexities, so it is worthwhile to discuss the main elements in detail and to explain how they typically are pleaded in a no-fault insurance anti-fraud lawsuit.

The plain language of the RICO statute defines "enterprise" as "any individual, partnership, corporation, association, or other legal entity, and any union or group of individuals associated in fact although not a legal entity."[22] Thus, virtually any type of business entity or unincorporated venture will qualify as a RICO enterprise. What is more, groups of people or entities acting together can count as a so-called "association-in-fact" RICO enterprise as long as the association-in-fact enterprise has a "structure" exhibiting three features: (i) a purpose, (ii) relationships among those associated with

---

[20] *See*, e.g., State Farm Mut. Auto. Ins. Co. v. Warren Chiropractic & Rehab Clinic P.C., 2015 U.S. Dist. LEXIS 104332 at *8 (E.D. Mich. 2015) (characterizing the standard, in abbreviated form, as requiring a plaintiff to plead "(1) conduct (2) of an enterprise (3) through a pattern (4) of racketeering activity.") (Internal quotations and citation omitted); Allstate Ins. Co. v. Khaimov, 2013 U.S. Dist. LEXIS 184872 at *10 (E.D.N.Y. 2013) (observing that, to plead a violation of Section 1962(c), a plaintiff must allege "(1) that the defendant (2) through the commission of two or more acts (3) constituting a 'pattern' (4) of 'racketeering activity' (5) directly or indirectly . . . participates in (6) an 'enterprise' (7) the activities of which affect interstate or foreign commerce.") (Internal quotations and citation omitted).

[21] *See*, e.g., Anza v. Ideal Steel Supply Corp., 547 U.S. 451, 461 (2006).

[22] *See* 18 U.S.C. § 1961(4).

the enterprise, and (iii) sufficient longevity to permit the associates to pursue the purpose.[23]

Against this backdrop, it generally will be easy to plead the existence of an enterprise in a no-fault insurance anti-fraud lawsuit. For example, and as discussed above, most no-fault fraud rings carry out their schemes through one or more professional entities. These types of professional corporations, partnerships, or limited liability companies qualify as "enterprises" for purposes of a RICO claim. Even a healthcare practice that is operated as an unincorporated sole proprietorship can qualify as a RICO enterprise.[24] Moreover, and as noted above, groups of people or entities acting together—for example, several related healthcare practices that work together to refer patients to one another for medically useless or illusory services—can constitute an association-in-fact RICO enterprise.

In this context, it is important to emphasize that the RICO statute makes a distinction between the defendant on a RICO claim—or, to use the statutory language, the "person"—and the racketeering "enterprise." To establish liability under Section 1962(c), a plaintiff "must allege and prove the existence of two distinct entities: (1) a 'person'; and (2) an 'enterprise' that is not simply the same 'person' referred to by a different name."[25] Thus, as a practical matter, anti-fraud litigators typically will not be able to name a healthcare practice that is alleged to be a RICO enterprise as a defendant on a RICO claim. Rather, in most cases, it will be the owners, managers, and employees of the healthcare practice—that is, the RICO "persons"—who will be named as defendants on the RICO claim, and the healthcare practice simply will do its duty as the requisite racketeering "enterprise."

Of course, it is not sufficient to merely allege the existence of a racketeering enterprise. Rather, a RICO plaintiff also must sufficiently allege that the defendants on a RICO claim "conducted" or "participated in" the enterprise. The Supreme Court has interpreted "conduct and participation" in the RICO context to mean "participation in the operation or management of the enterprise."[26] Under the

[23] *See*, e.g., Boyle v. United States, 556 U.S. 938, 946 (2009); Allstate Ins. Co. v. Etienne, 2010 U.S. Dist. LEXIS 113995 at *16 (E.D.N.Y. 2010).

[24] *See* City of New York v. Gordon, 1 F. Supp. 3d 94, 111 (S.D.N.Y. 2013).

[25] *See* Cedric Kushner Promotions, Ltd. v. King, 533 U.S. 158, 161 (2001).

[26] *See* De Falco v. Bernas, 244 F.3d 286, 309 (2d Cir. 2001); citing Reyes v. Ernst & Young, 507 U.S. 170, 179–185 (1993).

"operation or management" test, to conduct or participate, directly or indirectly, in the conduct of an enterprise's affairs, "one must have some part in directing those affairs."[27] RICO liability is not limited to those with primary responsibility, nor to those with a formal position in the enterprise, but some part in directing the enterprise's affairs is required.[28]

Accordingly, insurers pleading civil RICO claims against alleged no-fault fraud rings frequently focus on three classes of defendants whose "participation" in the RICO enterprises is sufficient to support RICO liability: (i) the physicians or other licensed healthcare professionals who own, or purport to own, the professional corporations through which the fraudulent billing is submitted, (ii) the physicians or other licensed health care professionals who purport to perform the services that are billed to insurers through the professional corporations, and/or (iii) the unlicensed laypersons or lay entities that in many cases are alleged to secretly and unlawfully control the professional corporations, often through complex financial arrangements meant to conceal their involvement in the schemes.[29]

Some anti-fraud litigators may be interested in broadening the scope of their RICO complaints, to include as defendants the attorneys who pursue collection on fraudulent no-fault billing, or even the no-fault insureds themselves. After all, there often will be some indication that an attorney who pursues collection on fraudulent no-fault billing is aware that the billing is fraudulent. Likewise, most insureds who receive medically unnecessary treatment for minimal or illusory "injuries" will know, at some level, that that some fraud is afoot. Even so, it usually will be difficult to colorably allege that an insured who simply seeks and receives unnecessary treatment from a healthcare practice/RICO enterprise actually has some role in directing the affairs of that enterprise. Likewise, courts typically are reluctant to hold that the mere provision of legal services to a

---

[27] *Id.*

[28] *Id.*

[29] *See*, e.g., Gov't Emples. Ins. Co. v. Korn, 310 F.R.D. 125 (D.N.J. 2015); Allstate Ins. Co. v. Tacoma Therapy, Inc., 2013 U.S. Dist. LEXIS 126399 (W.D. Wash. 2013); Allstate Ins. Co. v. Etienne, 2010 U.S. Dist. LEXIS 113995 (E.D.N.Y. 2010); and Allstate Ins. Co. v. Ahmed Halima, 2009 U.S. Dist. LEXIS 22443 (E.D.N.Y. 2009).

racketeering enterprise amounts to participation in the operation and management of the enterprise.[30]

The defendants on a Section 1962(c) RICO claim must not only "conduct or participate in" an "enterprise," they must do so through a "pattern of racketeering activity." Before moving on to discuss the "pattern" requirement, we should first understand what is meant by "racketeering activity."

The RICO statute defines "racketeering activity" to include a large number of specifically enumerated crimes, including mail fraud, wire fraud, money laundering, witness tampering, counterfeiting, crimes related to "white slave traffic," and so forth.[31] Most of the racketeering activity identified in the RICO statute will not arise in the context of no-fault insurance fraud. Instead, for our purposes, it is sufficient to focus on mail fraud and wire fraud, the two types of racketeering activity that most commonly give rise to RICO claims in no-fault insurance anti-fraud litigation. Mail and wire fraud are the most prevalent types of racketeering activity alleged in no-fault anti-fraud cases because most no-fault fraud rings will submit their fraudulent billing either by mail or by using some wire transmission device such as a fax machine or e-mail.

To state a claim for mail fraud, a plaintiff generally must show (i) the existence of a scheme to defraud, (ii) the defendant's knowing or intentional participation in the scheme, and (iii) the use of the mails in furtherance of the scheme.[32] Similarly, to state a claim for wire fraud, a plaintiff must allege (i) the existence of a scheme to defraud, (ii) the defendant's knowing or intentional participation in

---

[30] *See*, e.g., Azrielli v. Cohen Law Offices, 21 F.3d 512, 521–22 (2d Cir. 1994) (dismissing RICO claim against attorney who "acted as no more than [an] attorney"); Nolte v. Pearson, 994 F.2d 1311, 1316–17 (8th Cir.1993) (affirming a directed verdict in favor of a law firm that drafted documents sent to prospective clients based on information provided by client did not establish RICO liability and that there was no evidence that firm participated in the conduct of the affairs of the enterprise); Baumer v. Pachl, 8 F.3d 1341, 1344 (9th Cir. 1993) (dismissing a RICO claim against an attorney whose "role was limited to providing legal services"); Gilmore v. Berg, 820 F. Supp. 179, 183 (D.N.J. 1993) (lawyer's preparation of allegedly misleading tax opinion letter merely constituted the rendition of legal services, not participation in the direction of the affairs of the enterprise).

[31] *See* 18 U.S.C. § 1961(1).

[32] *See* 18 U.S.C. § 1341; *see also* Farmers Ins. Exch. v. First Choice Chiropractic & Rehab., 2016 U.S. Dist. LEXIS 51494 at *65 (D. Or. 016).

the scheme, and (iii) the use of the interstate wires in furtherance of the scheme.[33]

In this context, a plaintiff-insurer need not show that a defendant personally dropped a fraudulent bill into a mailbox, or personally faxed or otherwise transmitted a fraudulent bill using the interstate wires. Rather, it is sufficient to allege—and prove—that a defendant caused the mails or interstate wires to be used in furtherance of a fraudulent scheme.[34] Thus, for instance, it usually will be no defense for a fraudulent physician to contend that her billing company—rather than she, herself—was responsible for transmitting a fraudulent bill to an insurer.

Isolated acts of racketeering activity are insufficient to support RICO liability. Rather, the acts of racketeering activity must be sufficient to "constitute a pattern."[35] In particular, the RICO statute provides that a "pattern of racketeering activity" must consist of "at least two acts of racketeering activity" undertaken within 10 years.[36]

To establish a "pattern" sufficient to satisfy the statute, however, an insurer must not only allege at least two acts of racketeering activity within 10 years, but also must allege facts tending to show that "the racketeering predicates are related, and that they amount to or pose a threat of continuing criminal activity."[37] It generally will be easy for a plaintiff-insurer to satisfy the "relatedness" requirement because the defendants in an anti-fraud case typically will have submitted a large amount of fraudulent billing through a single healthcare practice or related group of healthcare practices and the individual bills typically will be fraudulent for the same or similar reasons.

As the Second Circuit has noted, "[t]he latter so-called 'continuity' requirement can be satisfied either by showing a 'closed-ended'

---

[33] *See* 18 U.S.C. § 1341; *see also* Liberty Mut. Fire Ins. Co. v. Acute Care Chiropractic Clinic P.A., 88 F. Supp. 3d 985, 998 (D. Minn. 2015).

[34] *See*, e.g., Pereira v. United States, 347 U.S. 1, 8 (1954) ("To constitute a [mail or wire fraud] violation . . . it is not necessary to show that [defendants] actually mailed [or wired] . . . anything themselves; it is sufficient if they caused it to be done.").

[35] See, e.g., United States v. Burden, 600 F.3d 204, 216 (2d Cir. 2010) (noting that the "pattern" requirement is meant to prevent application of RICO liability to perpetrators of isolated or sporadic criminal acts).

[36] *See* 18 U.S.C. § 1961(5).

[37] *See* H.J. Inc. v. Northwestern Bell Tel. Co., 492 U.S. 229, 239 (1989); S. Snow Mfg. Co. v. SnoWizard Holdings, Inc., 567 Fed. Appx. 945, 963 (Fed. Cir. 2014).

pattern—a series of related predicate acts extending over a substantial period of time—or by demonstrating an 'open-ended' pattern of racketeering activity that poses a threat of continuing criminal conduct beyond the period during which the predicate acts were performed."[38] While what constitutes a "substantial period of time" necessary to demonstrate a closed-ended pattern of racketeering activity varies somewhat from Circuit to Circuit, anti-fraud litigators generally should look for racketeering activity that extends over the course of at least two years.[39]

It is important to note that, when determining the temporal sufficiency of closed-ended pattern allegations, the relevant time period is the period when the actual predicate acts of racketeering activity occurred, not the period when the underlying scheme operated or the underlying dispute took place.[40] Thus, a plaintiff-insurer typically will not be able to plead a closed-ended pattern of racketeering activity unless it has received fraudulent claims from a prospective RICO defendant over the course of at least one year, and sometimes more than two years, depending on the jurisdiction.

---

[38] *See* Spool v. World Child Int'l Adoption Agency, 520 F.3d 178, 183 (2d Cir. 2008). Other Circuits generally are in accord. *See*, e.g., Kalitta Air, LLC v. GSBD & Assocs., 591 Fed. Appx. 338, 342 (6th Cir. 2014) (closed-ended continuity requires predicate acts over a "substantial period of time," while open-ended continuity may be established by showing "a distinct threat of long-term racketeering activity" or that the predicate acts or offenses are part of an ongoing entity's "regular way of doing business.") (Internal quotations and citations omitted); Coquina Invs. v. TD Bank, N.A., 760 F.3d 1300 (11th Cir. 2014) (same); Jennings v. Auto Meter Prods., 495 F.3d 466, 473 (7th Cir. 2007) (defining closed-ended continuity as "criminal behavior that has come to a close but endured for such a substantial period of time that the duration and repetition of the criminal activity carries with it an implicit threat of continued criminal activity in the future" and open-ended continuity as "a course of criminal activity which lacks the duration and repetition to establish continuity . . . [but] which by its nature projects into the future with a threat of repetition.") (Internal quotations and citations omitted).

[39] For example, the Second Circuit has indicated that it is disinclined to find closed-ended continuity where the predicate acts occurred over less than two years' time. *See* Spool, *supra* note 38, 520 F.3d at 184 (noting that while the two-year period is not a "bright-line requirement," conduct persisting for a shorter period of time rarely will be sufficient to establish closed-ended continuity). By contrast, in the Eighth Circuit and Eleventh Circuit, at least one year of racketeering activity may be sufficient. *See* Stonebridge Collection, Inc. v. Carmichael, 791 F.3d 811, 823 (8th Cir. 2015); Ferrell v. Durbin, 311 Fed. Appx. 253, 256 (11th Cir. 2009).

[40] *See*, e.g., Spool, *supra* note 38, 520 F.3d at 184.

Nonetheless, insurers should have little difficulty pleading closed-ended patterns of racketeering activity because the mechanics of no-fault insurance fraud generally require submission of fraudulent billing over the course of more than two years. As noted above, the typical no-fault fraud ring controls one or more professional entities, which are used as vehicles to submit fraudulent claims to insurers. However, most state no-fault laws cap the total amount of no-fault benefits that may be recovered for healthcare services provided to any individual insured, and only a fraction of these capped amounts typically can be recovered by a single healthcare provider.[41] As a result, the characteristic no-fault fraud ring must submit a large number of claims—and, by extension, submit those claims over an extended period of time—in order to realize the full fruits of its scheme.

Even so, when placed in the service of a no-fault fraud scheme, professional entities have a limited life span—inasmuch as large-scale fraudulent billing submitted through any individual professional entity inevitably will draw the attention of insurers. This, in turn, generally results in delayed or denied claims, as the insurers demand additional verification from a suspicious professional entity as a condition precedent to payment. Faced with insurers' investigations, no-fault fraud rings have increasingly elected to shutter whatever professional entities they previously used and carry on their scheme using one or more newly incorporated professional entities with new tax identification numbers. In other cases, rather than open and close a number of professional entities in sequence, a no-fault fraud ring will operate several professional entities at once, use them to simultaneously submit a large volume of fraudulent billing over a short period of time, and then decamp with the proceeds of the scheme when any one of the entities comes under suspicion.

These tactics can make it difficult for insurers to allege a closed-ended pattern of racketeering activity in support of their civil RICO claims, in that—increasingly—fraud rings do not submit billing through any one professional entity for the requisite "substantial period of time." Insurers therefore may be unable to plead a closed-ended pattern of racketeering activity, because the alleged "pattern

---

[41] For instance, in New York the cap is $50,000; *see* N.Y. Ins. Law § 5102. In New Jersey, the cap is $250,000; *see* N.J. Stat. § 39:6A-4.3. In Minnesota, it is $20,000; *see* Minn. Stat. § 65B.44. In contrast, in Michigan there is no cap; *see* MCLS § 500.3107.

of racketeering activity" generally must be specific to an individual professional entity, inasmuch as RICO requires that the defendant "conduct or participate in" the enterprise ***through*** the pattern of racketeering activity.[42]

However, to the extent that a plaintiff-insurer is unable to allege a closed-ended pattern of racketeering activity, the insurer typically will be able to allege an open-ended pattern. As noted above, an open-ended pattern of racketeering activity need not extend over a "substantial period of time" so long as it poses a threat of continuing criminal conduct beyond the period during which the predicate acts were performed.

RICO plaintiffs generally can meet their burden to show an open-ended pattern by alleging facts establishing either that the predicate acts of racketeering activity themselves include a specific threat of repetition extending indefinitely into the future or that the predicate acts or offenses are part of an ongoing entity's regular way of doing business.[43] This generally will be fairly easy in the context of a no-fault insurance fraud scheme. For example, federal courts in automobile insurance fraud cases have found an open-ended pattern to have been sufficiently alleged where (i) healthcare practices/RICO enterprises had illegal corporate structures, could not lawfully submit claims for no-fault benefits in the first instance, and therefore their "business [was] racketeering activity";[44] (ii) where a healthcare practice continued to operate in a fraudulent manner on an ongoing basis as of the date when the complaint was filed;[45] and (iii) where the sheer volume of fraudulent billing submitted through a healthcare practice made it reasonable to infer that the practice was operated for criminal purposes.[46]

---

[42] *See*, e.g., United States v. Pizzonia, 577 F.3d 455, 463 (2d Cir. 2009), quoting United States v. Russotti, 717 F.2d 27, 33 (2d Cir. 1983) ("it is neither the enterprise standing alone nor the pattern of racketeering activity by itself which RICO criminalizes," but "[r]ather, the combination of these two elements . . . .").

[43] *See*, e.g., Daedalus Capital LLC v. Vinecombe, 625 Fed. Appx. 973, 976 (11th Cir. 2015).

[44] *See*, e.g., Gov't Emples. Ins. Co. v. Simakovsky, 2015 U.S. Dist. LEXIS 135657 at *16 (E.D.N.Y. 2015); Gov't Emples. Ins. Co. v. Sanni-Thomas, 2015 U.S. Dist. LEXIS 135117 at *17 (E.D.N.Y. 2015).

[45] *See* State Farm Mut. Auto. Ins. Co. v. Universal Health Group, Inc., 2014 U.S. Dist. LEXIS 151213 at *15 (E.D. Mich. 2014).

[46] *See* Allstate Ins. Co. v. Lyons, 843 F. Supp. 2d 358, 369–70 (E.D.N.Y. 2012).

As discussed above, most RICO claims in no-fault anti-fraud litigation will be asserted under 18 U.S.C. §§ 1962(c) and (d) and 1964 and will allege that the plaintiff-insurer was injured "by reason of" a pattern of predicate acts of mail or wire fraud. While reliance is not an element of mail or wire fraud, the "by reason of" proximate causation requirement in Section 1964 means that—as a practical matter—plaintiffs attempting to predicate a civil RICO claim on mail or wire fraud will have to allege that someone, even a third party, relied on some misrepresentation or act of concealment.[47] In a no-fault insurance anti-fraud action, the plaintiff-insurer will generally be in a position to allege that it relied on the misrepresentations or material omissions in a fraudulent healthcare provider's billing and treatment reports. Otherwise, why would it have paid the provider's bills in the first place?

However—and as with the reliance element of a common law fraud claim—insurers should take care to allege facts in their complaints that support the reasonableness of their reliance. If the fraud goes to the corporate structure of a professional entity, the insurer should allege that the entity's corporate structure was facially valid and that the insurer was entitled to rely on its apparent legitimacy. If the fraud involves billing for medically useless or illusory services, then the insurer should allege that the underlying bills and treatment reports appeared to have been prepared and signed by a duly licensed professional in the pertinent discipline and appeared on their face to be legitimate. More generally, and again, it is useful to plead the expedited claims handling requirements that exist in no-fault states in order to put the reasonableness of the insurer's reliance into its proper context.

Of course, a RICO plaintiff must also sufficiently allege damages that were proximately caused by the racketeering activity. As a general rule, these RICO damages must be "clear and definite" rather than "speculative and amorphous."[48] In the context of no-fault insurance

---

[47] *See* Bridge v. Phoenix Bond & Indem. Co., 553 U.S. 639, 658 (2008) (noting that, although first-party reliance is not an element of RICO claims predicated on mail fraud, "none of this is to say that a RICO plaintiff who alleges injury 'by reason of' a pattern of mail fraud can prevail without showing that someone relied on the defendant's misrepresentations.") (Emphasis in original).

[48] *See, e.g.*, Evans v. City of Chicago, 434 F.3d 916 (7th Cir. 2006) ("Indeed, every court that has addressed this issue has held that injuries proffered by plaintiffs in order

anti-fraud litigation, this is usually an easy hurdle to clear. For example, plaintiff-insurers almost always will be able to allege a specific amount of damages in the form of no-fault payments that were made in reliance on a defendant's fraudulent billing. These damages are sufficiently concrete to support a RICO claim.[49]

(iv) State-Specific Statutory Claims

In addition to the common law and federal RICO claims that often are asserted against alleged no-fault insurance fraud rings, many states have enacted statutes that can provide a private right of action to insurers victimized by a fraud scheme. These statutes broadly break down into three general categories: (i) state anti-racketeering laws, also known as "little RICO" acts; (ii) consumer protection and unfair trade practices laws; and (iii) anti-insurance fraud laws that often seem to be specifically aimed at curbing no-fault insurance fraud. We will discuss each category in turn.

While many states have anti-racketeering statutes, and while those statutes generally criminalize the same types of conduct as the federal RICO Act, most of them do not provide a private right of action. However, to the extent that state little RICO acts do provide a private right of action, the statutes can differ significantly from their federal counterpart—often to the advantage of anti-fraud litigators.

For example, while the federal RICO Act has a four-year statute of limitations,[50] Florida's anti-racketeering law has a five-year limitations period for civil claims.[51] New Jersey's little RICO statute—which also

---

to confer RICO standing must be 'concrete and actual,' as opposed to speculative and amorphous."); First Nationwide Bank v. Gelt Funding Corp., 27 F.3d 763, 768 (2d Cir. 1994) ("[A]s a general rule, a cause of action does not accrue under RICO until the amount of damages becomes clear and definite.").

[49] *See*, e.g., Allstate Ins. Co. v. Lyons, 843 F. Supp. 2d 358, 374 (E.D.N.Y. 2012) (damages in the form of millions of dollars in payments to defendants "based upon their allegedly fraudulent claims for no-fault benefits" were sufficiently concrete to confer RICO standing); Allstate Ins. Co. v. Linea Latina De Accidentes, Inc., 781 F. Supp. 2d 837, 845 (D. Minn. 2011) (plaintiff-insurers' payments on allegedly fraudulent no-fault claims constituted damages that were sufficiently "concrete" to support RICO claims).

[50] *See* Agency Holding Corp. v. Malley-Duff & Associates, Inc., 483 U.S. 143, 156 (1987) (determining that the statute of limitations on a civil RICO claim is four years).

[51] *See* Fla. Stat. § 772.17.

provides a private right of action—does not place as much emphasis on continuity in establishing a pattern of racketeering activity and instead relies to a greater extent on whether the predicate acts were related to one another.[52] This, in turn, can be of assistance to insurers faced with no-fault fraud schemes that occurred over shorter periods of time. Although North Dakota is not known as a hotbed of automobile insurance fraud, it, too, has a little RICO act that offers a private right of action and a seven-year statute of limitations.[53]

To the limited extent that state anti-racketeering laws provide a private cause of action, these small differences may enable plaintiff-insurers to assert treble-damages racketeering claims that otherwise would be insufficient or time-barred under federal RICO. It is worthwhile to note, however, that if an insurer prefers to litigate in state court, it can assert a federal RICO claim whether or not the state in question has a little RICO act because state courts have concurrent jurisdiction with federal courts over civil RICO claims.[54]

Many states also have consumer protection or unfair trade practices laws that are sufficiently broad to provide a private right of action to insurers that are victimized by no-fault insurance fraud schemes. These statutes often allow for enhanced damages and fee-shifting similar to the treble damages and attorneys' fees available under RICO.

For example, the Florida Deceptive and Unfair Trade Practices Act provides a private right of action for actual damages, attorneys'

---

[52] *See*, e.g., Ford Motor Co. v. Edgewood Props., 2009 U.S. Dist. LEXIS 4172 at *44 to *45 (D.N.J. 2009) ("Unlike the federal statute, NJRICO, as interpreted by the New Jersey courts, does not place as much emphasis on 'continuity,' but instead, focuses on the 'relatedness' of the activity."); State v. Ball, 141 N.J. 142, 169 (1995) ("New Jersey's legislative discussions, unlike Congress', do not indicate a concern for reaching only long-term criminal activity. But short-term criminal activity, to be covered, must encompass incidents of criminal conduct that are not disconnected or isolated. Incidents of racketeering that occur sequentially, to overcome any inference that they are totally disconnected or isolated, must exhibit some temporal connection or continuity over time. Accordingly, we conclude that the primary criterion of New Jersey's 'pattern of racketeering activity' is 'relatedness.' That calls for the application of a broad standard involving the totality of all relevant circumstances, which may include 'continuity.'").

[53] *See* N.D. Cent. Code § 12.1-06.1-05.

[54] *See*, e.g., Tafflin v. Levitt, 493 U.S. 455, 458 (1990) (holding that state courts have concurrent jurisdiction over civil RICO claims).

fees, and costs to plaintiffs who can show a deceptive act or practice, causation, and actual damages. Courts interpreting the statute have held that fraudulent no-fault insurance billing qualifies as a "deceptive act" and that insurers can assert claims against no-fault insurance fraud rings under the statute.[55]

Along similar lines, Minnesota has enacted the Minnesota Consumer Protection Act, which prohibits any "fraud, false pretense, false promise, misrepresentation, misleading statement or deceptive practice, with the intent that others rely thereon in connection with the sale of any merchandise," and defines "merchandise" to include not only goods but also services.[56] While a plaintiff asserting a civil claim under the Minnesota Consumer Protection Act must demonstrate that the action is brought for the benefit of the public, lawsuits under the Act against alleged no-fault fraud rings will sufficiently benefit of the public where they seek not only damages, but also to enjoin future fraudulent conduct.[57]

Likewise, New York General Business Law § 349 provides a private right of action for actual damages, as well as attorneys' fees and penalties in the court's discretion, to any person injured by reason of "[d]eceptive acts or practices in the conduct of any business, trade or commerce or in the furnishing of any service in this state. . . ." However, the New York consumer protection statute generally requires that the offensive conduct be "consumer oriented," and there is some dissonance among the authorities as to whether insurance fraud

---

[55] *See* FLA. STAT. § 501.201, *et seq.*; State Farm Mut. Auto. Ins. Co. v. Med. Serv. Ctr. of Fla., 103 F. Supp. 3d 1343, 1354 (S.D. Fla. 2015) (collecting cases).

[56] MINN. STAT. § 325F.68, *et seq.*

[57] *See*, e.g., Liberty Mut. Fire Ins. Co. v. Acute Care Chiropractic Clinic, P.A., 88 F. Supp. 3d 985, 1011–12 (D. Minn. 2015) (plaintiff-insurer stated claim under Minnesota Consumer Protection Act where it sought not only damages, but also "a permanent injunction enjoining [Defendant Clinics] from further violations of the corporate practice of medicine doctrine and Minnesota Professional Firms Act" that would "have the effect of preventing the Defendant Clinics from continuing to misrepresent to the public that they are lawfully owned and operated."); Ill. Farmers Ins. Co. v. Mobile Diagnostic Imaging, Inc., 2014 U.S. Dist. LEXIS 114745 at *54 to *56 (D. Minn. 2014) (plaintiff-insurer did not state a claim under Minnesota Consumer Protection Act where it primarily sought compensatory damages, costs, and attorney's fees in connection with its consumer fraud claim, and although it also requested an injunction, the injunction would not colorably benefit the public).

directed at a no-fault insurer qualifies as consumer-oriented conduct.[58] Even so, at least two courts have permitted no-fault insurers to assert claims under Section 349 based on determinations that the effect of no-fault fraud on insurance rates was sufficient to show an impact on the consumer public at large.[59]

While, in most cases, consumer protection and unfair trade practices claims will not provide much of an advantage over the more typically asserted civil RICO, common law fraud, and unjust enrichment claims, they can occasionally make a difference in a close case. For instance, and in contrast to common law fraud or fraud-based civil RICO claims, state consumer protection laws often do not need to be pleaded with particularity.[60] By extension, consumer protection and unfair trade practices claims can provide for fee shifting in cases where a plaintiff-insurer is unable to obtain fee shifting through a sufficiently pleaded RICO claim. In addition to the more general consumer protection and unfair trade practices laws, some states have enacted laws that are specifically aimed at curbing insurance fraud and provide a private cause of action to insurers (and others) that are victimized by insurance fraud. For example, the New Jersey Insurance Fraud Prevention Act (the "IFPA") contains broad prohibitions against the knowing submission of insurance claims containing any "false or misleading information concerning any fact or thing material to the claim."[61] The IFPA also prohibits the concealment or deliberate nondisclosure of "an event which affects a person's initial or continued right or entitlement to (a) any insurance benefits or payment or (b) the amount of any benefit or payment to

---

[58] Compare Allstate Ins. Co. v. Lyons, 843 F. Supp. 2d 358, 375–76 (E.D.N.Y. 2012) and Allstate Ins. Co. v. Rozenberg, 590 F. Supp. 2d 384, 394–95 (E.D.N.Y. 2008) (permitting insurers to assert N.Y. Gen Bus. Law § 349 claims against alleged no-fault insurance fraud rings) with Allstate Ins. Co. v. Bogoraz, 818 F. Supp. 2d 544, 552 (E.D.N.Y. 2011) (finding that the alleged no-fault insurance fraud scheme did not have a sufficiently broad impact on the public at large to permit insurer to assert claim under Section 349).

[59] *See* Lyons, *supra* note 46; Rozenberg, *supra* note 58.

[60] *See, e.g.*, Tomasino v. Estee Lauder Cos., 44 F. Supp. 3d 251, 257 (E.D.N.Y. 2014) (noting that claims under N.Y. GEN. BUS. LAW § 349 do not need to be pleaded with particularity); Ward v. EZPawn Florida, Inc., 2015 U.S. Dist. LEXIS 176764 at *6 to *7 (M.D. Fla. 2015) (noting that courts are split as to whether Florida Deceptive and Unfair Trade Practices Act need to be pleaded with particularity).

[61] *See* N.J.S.A. § 17:33A-1, *et seq.*

which the person is entitled."[62] The IFPA provides a private right of action to insurers that are damaged through such misrepresentations or concealment and enables insurers to recover actual damages, attorneys' fees, and reasonable investigative costs.[63] What is more, an insurer that can prove a pattern of fraudulent behavior under the IFPA—defined as five or more related violations—can recover treble damages.[64]

Similarly, in Pennsylvania, an anti-insurance fraud statute makes it unlawful to knowingly submit "any statement forming a part of, or in support of, a claim that contains any false, incomplete or misleading information concerning any fact or thing material to the claim."[65] Like the IFPA, the Pennsylvania anti-fraud statute provides a private right of action to insurers and allows insurers to recover compensatory damages including reasonable investigation expenses, costs of suit, and attorney fees.[66] In addition—and, again, like the IFPA—the Pennsylvania statute permits recovery of treble damages if an insurer can prove a pattern of violations.[67]

For insurers in New Jersey and Pennsylvania, state anti-insurance fraud statutes can provide a considerable advantage over civil RICO and common law fraud claims. For instance, New Jersey's IFPA does not require an insurer to plead or prove reasonable reliance on a fraudulent claim or resulting damages,[68] nor does Pennsylvania's anti-insurance fraud statute.[69] Moreover, the burden to show a violation of the IFPA is a preponderance of the evidence, which is lower than

---

[62] *Id.*

[63] *See* N.J.S.A. § 17:33A-7(a).

[64] *See* N.J.S.A. § 17:33A-7(b); N.J.S.A. 17:33A-3.

[65] *See* 18 Pa. Cons. Stat. § 4117.

[66] *Id.*

[67] *Id.*

[68] *See*, e.g., Liberty Mut. Ins. Co. v. Land, 186 N.J. 163, 175 (N.J. 2006) ("[T]he statutory language of IFPA does not require proof of reliance on a false statement or resultant damages.").

[69] *See*, e.g., State Farm Mut. Auto. Ins. Co. v. Stavropolskiy, 2016 U.S. Dist. LEXIS 65234 at *8 (E.D. Pa. 2016) (noting that "it is not necessary to show reliance, let alone justifiable reliance, when pleading insurance fraud under Pennsylvania statutory law.").

the "clear and convincing evidence necessary to prove a common law fraud claim.[70]

(v) Declaratory Judgment Claims

Insurers typically want two things from an anti-fraud case. First, and most obvious, they want to recover the money that they already have paid on fraudulent charges. To do that, they can pursue the civil RICO, common law, and state statutory claims described above. Oftentimes, however, a fraudulent scheme will be ongoing at the time when the insurer prepares and files its anti-fraud complaint. As a result, in addition to fraudulent billing that it already has paid, an insurer may be faced with a substantial amount of fraudulent billing that remains pending and unpaid. What is more, the insurance fraud ring may be actively trying to collect on this pending, fraudulent billing, oftentimes at arbitration and in local civil courts, where insurers face the considerable procedural and systemic disadvantages described above.

In such cases, insurers should consider including a declaratory judgment claim in their anti-fraud complaints, seeking a declaration to the effect that—as a result of the defendants' fraud—they are not liable to pay any pending, fraudulent billing they have received from the defendants.

Pursuant to the federal Declaratory Judgment Act, "any court of the United States, upon the filing of an appropriate pleading, may declare the rights and other legal relations of any interested party seeking such declaration, whether or not further relief is or could be sought."[71] To the extent that a plaintiff-insurer wishes to litigate in state court, all of the no-fault states have similar declaratory judgment statutes.[72] The federal Declaratory Judgment Act and its state law analogues require plaintiffs to demonstrate the existence of an

---

[70] *See*, e.g., Horizon Blue Cross Blue Shield of N.J. v. Transitions Recovery Program, 2015 U.S. Dist. LEXIS 164116 at *12 to *13 (D.N.J. 2015) ("The burden of proof to show a violation of the IFPA is preponderance of the evidence, which is lower than the 'clear and convincing evidence' standard required to prove common law fraud."). Unlike the IFPA, the Pennsylvania anti-insurance fraud statute requires proof by clear and convincing evidence. *See*, e.g., State Auto Prop. & Cas. Ins. Co. v. Feger, 2009 U.S. Dist. LEXIS 46510 at fn. 1 (E.D. Pa. 2009) (collecting cases).

[71] *See* 28 U.S.C. § 2201.

[72] *See*, e.g., N.Y. C.P.L.R. § 3001 (New York); N.J. Stat. § 2A:16-52 (New Jersey); MCR 2.605 (Michigan); ALM GL ch. 231A, § 1 (Massachusetts); Fla. Stat. § 86.011 (Florida).

actual case or controversy, lest the courts become involved in issuing advisory opinions aimed at illusory disputes. Such cases and controversies generally must be real and actual rather than speculative or contingent.[73]

In this context, insurers typically will be able to meet the case or controversy requirement by alleging that they have received fraudulent billing from a no-fault insurance fraud ring, that the billing remains outstanding and unpaid, and that the no-fault fraud ring actively is pursuing collection on the fraudulent billing. Courts have been fairly consistent in holding these types of allegations sufficient to plead a case or controversy and—by extension—to support a declaratory judgment claim.[74]

---

[73] *See*, e.g., Malowney v. Federal Collection Deposit Group, 193 F.3d 1342, 1347 (11th Cir. 1999) (controversy "may not be conjectural, hypothetical, or contingent; it must be real and immediate, and create a definite, rather than speculative threat of future injury.") (Internal quotations and citation omitted).

[74] *See*, e.g., Allstate Ins. Co. v. Williams, 2015 U.S. Dist. LEXIS 126020 at *13 to *16 (E.D.N.Y. 2015), adopted by Allstate Ins. Co. v. Dublin, 2015 U.S. Dist. LEXIS 125763 (E.D.N.Y. 2015) (recommending default judgment on a declaratory judgment claim in a no-fault fraud case based on the pendency of fraudulent no-fault insurance claims); State Farm Mut. Auto. Ins. Co. v. Warren Chiropractic & Rehab Clinic P.C., 2015 U.S. Dist. LEXIS 104332 at *52 to *56 (E.D. Mich. 2015) (denying a motion to dismiss the insurer's declaratory judgment claim, where the plaintiff-insurer sought to avoid liability on pending billing that was alleged to be fraudulent); State Farm Mut. Auto. Ins. Co. v. Physicians Group of Sarasota, LLC, 9 F. Supp. 3d 1303, 1313-1314 (M.D. Fla. 2014) (same).

7

Motions to Dismiss in No-Fault Insurance Anti-Fraud Litigation

In the best-case scenario, a defendant confronted with a detailed fraud complaint will know the game is up and immediately pursue settlement discussions. More commonly, however, defendants in no-fault insurance fraud cases will either file a pre-answer motion to dismiss or will file an answer and then immediately move for judgment on the pleadings. Given the weight of authority denying motions to dismiss in no-fault insurance fraud cases—or granting motions to dismiss without prejudice and with leave to replead—these motions are often an exercise in futility. Indeed, in their decisions denying motions to dismiss no-fault anti-fraud claims, judges have often cited the large body of authority from analogous actions in which substantively identical arguments for dismissal have been rejected.[1]

[1] *See*, e.g., State Farm Mut. Auto. Ins. Co. v. Warren Chiropractic & Rehab Clinic P.C., 2015 U.S. Dist. LEXIS 104332 at *14 to *23 (E.D. Mich. 2015) (rejecting the motion to dismiss a plaintiff-insurer's civil RICO claims, noting "the large number of federal courts that have rejected similar arguments," and collecting analogous no-fault anti-fraud cases where similar motions to dismiss were denied); Gov't Emples. Ins. Co. v. Korn, 310 F.R.D. 125, 130 (D.N.J. 2015) (denying a motion to dismiss the plaintiff-insurers' civil RICO claims as insufficiently pleaded, noting that "[m]any other courts have held the same in cases involving very similar facts" and collecting cases).

Even so, motions to dismiss are the rule rather than the exception in no-fault anti-fraud cases. There are many reasons why this is so. A no-fault fraud ring, or an individual member of the ring, may believe that the pendency of a dispositive motion will provide some leverage in settlement negotiations. Defendants in no-fault fraud cases may want to use the pendency of a motion to dismiss as a basis to seek a stay of discovery, so as to slow down the insurer's case and provide a window in which to secrete or dissipate their assets. They even may have a legitimate belief that they have done nothing wrong.

While there may be many reasons why defendants in no-fault fraud cases file motions to dismiss, the universe of arguments for dismissal is fairly limited. It therefore is possible to set forth the most common arguments for dismissal that recur in no-fault anti-fraud cases and the counterarguments that usually prevail.

A. Motions to Dismiss Common Law Fraud Claims

While there is no end to the creativity with which no-fault insurance fraud rings have responded to common law fraud claims, their arguments for dismissal typically boil down to the classics: (i) lack of particularity, (ii) lack of reliance, and (iii) lack of injury. We will discuss each of these arguments in turn.

1. Lack of Particularity

As discussed above, fraud-based claims—including, of course, common law fraud claims and RICO claims with mail or wire fraud predicates—must be pleaded with particularity. Plaintiff-insurers will typically be able to meet this particularity requirement by (i) detailing the overall mechanics of the fraudulent scheme—in other words, explaining why the defendants' claims were fraudulent; (ii) pleading a representative sample of the individual fraudulent claims in detail; and (iii) attaching, as an exhibit to the complaint, a chart identifying all of the claims that were submitted pursuant to the scheme by claim number, CPT code, amount charged, and the dates on which each claim was sent or received. Numerous courts in no-fault anti-fraud cases have held this level of detail sufficient to satisfy the particularity requirements of Rule 9(b) and its state law analogues.[2]

Even so, many alleged no-fault fraud rings persist in raising specificity challenges. Generally, these challenges are either based on the plaintiff-insurer's putative failure to plead the who, what, when, where, and why of each discrete fraudulent act or on the insurer's supposedly improper use of "group pleading." Neither of these arguments has found much traction in the courts.

For example, virtually every no-fault insurance fraud scheme will involve hundreds or even thousands of discrete fraudulent acts over the course of an extended period of time. As a practical matter, it would be unwieldy—if not outright impossible—for a plaintiff-insurer to plead the granular details of each misrepresentation or act of fraudulent concealment within the body of a complaint.

For instance, imagine a fraudulent healthcare provider that submitted hundreds of fraudulent bills over the course of a three-year period. Each bill sought reimbursement for seven or eight discrete services and falsely represented that the services were medically necessary and reimbursable, when in fact they were not. If all of the services

---

[2] *See*, e.g., Gov't Emples. Ins. Co. v. Korn, 310 F.R.D. 125, 131 (D.N.J. 2015) (rejecting the argument for dismissal pursuant to Rule 9(b), where "the Complaint gives numerous specific examples of Defendants' allegedly fraudulent conduct—complete with dates, patient identifiers, diagnoses, and the type of treatment involved" and "attached as exhibits to the Complaint are voluminous spreadsheets, itemizing specific bills by provider, claim number, and date."); State Farm Mut. Auto. Ins. Co. v. Warren Chiropractic & Rehab Clinic P.C., 2015 U.S. Dist. LEXIS 104332 at *20 to *21 (E.D. Mich. 2015) (collecting cases in which an explanation of the mechanics of a no-fault insurance fraud scheme, together with spreadsheets identifying individual fraudulent claims submitted pursuant to the scheme, were held sufficient under Rule 9(b); State Farm Mut. Auto. Ins. Co. v. Comprehensive Physician Servs., 2014 U.S. Dist. LEXIS 172824 at *5 (M.D. Fla. 2014) (rejecting the argument that the automobile insurer's anti-fraud complaint was insufficiently particularized under Rule 9(b), where the complaint alleged "that the Defendants submitted claims and charges to State Farm as services lawfully rendered, knowing that the claims or charges were not lawfully rendered" and where the complaint contained a chart identifying "over 400 claims in which Defendants made these false statements, along with the State Farm claim number and amount paid on each claim" and "further explain[ed] why the services are not lawfully rendered because they violate Florida law, are not in compliance with generally accepted standards of medical practice, and are not related or medically necessary.").

were medically unnecessary and unreimbursable for the same or similar reasons, should the insurer be required to include an extended narrative discussion in the complaint regarding why each individual service was unnecessary and unreimbursable, the date it was submitted for reimbursement, and the identity of each individual who dropped each fraudulent claim into the mailbox? Would the resulting complaint—which would probably run to several hundred pages at least—comport with Fed. R. Civ. P. 8's requirement of "a short and plain statement of the claim"?

Similarly, imagine a fraudulent healthcare provider with an illegal corporate structure—such as a medical practice that secretly and unlawfully is owned or controlled by an unlicensed non-physician. Because the healthcare provider has an illegal corporate structure, none of its billing is eligible for no-fault reimbursement, and every claim that the provider submits will misrepresent its eligibility to collect no-fault benefits in the first instance. In such a case, should an insurer be required to describe every single bill it received from the provider within the body of the complaint and include a claim-specific narrative as to why each individual bill is fraudulent?

The answer—in case after case—is no. Though alleged no-fault fraud rings often argue that plaintiff-insurers have not pleaded fraud with particularity because they have not alleged each individual fraudulent act in exacting detail within the body of the complaint, courts tend to take a more forgiving view. As discussed above, no-fault anti-fraud complaints will usually be held sufficient under Rule 9(b) or its state law equivalents if the complaints (i) detail the overall mechanics of the fraudulent scheme—in other words, explain why the defendants' claims were fraudulent; (ii) plead a representative sample of the individual fraudulent claims in detail; and (iii) attach, as an exhibit to the complaint, a chart identifying all of the claims that were submitted pursuant to the scheme.

What does this look like in practice? To take one example, in the case of a no-fault fraud ring that bills for medically unnecessary diagnostic tests, the complaint should provide considerable detail regarding the general nature of the insureds' injuries and why the diagnostic tests have no legitimate value in the diagnosis or treatment of those injuries.

For instance, in the case of VNG testing to diagnose unexplained dizziness or balance disorders, the complaint might explain that the insured patients at issue were involved in relatively minor fender benders that could not have caused them to suffer any dizziness or balance disorders. The complaint might go on to set forth the extremely rare circumstances in which minor automobile accidents were found to cause dizziness or balance disorders. Against this backdrop, the complaint could discuss how every single patient whom the defendants purported to treat received a medically unnecessary VNG test, ostensibly to ascertain the cause of dizziness or balance disorders that could not in any event have been caused by the underlying automobile accidents. To lend color to these general allegations regarding lack of medical necessity, the complaint should include a meaningful number of claim-specific examples—20 or 30 is usually more than sufficient—within the body of the complaint. In these claim-specific examples, the plaintiff-insurer can set forth the who, what, when, where, and why of the discrete claims by recounting the trivial nature of the insured patients' automobile accidents, the absence of any plausible circumstances that would lead to dizziness or balance disorders in the insureds, the dates on which the defendants nonetheless purported to provide medically unnecessary VNG testing to the insureds, and the dates on which the resulting charges were submitted, with the attendant false representations that the underlying services were medically necessary. Then, as an exhibit to the complaint, the plaintiff-insurer should attach a spreadsheet identifying—by claim number, CPT code, amount charged, and the dates on which each claim was sent or received—every claim for VNG testing that fits the pattern illustrated by the claim-specific examples. This usually will be sufficient, provided—as generally is the case—that all of the claims at issue were submitted by the same person or group of people.

Insurers can take a similar approach where a healthcare provider's billing misrepresents the legitimacy of its corporate structure. First, the complaint should set forth the pertinent state law prohibiting unlicensed parties from owning or controlling healthcare practices.

Second, the complaint should explain that healthcare providers with an illegal corporate structure are not eligible for no-fault reimbursement and that every bill submitted through an unlawfully organized provider therefore falsely represents that the provider is eligible for reimbursement in the first instance.

Third, the complaint should explain—in detail—exactly why the healthcare provider in question has an illegal corporate structure. For example, does the provider list unlicensed people as directors, members, or officers in its corporate filings? Does the provider have a "management agreement" with an unlicensed person that obligates the provider to pay over the vast majority of its revenues to the unlicensed person? Is an unlicensed person in de facto, day-to-day control of the practice?

Fourth, the complaint should set forth a reasonable number of claim-specific examples—again, 20 or 30 usually is sufficient—setting forth the who, what, when, where, and why of discrete claims that misrepresented the provider's entitlement to collect no-fault benefits.

Finally, the complaint should include a spreadsheet as an exhibit that specifically identifies every fraudulent claim that was submitted through the provider. If these general rules of thumb are followed and if all of the claims at issue were submitted by the same person or group of people, there will generally be no need to plead each fraudulent claim submission in detail within the body of the complaint itself.

As a variation on the "lack of specificity" arguments, some alleged no-fault fraud rings will argue that a plaintiff-insurer's complaint fails to sufficiently particularize each individual defendant's role in a scheme. This situation often arises in cases where several defendants act together to submit fraudulent billing.

For example, a corrupt physician may employ several subordinate physicians in a medical practice. If an insurer receives a fraudulent bill that misrepresents the medical necessity of a service that one of those employee-physicians purported to provide, who is responsible for the misrepresentation? Is it the employee-physician who purported to provide the underlying service, the medical practice through which the bill was submitted, or the corrupt physician who owns the practice? Oftentimes, all three will have colluded with one another to submit the fraudulent bill. While the employee-physician may not have personally mailed the fraudulent bill to the insurer, she purported to perform the service with the knowledge that it was medically useless and with the knowledge that it would be billed to the insurer. Similarly, while the physician who owns the practice may not have personally performed the medically unnecessary service, he knew it was unnecessary and caused his medical practice to bill the insurer for it anyway.

Along similar lines, imagine a medical practice that is unlawfully owned or controlled by unlicensed non-physicians. Who is responsible for billing that misrepresents the practice's corporate legitimacy and eligibility to collect no-fault insurance benefits? Is it the unlicensed non-physicians who secretly and illegally own and control the practice, the licensed physician who falsely purports to own and control the practice, the practice itself, or all three? Considering that all of the defendants arguably colluded with each other to submit each fraudulent charge, it will usually be appropriate to allege that each fraudulent bill was submitted collectively by the unlicensed non-physicians, the nominal physician "owner," and the practice itself.

In many cases, defendants in no-fault anti-fraud cases have argued that allegations such as these constitute improper "group pleading" because they fail to sufficiently particularize each defendant's individual role in the submission of fraudulent billing. These arguments usually fail, for two reasons. First, and as discussed above, the fraud pleading requirements will often be relaxed in cases where the information necessary to plead with greater particularity is peculiarly within the knowledge of a defendant. Especially when fraud is carried out in a corporate context, the precise internal workings of the fraud can be difficult for outsiders to discern. Second, and relatedly, most insurers will—even at the pleading stage—have sufficient information to plead each defendant's general role in the overall scheme even if they cannot specify which of several defendants dropped each individual fraudulent bill into the mailbox.

So long as a complaint sets forth the overall mechanics of a scheme and specifies each individual defendant's role in the scheme, courts will usually discount "group pleading" arguments and find that the complaint provides the defendants with adequate notice of the claims against them.[3]

---

[3] *See*, e.g., GEICO v. KJ Chiropractic Ctr. LLC, 12-cv-1138-Orl-36DAB, 2014 U.S. Dist. LEXIS 28913 at *12 to *18 (M.D. Fla. 2014) (complaint sufficient under Rule 9(b), where—although GEICO "has lumped the Defendants together in certain portions of the Second Amended Complaint"—it delineated each defendant's overall role in the scheme); State Farm Mut. Auto. Ins. Co. v. Universal Health Group, Inc., 2014 U.S. Dist. LEXIS 151213 at *6 to *9 (E.D. Mich. 2014) (rejecting the "group pleading" argument where each of the defendants was "alleged to have contributed to or orchestrated" the overall scheme); Allstate Ins. Co. v. Ahmed Halima, 2009 U.S. Dist. LEXIS 22443 at *18 to *20 (E.D.N.Y. 2009) (rejecting the defendants' contention that the plaintiff-insurers "merely have grouped the . . . Defendants with other Management Defendants and, thus, fail to particularize the specific role and acts of the . . . Defendants," where the complaint alleged that the defendants acted in concert to submit fraudulent claims).

2. Lack of Reliance

Justifiable reliance is an element of fraud, and a plaintiff's failure to allege justifiable reliance can warrant dismissal of a fraud claim. As a result, anti-fraud plaintiffs should make sure to allege that they justifiably relied on a defendant's misrepresentations or fraudulent concealment and to plead some facts to show that their reliance was, in fact, justifiable.

As a general rule, whether or not a party justifiably relied on some misrepresentation is a fact-intensive inquiry that will usually not be suitable for resolution on a motion to dismiss.[4] Even so, defendants in no-fault insurance anti-fraud cases have in the past argued that the claims verification tools that are available to insurers under state no-fault regulations—such as examinations under oath, peer reviews of suspect claims, and independent medical examinations of insured claimants—should preclude any allegation of justifiable reliance. In other words, alleged no-fault fraud rings have argued that because insurers have the tools to detect fraudulent claims, insurers cannot, as a matter of law, justifiably rely on a fraudulent claim. As a variation on this theme, some defendants in anti-fraud cases have argued that insurers are inherently large, well-resourced, and sophisticated businesses, and therefore should not be heard to claim that they were deceived by a no-fault insurance fraud scheme.

By and large, courts have rejected these types of "sophisticated insurer" arguments. In some cases, courts have noted that justifiable

---

[4] *See*, e.g., State Farm Mut. Auto. Ins. Co. v. Fayda, 2015 U.S. Dist. LEXIS 86795 at *7 (E.D.N.Y. 2015) (the insurer sufficiently alleged justifiable reliance by alleging that it paid defendants' allegedly fraudulent no-fault charges and holding that further inquiry into whether the reliance was justifiable was "a fact question for discovery"); Farmers Ins. Exch. v. First Choice Chiropractic & Rehab., 2014 U.S. Dist. LEXIS 98815 at *18 to *19 (D. Or. 2014) (rejecting the argument that plaintiff-insurers' complaint was subject to dismissal for lack of justifiable reliance and determining that it was "premature" to decide, at the pleading stage, "when plaintiffs were aware, or should have been aware, of defendants' alleged fraudulent scheme"); Allstate Ins. Co. v. Valley Physical Med. & Rehab., P.C., 2009 U.S. Dist. LEXIS 91291 at *13 to *16 (E.D.N.Y. 2009) (rejecting the argument, raised by defendants on motion to dismiss, that the plaintiff-insurer could not have justifiably relied on their alleged misrepresentations, considering the "highly fact dependent" nature of the inquiry).

reliance has to be assessed in the context of the short claims-handling time frames imposed by state no-fault systems, which as a practical matter force insurers to rely on incoming claims.[5] In other cases, courts have determined that insurers have a right to rely on facially valid claims submitted by licensed professionals through apparently legitimate professional entities and that such reliance is by its very nature justifiable.[6]

Overall, unless a defendant is able to show that an insurer had actual knowledge that a bill was fraudulent and paid it anyway, the defendant will find it almost impossible to secure a dismissal based on lack of justifiable reliance. Even then, plaintiff-insurers may have an argument that justifiable reliance is a question that must be determined in context.

If, for example, an insurer's internal records show that it had suspicions regarding a healthcare provider but nonetheless continued paying the provider's bills, the insurer still may be able to argue that state no-fault claims handling requirements forced it to rely on the provider's billing. For instance, the insurer's suspicious may not have been sufficient to deny payment on the bill or even to delay payment of the bill pending further investigation. What is more, absent a sufficient basis to deny or delay payment on the bill, the insurer may well have faced stiff and progressively escalating interest and penalties if it did not make prompt payment on the bill. Under such circumstances, courts may be willing to deny a motion to dismiss for lack of reliance and to let the jury decide the question.

---

[5] *See*, e.g., Allstate Ins. Co. v. Lyons, 843 F. Supp. 2d 358, 375 (E.D.N.Y. 2012) (rejecting the argument that the plaintiff—as a "sophisticated insurer"—could not justifiably have relied on the defendants' alleged misrepresentations and noting that "regardless of the strength of [plaintiff's] investigatory capabilities, it is not barred from asserting fraud claims solely for failing to detect—within the no-fault law's 30-day window, no less—the complex fraudulent schemes attributed to defendants here").

[6] *See*, e.g., Allstate Ins. Co. v. Ahmed Halima, 2009 U.S. Dist. LEXIS 22443 at *15 (E.D.N.Y. 2009) (rejecting the motion to dismiss predicated on putative lack of justifiable reliance and observing that "[o]n a motion to dismiss, the court cannot say definitively that an insurance company that receives thousands of insurance claims could not reasonably rely on facially valid claims submitted by a licensed professional corporation and accompanied by reports from licensed physicians").

3. Lack of Injury

Of course, it is not sufficient for an insurer to allege that it justifiably relied on a misrepresentation. The insurer also must allege that it suffered some cognizable injury as the result of its reliance. In most cases, this will be a fairly straightforward allegation to make—the insurer will simply allege that it paid money to a no-fault insurance fraud ring in reliance on fraudulent billing and that the payments constitute the resulting injury.

However, the issue becomes more complicated where a case involves misrepresentations as to the legitimacy of a healthcare provider's corporate structure as opposed to misrepresentations as to the legitimacy of the underlying healthcare services. For example, what if a healthcare provider has an illegal corporate structure in that it is unlawfully owned and controlled by unlicensed nonprofessionals but all of the services billed through that healthcare provider were medically necessary and actually performed? Under such circumstances, can a plaintiff-insurer really allege that it suffered some cognizable injury by paying a bill for medically necessary services that actually were provided to one of its insureds?

The answer usually will be "yes." Though defendants in corporate structure fraud cases have repeatedly argued that plaintiff-insurers were not injured by the fraud because—after all—the insured patients actually received medically necessary services, these arguments have generally been unavailing. Courts have determined that payments to an illegally organized healthcare practice are sufficient to constitute a fraud injury because insurers are under no obligation to pay an illegally organized healthcare practice at all, whether or not the underlying services were medically necessary.[7]

---

[7] *See*, e.g., Liberty Mut. Fire Ins. Co. v. Acute Care Chiropractic Clinic P.A., 88 F. Supp. 3d 985, 1008–09, 1012–13 (D. Minn. 2015) (rejecting the argument that the plaintiff-insurer failed to state fraud-based claims predicated on healthcare providers' illegal corporate structure); Gov't Emples. Ins. Co. v. Zuberi, 2015 U.S. Dist. LEXIS 133789 at *15 to *16 (D.N.J. 2015) (rejecting the motion to dismiss a complaint alleging that healthcare providers misrepresented the legitimacy of their corporate structure); State Farm Mut. Auto. Ins. Co. v. Rabiner, 749 F. Supp. 2d 94, 103 (E.D.N.Y. 2010) (rejecting the argument that the plaintiff-insurer failed to state fraud-based claims "because it has not alleged that the medical services that were the subject of the challenged claims were medically unnecessary or not rendered," where the insurer was not required in the first instance to "pay monies to an improperly licensed professional corporation").

B. Motions to Dismiss Unjust Enrichment Claims

By and large, arguments for dismissal of unjust enrichment claims will run parallel to arguments for dismissal of common law fraud claims because proof of unjust enrichment in a no-fault insurance fraud case will depend—at least to a large extent—on proof of fraud. As a result, if an insurer cannot colorably allege that a defendant engaged in fraudulent conduct, it is likely to have difficulty colorably alleging that the defendant was unjustly enriched.

Nonetheless, there are at least some common arguments for dismissal that are peculiar to unjust enrichment claims, specifically (i) arguments to the effect that the existence of a contractual relationship between the parties precludes an unjust enrichment claim and (ii) arguments to the effect that a given defendant was not directly enriched by the underlying scheme.

Although these arguments are commonly raised by alleged no-fault fraud rings, they need not detain us long. Although an insurer arguably may have a contractual relationship with a healthcare provider that takes an assignment of no-fault benefits from an insured patient, the healthcare provider will have some difficulty arguing that the contract precludes fraud-based unjust enrichment claims. This is because the insurer's fraud-based claims—including any unjust enrichment claims—will typically be predicated on misrepresentations that are collateral and extraneous to the contract at issue.[8]

For example, the healthcare provider will be unable to point to any contractual provision—whether in the assignment of no-fault insurance benefits it takes from an insured patient, in the underlying insurance policy, or anywhere else—whereby it agreed to refrain from misrepresenting the medical necessity of its services or its corporate structure and legitimacy. More generally, some classes of defendants in no-fault insurance fraud litigation—such as unlicensed individuals

[8] *See*, e.g., State Farm Mut. Auto. Ins. Co. v. Pointe Physical Therapy, LLC, 107 F. Supp. 3d 772, 793 (E.D. Mich. 2015) (unless it is undisputed that there is an express contract between the same parties covering the same subject matter, an unjust enrichment claim will lie); Allstate Ins. Co. v. Ahmed Halima, 2009 U.S. Dist. LEXIS 22443 at *22 to *28 (E.D.N.Y. 2009) (rejecting the argument that the contractual relationship between the parties barred the plaintiff-insurer's common law fraud and unjust enrichment claims against alleged no-fault insurance fraud ring, where the alleged fraud was collateral and extraneous to any contract between the parties).

who secretly and illegally own and control professional practices—will not have any claim to a contractual relationship with a plaintiff-insurer. Indeed, unlicensed individuals and entities that secretly and illegally own and control professional practices typically do everything that is in their power to conceal their existence from insurers, rendering any claim to a contractual relationship with the insurers specious at best.

The other common argument for dismissal of unjust enrichment claims in the no-fault context is an argument to the effect that the defendant did not directly benefit from the fraudulent scheme. This argument is typically accompanied by a claim by the defendant that she was only an employee or independent contractor of the fraudulent practice and that the insurer's payments went directly to the practice and its owners, not to the employees or independent contractors of the practice. Most courts that have considered this argument have rejected it, holding that an unjust enrichment claim will lie when it can be inferred that a defendant shared in a benefit—however indirectly—that was directly conferred on others.[9]

C. Motions to Dismiss Civil RICO Claims

Many federal courts are sensitive to the stigmatizing effect of RICO claims and actively look for reasons to dismiss defective RICO complaints.[10] Some courts go so far as to require RICO plaintiffs to file

---

[9] *See*, e.g., State Farm Mut. Auto. Ins. Co. v. B&A Diagnostic, Inc., 104 F. Supp. 3d 1366, 1375–76 (S.D. Fla. 2015) (a defendant is not required to individually receive payments in order for a cause of action for unjust enrichment to exist); State Farm Mut. Auto. Ins. Co. v. Rabiner, 2010 U.S. Dist. LEXIS 119961 at *18 (E.D.N.Y. 2010) (benefit necessary to support unjust enrichment claim can be either direct or indirect); AIU Ins. Co. v. Olmecs Med. Supply, Inc., 2005 U.S. Dist. LEXIS 29666 at *47 to *49 (E.D.N.Y. 2005) (rejecting the "no direct benefit" argument and denying the motion to dismiss where it could be inferred that the moving defendants shared in the benefit directly conferred upon other defendants).

[10] *See*, e.g., Ruiz v. Alegria, 896 F.2d 645, 650 (1st Cir. 1990) ("The mere assertion of a RICO claim consequently has an almost inevitable stigmatizing effect on those named as defendants. In fairness to innocent parties, courts should strive to flush out frivolous RICO allegations at an early stage of the litigation."); Katzman v. Victoria's Secret Catalogue, 167 F.R.D. 649, 655 (S.D.N.Y. 1996) (designating civil RICO the litigation equivalent of a "thermonuclear device" for its "inevitable stigmatizing effect on those named as defendants" and asserting that courts should therefore

so-called "RICO case statements" when asserting RICO claims. Such RICO case statements, when required, must typically be filed together with a RICO complaint or shortly thereafter and generally obligate a plaintiff to demonstrate that it has met the technical pleading requirements for asserting a RICO claim.

For example, a RICO case statement will usually require a plaintiff to set forth each predicate act of racketeering activity that is alleged to support a RICO claim, how the predicate acts amount to a pattern of racketeering activity, the structure of the alleged enterprise, how the various defendants were associated with the alleged enterprise, and so forth. To the extent that they are required, RICO case statements are usually considered to be part of the complaint, so the court can consider them on a motion to dismiss.[11]

In this setting, and given the hyper-technical RICO pleading requirements, there are numerous potential arguments that defendants can raise in support of motions to dismiss civil RICO claims. However, certain arguments tend to recur more often than others in the context of no-fault anti-fraud litigation. In particular, arguments (i) that mail or wire fraud–based RICO claims are not pleaded with the requisite specificity, (ii) that the plaintiff-insurer did not justifiably rely on any misrepresentations in the context of mail or wire fraud–based RICO claims, (iii) that the predicate acts of racketeering activity are not sufficient to constitute an open- or closed-ended pattern of racketeering activity, (iv) that the alleged racketeering enterprise is not sufficiently distinct from the defendants on the underlying RICO claim, and (v) that one or another of the defendants did not sufficiently participate in the operation and management of the alleged RICO enterprise.

"strive to flush out frivolous RICO allegations at an early stage of the litigation") (Internal citation omitted), *aff'd sub nom.* Katzman v. Victoria's Secret Catalogue Div. of The Ltd., Inc., 113 F.3d 1229 (2d Cir. 1997).

[11] *See*, e.g., Mackin v. Auberger, 59 F. Supp. 3d 528, 541 (W.D.N.Y. 2014) ("The Local Rule mandating the provision of a RICO case statement does not state that a case statement may be treated as part of the allegations in the complaint. . . . However, the Second Circuit Court of Appeals directs that a RICO case statement should be read together with a complaint on a motion to dismiss."); Macauley v. Estate of Nicholas, 7 F. Supp. 3d 468 at fn. 4 (E.D. Pa. 2014) ("The RICO Case Statement is a pleading that may be considered part of the operative complaint for the purposes of a motion to dismiss or a motion for judgment on the pleadings.") (Internal quotations and citation omitted).

While we have previously alluded to some of these arguments in other contexts, it is worthwhile to address them in the specific context of motions to dismiss civil RICO claims.

1. Lack of Particularity

While there are a large number of activities that can, for purposes of a civil RICO claim, constitute predicate acts of racketeering activity, the most common predicate acts alleged by automobile insurers in no-fault insurance anti-fraud cases are mail fraud and wire fraud. As discussed above, this is because most no-fault fraud rings will submit their fraudulent billing via the mail, through the use of a fax machine, or through some electronic claims submission system. Like common law fraud, mail and wire fraud must be pleaded with particularity under Fed. R. Civ. P. 9(b) or its state law equivalents.

As with common law fraud claims, many defendants in no-fault fraud cases will argue for dismissal of insurers' mail or wire fraud–based RICO claims by contending that the claims are not pleaded with the requisite specificity. These types of arguments will, as a general rule, track the common particularity arguments that are raised against common law fraud claims. In particular, insurers often will be confronted with contentions that their complaints fail to plead the who, what, when, where, and why of each discrete fraudulent act or that the attribution of a discrete fraudulent act to more than one defendant constitutes defective "group pleading."

Again, these arguments will generally fail as long as the plaintiff-insurer's complaint (i) details the overall mechanics of the fraudulent scheme—in other words, explains why the defendants' claims were fraudulent; (ii) pleads a representative sample of the individual fraudulent claims in detail; and (iii) attaches, as an exhibit to the complaint, a chart identifying all of the claims that were submitted pursuant to the scheme. As with common law fraud claims, numerous courts considering civil RICO claims have held this level of detail sufficient to satisfy the fraud pleading requirements.[12]

---

[12] *See*, e.g., State Farm Mut. Auto. Ins. Co. v. Warren Chiropractic & Rehab Clinic P.C., 2015 U.S. Dist. LEXIS 104332 at *18 to *23 (E.D. Mich. 2015) (finding a RICO complaint containing these elements to satisfy the fraud pleading requirements and collecting cases); Allstate Ins. Co. v. Lyons, 843 F. Supp. 2d 358, 372–73 (E.D.N.Y. 2012) (RICO complaint sufficient under Rule 9(b), where it

What is more, and as with common law fraud claims, courts in no-fault fraud cases typically discount arguments that civil RICO claims are based on improper group pleading. Usually, this is because the information necessary to particularize each defendant's discrete role in a complex no-fault fraud scheme is going to be peculiarly within the knowledge of the defendants—especially in cases, like most no-fault fraud cases, where the fraud is enacted through a professional corporation. Provided that a complaint sets forth the overall operation of the scheme and particularizes each individual defendant's general role in the scheme, courts generally find that the complaint gives the defendants adequate notice of the claims against them.[13]

2. Lack of Reliance

Unlike common law fraud claims, civil RICO claims that are predicated on mail or wire fraud do not require first-party reliance.[14] In other words, where a RICO claim is predicated on mail or wire fraud, a plaintiff-insurer does not have to plead or prove that it individually

---

"explain[ed] in detail the contours of the fraudulent scheme it alleges," "provide[d] several representative examples of the thousands of claims at issue in this case," and where the plaintiff-insurer "attache[d] to its Complaint a series of charts that include each of the charges submitted by the defendants that it believe[d] were fraudulent," with each chart "detail[ed] the entity that submitted each claim, as well as the corresponding claim number, the year [the plaintiff] paid the claim, and the amount paid").

[13] *See*, e.g., GEICO v. KJ Chiropractic Ctr. LLC, 12-cv-1138-Orl-36DAB, 2014 U.S. Dist. LEXIS 28913 at *12 to *18 (M.D. Fla. 2014) (complaint sufficient under Rule 9(b) where—although GEICO "has lumped the Defendants together in certain portions of the Second Amended Complaint"—it delineated each defendant's overall role in the scheme); State Farm Mut. Auto. Ins. Co. v. Universal Health Group, Inc., 2014 U.S. Dist. LEXIS 151213 at *6 to *9 (E.D. Mich. 2014) (rejecting the "group pleading" argument where each of the defendants was "alleged to have contributed to or orchestrated" the overall scheme); Allstate Ins. Co. v. Ahmed Halima, 2009 U.S. Dist. LEXIS 22443 at *18 to *20 (E.D.N.Y. 2009) (rejecting the defendants' contention that the plaintiff-insurers "merely have grouped the Palter Defendants with other Management Defendants and, thus, fail to particularize the specific role and acts of the Palter Defendants," where the complaint alleged that the defendants acted in concert to submit fraudulent claims).

[14] *See*, e.g., Bridge v. Phoenix Bond & Indem. Co., 553 U.S. 639, 661 (2008) (first-party reliance not required to assert a RICO claim predicated on mail fraud).

relied on any misrepresentation. Although the Supreme Court, in *Bridge v. Phoenix Bond & Indem. Co.*, 553 U.S. 639 (2008), made clear that first-party reliance is not required to support a RICO claim predicated on mail or wire fraud, it did note, in dicta, that the proximate causation requirement inherent in 18 U.S.C. § 1964(c), which provides a private RICO claim to anyone injured "by reason of" a RICO violation, probably means that someone has to rely on a misrepresentation for a RICO claim to lie.[15]

In no-fault insurance anti-fraud litigation, the distinction between first-party reliance and third-party reliance will usually be academic. Most plaintiff-insurers will be in a position to allege that they themselves relied on a no-fault fraud ring's fraudulent billing. They will not need to allege that some third party relied on any misrepresentations attendant to the underlying scheme.

Even so, if an insurer is for some reason unable to colorably allege that it relied on a defendant's fraudulent misrepresentations, it may be possible to show that some third party relied on a misrepresentation in relation to the scheme. For example, in a case alleging that a healthcare provider misrepresented the legitimacy of its corporate structure, the insurer may be able to show that the state licensing authorities relied on the healthcare provider's misrepresentations in issuing a license to the provider.

Along similar lines, in a case focused on medical necessity, the insurer may be able to show that the insured patients themselves relied on a healthcare provider's false representations that a given type of service was medically necessary.

As with common law fraud claims, on a motion to dismiss a civil RICO claim, the most common reliance argument will be to the effect that the insurer has not sufficiently alleged that it justifiably relied on any misrepresentations. As discussed previously, these arguments are usually based, in turn, on contentions that the insurers' investigative capabilities preclude any claim that their reliance was justifiable. Courts typically reject these arguments and hold that justifiable reliance in the RICO context, as in the common law fraud

[15] *See Id.*, 553 U.S. at 658 (Although the Supreme Court held that first-party reliance was not required for a RICO claim predicated on mail fraud, it observed that, "[o]f course, none of this is to say that a RICO plaintiff who alleges injury 'by reason of' a pattern of mail fraud can prevail without showing that someone relied on the defendant's misrepresentations.") (Emphasis in original).

context, is a fact question that is not suitable for resolution at the pleading stage.

3. Lack of a Pattern of Racketeering Activity

As discussed previously, insurers will usually be able to allege a closed-ended pattern of racketeering activity in support of their civil RICO claims because most no-fault insurance fraud rings will have operated on a consistent basis for a number of years and will have committed numerous predicate acts of mail or wire fraud over the course of those years. To the extent that an insurer is unable to allege a closed-ended pattern—a situation that can arise if a no-fault fraud ring operated for only a short period of time prior to the commencement of the insurer's anti-fraud litigation—the insurer may be able to plead an open-ended pattern of racketeering activity, especially if the scheme is ongoing at the time when the complaint is filed.

Against this backdrop, most defendants in no-fault anti-fraud cases will not bother to argue that a plaintiff-insurer has failed to sufficiently allege the requisite pattern of racketeering activity in support of its RICO claims. It is simply too difficult to rebut the notion that hundreds of discrete fraudulent claims submitted via the mails or wires over the course of months or years are inadequate to constitute a pattern. To the extent that a defendant does argue that a plaintiff has failed to plead a RICO pattern, the argument will usually appear as a contention that multiple acts of mail or wire fraud involving a single victim or a single type of misrepresentation are insufficient to constitute a pattern of racketeering activity. These contentions rely, in turn, on arguments regarding the purpose of the RICO statute—namely to combat organized crime. Defendants may posit that a statute aimed at combatting organized crime should not be used as a sword against inherently limited schemes aimed at a single plaintiff. Were it otherwise, the argument goes, then virtually any garden-variety fraud could give rise to RICO liability.

There certainly are cases in which courts have held that mail or wire fraud schemes involving a single victim or a single type of misrepresentation did not involve the requisite pattern of racketeering activity. However, these cases generally involved open-ended patterns of racketeering activity because the plaintiffs had not alleged that the underlying predicate acts of racketeering activity occurred over a "substantial period of time."[16] Because the continuity necessary to establish a pattern of racketeering activity is "centrally a temporal concept,"[17] most insurers will be in a good position to argue that the number of victims or varieties of misrepresentations are irrelevant in the context of closed-ended patterns of racketeering activity that extend over a term of years.

Indeed, to the extent that defendants in no-fault fraud cases have raised "single victim" arguments in an attempt to show the absence of a closed-ended pattern of racketeering activity, the arguments have been rejected.[18]

4. Lack of "Distinctiveness" Between the RICO Defendants and the Alleged RICO Enterprise

As previously noted, the RICO statute makes a distinction between the defendant on a RICO claim—or, in the language of the RICO statute, the "person"—and the racketeering "enterprise." Thus, to establish liability under Section 1962(c), a plaintiff "must allege and

[16] *See*, e.g., Antonacci v. City of Chicago, 640 Fed. Appx. 553, 557 (7th Cir. 2016) (where the alleged scheme lasted only 21 months, and the "combination of such a short period with only a single victim of a single scheme" was insufficient to establish the requisite pattern); Terry A. Lambert Plumbing, Inc. v. Western Sec. Bank, 934 F.2d 976, 981 (8th Cir. 1991) (a single transaction that involves only one victim and takes place over a short period of time does not constitute a pattern; the complaint was dismissed where the case involved, at most, a plan to defraud a single company in connection with a single set of loan agreements); Baldwin v. Twp. of Union, 2005 U.S. Dist. LEXIS 37534 (D.N.J. 2005) ("Courts often hold that a single scheme involving a single injury to a single victim within a short period of time falls outside of RICO due to lack of pattern, even though all aspects are entirely related.") (Emphasis added).

[17] H. J. Inc. v. Northwestern Bell Tel. Co., 492 U.S. 229, 242 (1989).

[18] *See*, e.g., State Farm Mut. Auto. Ins. Co. v. Warren Chiropractic & Rehab Clinic P.C., 2015 U.S. Dist. LEXIS 104332 at *23 to *26 (E.D. Mich. 2015) (rejecting the argument that the plaintiff-insurer's complaint failed to allege the requisite RICO pattern because it alleged "a single fraudulent scheme to defraud a single company," where the scheme had gone on for years, was not inherently terminable, and could continue indefinitely); Gov't Emples. Ins. Co. v. Hollis Med. Care, P.C., 2011 U.S. Dist. LEXIS 130721 at *28 to *30 (E.D.N.Y. 2011) (rejecting the argument that the plaintiff-insurer's complaint alleging "predicate acts of mail fraud by a small number of participants against a single victim" was insufficient to establish a closed-ended pattern, where complaint alleged thousands of fraudulent charges were submitted over a six-year period).

prove the existence of two distinct entities: (1) a 'person'; and (2) an 'enterprise' that is not simply the same 'person' referred to by a different name."[19]

In practice, this means that an entity that is identified in a complaint as a racketeering enterprise usually cannot be named as a defendant on the underlying RICO claim. To the extent that a defendant on a RICO claim is also doing double-duty as the alleged RICO enterprise, the claim is almost certain to be dismissed. In no-fault anti-fraud cases, this can limit an insurer's ability to obtain a treble-damages judgment against a healthcare practice itself because the healthcare practice through which fraudulent billing is submitted usually is named as the RICO enterprise, which means that it cannot be named as a defendant on the RICO claim.

Even so, plaintiff-insurers can still name all of the owners and associates of a healthcare practice as defendants on a RICO claim even if they cannot name the practice itself as a defendant on the claim. This usually is satisfactory considering that the practices can be named as defendants on other claims, including common law fraud claims that permit punitive damages.

PRACTICE POINTS

Distinctiveness and Association-in-Fact Rico Enterprises

- ✓ Although in theory a plaintiff-insurer could name a healthcare practice and its associates as an association-in-fact RICO enterprise and then name the healthcare practice and its associates as the defendants on the underlying RICO claim, this should be avoided where possible.
- ✓ While such an association-in-fact enterprise might constitute something more than the sum of its parts, it can open the plaintiff-insurer up to a distinctiveness challenge.

Even where insurers do not name a healthcare practice/RICO enterprise as a defendant on a RICO claim, some defendants may argue that a closely held healthcare practice, such as a sole-shareholder professional corporation, is not sufficiently distinct from its owner to

[19] Cedric Kushner Promotions, Ltd. v. King, 533 U.S. 158, 161 (2001).

constitute a sufficiently separate racketeering enterprise. Courts have rejected these types of arguments and have held that a professional entity is sufficiently separate from its owner to constitute a RICO enterprise in a complaint alleging its owner to be the RICO defendant.[20]

5. Lack of Participation in the Operation and Management of the RICO Enterprise

Because a RICO defendant must have participated in the operation and management of the RICO enterprise[21] and because this "participation" has been interpreted to require some part in directing the enterprise's affairs,[22] insurers should take care to ensure that the defendants on their RICO claims actually had some legitimate managerial role in the underlying scheme. Minor clerical employees, outside service providers such as lawyers and accountants, and the patients who received medically useless or illusory "treatment" from a fraudulent healthcare practice alleged to be a RICO enterprise will typically not meet the "participation in the operation and management" test even if they knew some fraud was afoot.

By contrast, the owners of a corrupt healthcare practice, its managers, and its higher-level employees—including the professionals who rendered fraudulent services from the practice—will generally fit the "participation" bill, at least at the pleading stage. These categories of individuals may attempt to argue, on a motion to dismiss, that their role in the enterprise was too subordinate to constitute participation in its operation and management. However, as long as the insurer has pleaded some facts to establish a defendant's ability to direct some meaningful aspect of the enterprise's affairs, courts will likely be reluctant to resolve fact-intensive operation and management questions on a pre-answer motion to dismiss.

---

[20] *See*, e.g., Allstate Ins. Co. v. Rozenberg, 590 F. Supp. 2d 384, 391 (E.D.N.Y. 2008) (where the plaintiff-insurers alleged that "the corporate officers and employees are the RICO persons while the corporations are the RICO enterprise," and the "legal distinction between the RICO enterprise . . . and the RICO persons . . . [was] sufficient to satisfy the distinctiveness requirement").

[21] *See* De Falco v. Bernas, 244 F.3d 286, 309 (2d Cir. 2001), citing Reyes v. Ernst & Young, 507 U.S. 170, 179–85 (1993).

[22] *Id.*

Indeed, in the context of no-fault insurance fraud cases, a RICO defendant's participation in the operation and management of the alleged enterprise—usually a healthcare practice or related group of practices—will usually be so manifest that the defendant will not even bother to make a nonparticipation argument on a motion to dismiss.

For example, the record owner of an allegedly corrupt healthcare practice/RICO enterprise cannot seriously contend that she lacks an operational or managerial role. Nor, for that matter, can an unlicensed individual or entity alleged to secretly and unlawfully own and control the practice—provided that the plaintiff-insurer can plead some facts to lend color to its allegations of illegal corporate structure.

Similarly, though a physician or other licensed healthcare provider who is associated with a corrupt practice as an employee or independent contractor may contend that they "just work there" and have no management role, these types of contentions are unlikely to prevail on a motion to dismiss at the pleading stage. Rather, the insurer will be well positioned to argue that even if these professionals were just employees or independent contractors of a corrupt healthcare practice/RICO enterprise, the practice could not have operated without their involvement. They were, after all, professionals, and the fraudulent billing that was submitted through the practice was for services that they themselves performed.

Perhaps the most novel nonparticipation argument is one that has been repeatedly advanced by licensed professionals—typically physicians—who allegedly permitted unlicensed nonprofessionals to secretly and illegally own and control their healthcare practices. These professionals have argued, in substance, that because they were alleged to have ceded total control over their professional practices to unlicensed third parties, they could not possibly have personally participated in the operation and management of the healthcare practices in a manner sufficient to support RICO liability.

However, without a licensed professional willing to falsely pose as the "owner" of an illegally organized healthcare practice, no healthcare practice could ever be unlawfully owned and controlled by unlicensed nonprofessionals or used by those nonprofessionals to submit fraudulent no-fault billing that misrepresents the legitimacy of the practice's corporate structure. As such, courts have rejected this type of nonparticipation argument.[23]

D. Motions to Dismiss Declaratory Judgment Claims

In some cases, a no-fault insurance fraud scheme will be over and done with by the time a plaintiff-insurer completes its investigation, realizes it has been defrauded, and prepares and files its complaint. In such cases, where a fraud ring no longer is submitting fraudulent billing or pursuing collection of its unpaid fraudulent billing, the claims in the insurer's complaint—like RICO, common law fraud, or unjust enrichment claims—will focus exclusively on recovering money that has already been paid out.

As we have seen, however, many no-fault insurance fraud schemes are active and continuing at the time when an insurer is contemplating litigation. A corrupt healthcare practice and its associates may be submitting fraudulent billing on an ongoing basis. Even if a no-fault fraud ring has stopped submitting new billing, it may still be attempting to collect on its outstanding charges through collections litigation and arbitration. As discussed above, the deck often can be stacked against insurers in no-fault collections suits or arbitration, where discovery is limited and insurers often come under pressure from judges and arbitrators to settle cases that—in the fullness of time and with reasonable discovery—would be defensible. Under such circumstances, many insurers include declaratory judgment claims in their anti-fraud complaints, seeking a declaration to the effect that they are not liable to pay any of a no-fault fraud ring's

[23] *See*, e.g., Liberty Mut. Ins. Co. v. Excel Imaging, P.C., 2012 U.S. Dist. LEXIS 86303 at *63 to *64 (E.D.N.Y. 2012) ("In the present case, Liberty Insurance's allegations that . . . that the Nominal Owner Defendants agreed to serve as the 'paper' owners of Excel in exchange for a fee are sufficient to support the claim that the defendants actively participated in the creation or management of Excel."); Allstate Ins. Co. v. Bogoraz, 818 F. Supp. 2d 544, 553 (E.D.N.Y. 2011) ("Defendant's argument that the allegations of his failure to operate, manage or control [the professional corporation] mandates dismissal [are] unavailing. These allegations are foundational to plaintiffs case; as a medical professional, had defendant been the sole owner, operator and manager as he represented himself to be, there would be no fraud and he would have been entitled to receive no-fault benefits.").

outstanding charges. Typically, these declaratory judgment claims are asserted alongside civil RICO, common law fraud, unjust enrichment, and other related causes of action aimed at recovering whatever money already has been paid pursuant to fraudulent no-fault charges.

These types of declaratory judgment claims can give an insurer considerable leverage in the context of settlement negotiations because they can provide the basis for a motion to stay and enjoin a fraud ring's attempts to collect on its billing during the pendency of the lawsuit. Oftentimes, a dishonest healthcare provider will attempt to fund her defense of an insurer's fraud claims with the ongoing proceeds of the underlying scheme. If the insurer asserts a claim for a declaratory judgment and can obtain a stay of the healthcare provider's collections activity pending the resolution of the declaratory judgment claim, then the healthcare provider may find herself deprived of resources with which to mount a defense, and the case may settle quite quickly. In addition, where it appears that a plaintiff-insurer has a viable declaratory judgment claim, a corrupt healthcare practice may decide not to invest resources in continuing to submit fraudulent billing to that insurer in the expectation that declaratory relief could render its investment worthless. This, too, can facilitate a settlement.

Even outside of the settlement context, there are considerable advantages to declaratory judgment claims in no-fault anti-fraud cases, including—most obviously—that a successful declaratory judgment claim can obviate the need for an insurer to pay large amounts of outstanding fraudulent billing. In some cases, the potential benefit of a declaratory judgment in the form of avoidance of a massive amount of potential liability on outstanding fraudulent billing can exceed the potential recovery on common law fraud, civil RICO, unjust enrichment, or other claims. For example, an insurer may have denied the bulk of a healthcare provider's fraudulent billing, resulting in a low amount of prospective damages on fraud-based claims relative to the amount of outstanding and unpaid billing that could be the subject of a declaratory judgment claim.

As a result, declaratory judgment claims are often as hotly contested as civil RICO and other fraud-based claims. Defendants in no-fault fraud cases often seek to dismiss declaratory judgment claims and may put somewhat different glosses on their dismissal arguments.

However, all of the arguments tend to fall into one of three related categories: (i) arguments to the effect that the court should abstain from exercising jurisdiction over the declaratory judgment claims, (ii) arguments to the effect that the declaratory judgment claims must be dismissed in favor of arbitration procedures that are in place in some no-fault states, and/or (iii) arguments to the effect that the insurer's declaratory judgment claims are moot because the defendants are no longer engaging in the practices that gave rise to the declaratory judgment claims.

1. Common Abstention Arguments and Counterarguments

Although some states have rules in place that permit state courts to abstain from entertaining disputes that are pending in other forums, the main abstention doctrines are primarily federal. For a number of reasons, many insurers and anti-fraud litigators prefer to file their cases in federal court. These reasons can include—as discussed previously—a belief that the quality of the federal bench may be higher or that discovery will proceed more quickly with the assistance of a magistrate judge and the expedited briefing schedule on discovery motions that is in place in many federal courts.

Conversely, many defendants in no-fault fraud cases prefer for their outstanding billing to be adjudicated in state court collections actions, or in arbitration, where the environment is more favorable for them. As a result, they will often argue that federal courts should abstain from exercising jurisdiction over insurers' declaratory judgment claims so they can pursue collection on their outstanding fraudulent billing in state court or at arbitration.

On the face of things, it might appear as if an alleged no-fault fraud ring's abstention arguments would find little traction in the federal courts. Insurers will usually have little difficulty satisfying the diversity jurisdiction requirements of 28 U.S.C. § 1332 because the amount in controversy typically will be more than $75,000, exclusive of interest and costs, and the plaintiff-insurer generally will be a citizen of a different state than each of the defendants. To the limited extent that the insurer and the defendants are not completely diverse, the insurer often will be able to obtain federal question jurisdiction under 28 U.S.C. § 1331 via civil RICO claims. Moreover, for generations the Supreme Court has emphasized the duty of the federal courts to exercise the jurisdiction conferred upon them.[24] Therefore, abstention is "an extraordinary and narrow exception to the duty of a District Court to adjudicate a controversy properly before it."[25]

Nonetheless, some federal judges can give the impression that they would prefer no-fault insurance disputes to be adjudicated elsewhere. They may feel that a no-fault insurance fraud case involving a few million dollars is "small beer" next to a massive securities fraud or terrorism case. Or they may make note of the high volume of no-insurance fraud cases that are filed in other federal districts and shudder to imagine their increased workload if their district is next. Whatever the reason, some no-fault fraud defendants have prevailed—at least initially—on what appear to be defective abstention arguments. As a result, it is important to discuss the most common abstention arguments and counterarguments.

(i) Abstention Pursuant to Burford v. Sun Oil Co. *and its Progeny*

Pursuant to the abstention doctrine announced in *Burford v. Sun Oil Co.*, 319 U.S. 315 (1943) and its progeny, "[w]here timely and adequate state-court review is available, a federal court sitting in equity must decline to interfere with the proceedings or orders of state administrative agencies: (1) when there are difficult questions of state law bearing on policy problems of substantial public import whose importance transcends the result in the case then at bar; or (2) where the exercise of federal review of the question in a case and in similar cases would be disruptive of state efforts to establish a coherent policy with respect to a matter of substantial public concern."[26]

---

[24] *See*, e.g., Cohens v. Virginia, 19 U.S. 264, 404 (1821) ("We have no more right to decline the exercise of jurisdiction which is given, than to usurp that which is not given. The one or the other would be treason to the Constitution"); *See also* Chicot County v. Sherwood, 148 U.S. 529, 534 (1893) ("[T]he courts of the United States are bound to proceed to judgment and to afford redress to suitors before them in every case to which their jurisdiction extends. They cannot abdicate their authority or duty in any case in favor of another jurisdiction. . . .") (internal quotations and citations omitted); Willcox v. Consolidated Gas Co., 212 U.S. 19, 39 (1909) ("When a Federal court is properly appealed to in a case over which it has by law jurisdiction, it is its duty to take such jurisdiction. . . . The right of a party plaintiff to choose a Federal court where there is a choice cannot be properly denied").

[25] Colorado River Water Conservation Dist. v. United States, 424 U.S. 800, 813 (1976).

[26] New Orleans Pub. Serv., Inc. v. Council of New Orleans, 491 U.S. 350, 361 (1989).

Thus, Burford abstention is a two-step process. First, a court must determine whether timely and adequate state court review is available.[27] Second, the court must determine "(i) whether the particular regulatory scheme involves a matter of substantial public concern; (ii) whether it is the sort of complex technical regulatory scheme to which the Burford abstention doctrine usually is applied; and (iii) whether federal review of a party's claims would interfere with the state's efforts to establish and maintain a coherent regulatory policy."[28]

Against this backdrop, defendants in several no-fault insurance fraud cases across the country have argued that federal courts should abstain from adjudicating insurers' declaratory judgment claims. For this proposition, they generally have argued that the first step of the Burford analysis—the availability of timely and adequate state court review—is satisfied because state courts can generally oversee and review decisions in no-fault litigation and arbitration. Moving to the second step of the Burford analysis, these defendants have argued that state no-fault systems involve matters of substantial public concern and that the exercise of federal jurisdiction over an insurer's declaratory judgment claim would interfere with the state's efforts to establish and maintain a coherent no-fault system. These arguments contend that because no-fault systems are a creation of state law, a healthcare provider's right to collect no-fault insurance benefits should be decided by a state court or by an arbitration acting under color of state no-fault law.

As a general matter, these types of Burford abstention arguments have foundered in the second step of the Burford analysis. For instance, in *State Farm Mut. Auto. Ins. Co. v. Warren Chiropractic & Rehab Clinic P.C.*, 2015 U.S. Dist. LEXIS 104332 (E.D. Mich. 2015), the plaintiff-insurer alleged that the defendants engaged in a concerted scheme to defraud through the submission of no-fault insurance claims for medically unnecessary and illusory services.[29] The

---

[27] *See*, e.g., Raritan Baykeeper v. NL Indus., 660 F.3d 686, 693 (3d Cir. 2011); Gov't Emples. Ins. Co. v. Uptown Health Care Mgmt., 945 F. Supp. 2d 284, 289 (E.D.N.Y. 2013).

[28] Hi-Tech Trans., LLC v. New Jersey, 382 F.3d 295, 304 (3d Cir. 2004); Allstate Ins. Co. v. Elzanaty, 916 F. Supp. 2d 273, 289–92 (E.D.N.Y. 2013).

[29] *See* State Farm Mut. Auto. Ins. Co. v. Warren Chiropractic & Rehab Clinic P.C., 2015 U.S. Dist. LEXIS 104332 at *2 (E.D. Mich. 2015).

insurer alleged civil RICO, common law fraud, and unjust enrichment claims, as well as a declaratory judgment claim seeking a declaration to the effect that it was not liable to pay any of the defendants' pending bills.[30] The defendants argued for Burford abstention, contending that Michigan's no-fault insurance system was a "unique" regime and that intervention by the federal court risked "thwarting the state's attempt to manage its own affairs" and "inconsistent decisions on how the scheme applies."[31]

However, the Warren Chiropractic court rejected these arguments, holding that:

> Federal courts regularly decide issues concerning Michigan's no-fault scheme without raising the conflict issues Burford abstention is intended to address. Indeed, Defendants have not provided any real basis for concluding that a decision in this case presents "difficult questions of state law bearing on policy problems of substantial public import," or would be "disruptive of state efforts to establish a coherent policy with respect to a matter of substantial public concern."
>
> Furthermore, despite Defendants' protestations to the contrary, this case challenges purportedly fraudulent conduct by Defendants under a federal statute: RICO. Plaintiff does not challenge the no-fault scheme itself, or any state decision—administrative or otherwise—based on those statutory provisions. Instead, Plaintiff claims that Defendants acted fraudulently—conduct the no-fault scheme also seeks to prevent.[32]

Along similar lines, in *State Farm Mut. Auto. Ins. Co. v. Mallela*, 175 F. Supp. 2d 401 (E.D.N.Y. 2001), the plaintiff-insurer alleged that various professional corporations were illegally organized, and—among other things—sought a declaratory judgment to the effect that the defendants were not entitled to recover on any of the billing that

---

[30] *Id.* at *7.

[31] *Id.* at *43.

[32] *Id.* at *44 to *45; *see also* State Farm Mut. Auto. Ins. Co. v. Universal Health Group, Inc., 2014 U.S. Dist. LEXIS 151213 (E.D. Mich. 2014) (in a similar case involving RICO, fraud, and declaratory judgment claims based on fraudulent PIP billing, rejecting Burford abstention argument that was based on the same argument that Michigan's no-fault law was "unique").

they had submitted through the professional corporations.[33] The *Mallela* defendants argued for *Burford* abstention, contending that such abstention was "appropriate in order to avoid interference with New York's 'extensive statutory [no-fault insurance] scheme.'"[34] However, the *Mallela* court rejected that argument, holding that:

> The mere fact that this action involves questions of state law insurance coverage does not, however, imply that abstention is appropriate. In *Alliance of American Insurers* [854 F.2d 591, 599 (2d Cir. 1988)], an insurance industry cooperative group brought an action challenging the constitutionality of a provision of the New York Medical and Dental Malpractice and Professional Conduct Act that imposed a moratorium on medical malpractice insolvencies. The defendants moved to dismiss, arguing that "the insurance industry is subject to . . . a specialized, comprehensive state regulatory system under the New York Insurance Law." *Alliance of American Insurers*, 854 F.2d at 600. The district court granted the motion, ruling in favor of abstention, but the Court of Appeals reversed, holding that because plaintiffs did not "challenge . . . a state administrative or judicial order made pursuant to state law, [and because the] case does not involve the federal courts in disrupting any ongoing state judicial or administrative proceedings," abstention was inappropriate. *Id.*
>
> In the case at bar, plaintiff alleges fraud on the part of several private health care providers. Adjudication of plaintiff's claims will not unduly disrupt New York's regulatory scheme. If plaintiff succeeds, the PC Defendants will not be able to provide medical services and bill plaintiff for those services; if plaintiff fails, the PC Defendants will likely obtain compensation for services already rendered to plaintiff's insureds. As in *Alliance of American Insurers*, "the considerations warranting invocation of *Burford* abstention are absent in the case now before the Court," because "this case [will] not involve

[33] See State Farm Mut. Auto. Ins. Co. v. Mallela, 175 F. Supp. 2d 401, 407–8 (E.D.N.Y. 2001).

[34] *Id.*, 175 F. Supp. 2d at 411.

federal courts in supervising, interrupting, or meddling in state policies by interfering in state regulatory matters." *Id.*

Most recently, in *Gov't Emples. Ins. Co. v. Tri-Cnty. Neurology & Rehab.*, LLC, 2016 U.S. Dist. LEXIS 101494 (D.N.J. 2016), a district court initially had dismissed an insurer's declaratory judgment claim based on a determination that adjudication of the claim would interfere with New Jersey's no-fault arbitration procedures, which permitted healthcare providers to compel arbitration of their no-fault claims.[35] On reconsideration, however, the court reversed itself, reinstated the declaratory judgment claim, and determined that federal review of the insurer's declaratory judgment claim would not interfere with New Jersey's no-fault arbitration procedures:

> Here, Plaintiffs are not challenging the validity of New Jersey's no-fault automobile insurance statute or the PIP regulations but rather the application of the statute to Defendants. This distinction is crucial.
>
> . . .
>
> The Third Circuit has held that "[t]o implicate the sort of technical, complex regulatory scheme to which Burford abstention is usually applied, the action must challenge the scheme itself, rather than just actions taken under color of the scheme." . . . Here, Plaintiffs are seeking a declaration that Defendants were not entitled to collect on any of its pending no-fault insurance billing because of Defendants' fraudulent conduct, including, but not limited to, an illegal practice structure, improper referrals, miscoded examinations, and unnecessary testing. This is not a challenge to the validity of New Jersey's no-fault automobile insurance statute or the PIP regulations.[36]

Indeed, as the *Tri-County* aptly observed, "if Burford abstention was appropriate here, then an insurer would be able to sue an allegedly illegally-organized healthcare provider under the [New

---

[35] *See* Gov't Emples. Ins. Co. v. Tri-County Neurology & Rehab., LLC, 2015 U.S. Dist. LEXIS 162630 at *6 to *7, *9 to *12 (D.N.J. 2015).

[36] Gov't Emples. Ins. Co. v. Tri-Cnty. Neurology & Rehab., LLC, 2016 U.S. Dist. LEXIS 101494 at *10 to *11 (D.N.J. 2016).

Jersey Insurance Fraud Prevention Act] or RICO and seek to recover money it already paid to the healthcare provider, but then would be without any remedy to prevent the healthcare provider from continuing its fraudulent scheme and collecting outstanding unpaid bills. This is illogical."[37]

Accordingly, it seems increasingly clear that courts will reject requests to abstain from exercising jurisdiction over insurer's declaratory judgment claims under *Burford* and its progeny.

(ii) Abstention Pursuant to Brillhart v. Excess Ins. Co. of America *and* Wilton v. Seven Falls Co. *and Their Progeny*

Another abstention doctrine that can apply to claims for declaratory relief is the so-called *Brillhart-Wilton* doctrine, named for the Supreme Court's decisions in *Brillhart v. Excess Ins. Co. of America*, 316 U.S. 491 (1942) (generally holding that where a suit is pending in state court presenting identical issues governed by state law, a federal court ought to abstain from entering declaratory relief) and *Wilton v. Seven Falls Co.*, 515 U.S. 277 (1995) (holding that the standard for determining whether to abstain from a case presenting identical issues to those pending in state court is highly discretionary).

Alleged no-fault insurance fraud rings have often asked courts to abstain from exercising jurisdiction over insurers' declaratory judgment claim under the *Brillhart-Wilton* doctrine based on a contention that they are attempting to collect on their outstanding billing in state court collections suits. Because the state court collections suits supposedly present identical issues to the insurers' declaratory judgment claims (i.e., whether or not a healthcare provider is entitled to collect on its pending no-fault insurance billing), these defendants claim that *Brillhart-Wilton* abstention is appropriate.

However, these arguments tend to ignore a critical issue with respect to *Brillhart-Wilton* abstention—namely, that it is only appropriate where a lawsuit exclusively seeks declaratory relief.[38] Where—as in

---

[37] *Id.* at fn. 7.

[38] *See*, e.g., Adrian Energy Assoc. v. Michigan Pub. Serv. Comm'n, 481 F.3d 414, 422 (6th Cir. 2007) ("When a plaintiff seeks relief in addition to a declaratory judgment, such as damages or injunctive relief, both of which a court must address, then the entire benefit derived from exercising discretion not to grant declaratory relief is frustrated, and a stay or dismissal would not save any judicial resources. The claims in this case for which declaratory relief is requested and those for which injunctive

most no-fault insurance fraud litigation—an insurer asserts common law fraud, civil RICO, unjust enrichment, or other claims in tandem with its declaratory judgment claim, a defendant will have no colorable argument for *Brillhart-Wilton* abstention.[39]

(iii) Abstention Pursuant to Colorado River Water Conservation District v. United States *and its Progeny*

Some defendants in no-fault insurance fraud cases have argued for abstention under the abstention doctrine set forth in *Colorado River Water Conservation District v. United States*, 424 U.S. 800 (1976) and the cases that have followed it. Pursuant to *Colorado River*, a federal court may stay or dismiss a suit in federal court when a concurrent state court case is under way but only under exceptional circumstances and if it would promote wise judicial administration.[40] The primary purpose of the *Colorado River* doctrine is to conserve both state and federal judicial resources and prevent inconsistent results.[41]

In the no-fault insurance fraud litigation context, defendants typically argue that, under *Colorado River*, federal courts should abstain from exercising jurisdiction over insurers' declaratory judgment claims because (i) the insurers' declaratory judgment claims concern the defendants' pending and unpaid no-fault insurance billing and are an attempt to avoid liability on that billing, yet (ii) the billing is the

---

relief is requested are so closely intertwined that judicial economy counsels against dismissing the claims for declaratory judgment relief while adjudicating the claims for injunctive relief."); State Farm Mut. Auto. Ins. Co. v. Physicians Group of Sarasota, LLC, 9 F. Supp. 3d 1303, 1308–9 (M.D. Fla. 2014) (denying a motion for Brillhart-Wilton abstention where the complaint contained stand-alone damage claims in addition to claims for declaratory relief); State Farm Mut. Auto. Ins. Co. v. Schepp, 616 F. Supp. 2d 340, 347 (E.D.N.Y. 2008) ("Brillhart/Wilton abstention, which only applies to declaratory judgment actions, also merits little discussion: it does not apply because plaintiffs seek, in addition to declaratory relief, damages based on theories of fraud and unjust enrichment."); Allstate Ins. Co. v. Smirnov, 2013 U.S. Dist. LEXIS 138180, 2013 WL 5407224 at *8 n.6 (E.D.N.Y. Aug. 21, 2013) (Gold, M.J.) (suggesting that "Wilton/Brillhar[t] abstention does not apply where . . . the plaintiff seeks damages and declaratory relief, as opposed to declaratory relief alone") (Alteration added).

[39] *Id.*

[40] *See* Colorado River, 424 U.S. at 817–18.

[41] *See*, e.g., Day v. Union Mines, 862 F.2d 652, 657 (7th Cir. 1988).

subject of pending collections proceedings in state courts, where the defendants in the no-fault fraud case are the plaintiffs.

However, in seeking abstention pursuant to *Colorado River*, defendants in no-fault anti-fraud cases usually will founder on the threshold requirement for application of the doctrine. In particular, pursuant to *Colorado River*, the threshold inquiry in determining whether a federal court should abstain and defer to a state court is whether the concurrent federal and state cases are "parallel."[42] State court proceedings will be parallel to federal proceedings for *Colorado River* abstention purposes only when "the two proceedings are essentially the same; that is, there is an identity of parties, and the issues and relief sought are the same."[43]

While, in some no-fault fraud cases, there will be an identity of parties with pending state court no-fault insurance collections suits, parallelism generally requires a substantial likelihood that the state litigation will dispose of all claims presented in the federal case.[44] Under this standard, it usually cannot be said that a healthcare provider's state court collections suits are parallel to an insurer's federal anti-fraud litigation, even if there is some overlap between the issues in the insurer's federal declaratory judgment claim (in which it seeks to avoid paying a defendant's pending fraudulent no-fault charges) and state court no-fault collections lawsuits (in which the federal

---

[42] *See*, e.g., State Farm Mut. Auto. Ins. Co. v. Warren Chiropractic & Rehab Clinic P.C., 2015 U.S. Dist. LEXIS 104332 at *39 (E.D. Mich. 2015) ("A two-part test is used in determining whether abstention is proper under Colorado River. First, the district court must find that the concurrent state and federal actions are parallel. . . . If the cations are parallel, the district court must consider a number of factors in determining whether abstention is warranted."); Gov't Emples. Ins. Co. v. Leica Supply, Inc., 2014 U.S. Dist. LEXIS 42525 at *12 (E.D.N.Y. 2014) ("The threshold question in determining whether a federal court should abstain under Colorado River is whether the state court proceedings are 'parallel.'").

[43] National Union Fire Ins. Co. v. Karp, 108 F.3d 17, 22 (2d Cir. 1997); *see also* Warren Chiropractic, *supra* note 1, at *39 to *40 ("[T]o show parallelism, Defendants must demonstrate that (1) the parties are substantially similar and (2) [Plaintiff's] claims against [Defendants] are predicated on the same allegations as to the same material facts.") (Internal quotations and citation omitted).

[44] *See*, e.g., Allstate Ins. Co. v. Elzanaty, 916 F. Supp. 2d 273, 287–8 (E.D.N.Y. 2013) (observing that, while "[p]erfect symmetry of parties and issues is not required" for Colorado River abstention, "[r]ather, parallelism is achieved where there is a substantial likelihood that the state litigation will dispose of all claims presented in the federal case.") (Internal quotations and citation omitted; emphasis in original).

defendants, in the role of plaintiffs, are pursuing collection on those same fraudulent charges). This is because the insurer typically will be asserting common law fraud, civil RICO, unjust enrichment, or similar claims in tandem with its declaratory judgment claim, and those claims—which are aimed at recovering money that an insurer already paid on fraudulent no-fault charges—will not be at issue in the defendant healthcare provider's state court collections suits.[45]

Even assuming for argument's sake that a healthcare provider can show that its state court collections actions are parallel to an insurer's declaratory judgment claim—which sometimes, albeit rarely, occurs[46]—that does not end the *Colorado River* abstention inquiry. Specifically, once a defendant shows the requisite parallelism, federal courts contemplating *Colorado River* abstention apply a six-factor test to determine whether abstention would be appropriate: (i) whether the controversy involves a res over which one of the courts has assumed jurisdiction, (ii) whether the federal forum is less inconvenient than the other for the parties, (iii) whether staying or dismissing the federal actions will avoid piecemeal litigation, (iv) the order in which the actions were filed and whether proceedings have advanced more in one forum than in the other, (v) whether federal law provides the rule of decision, and (vi) whether the state procedures are adequate to protect the plaintiff's rights.[47] The six-factor test is a balancing test and "[t]he weight to be given any one factor may vary greatly depending on the case; however, the balance is 'heavily weighted' in favor of the federal court exercising jurisdiction."[48] As a

[45] *See*, e.g., Leica Supply, Inc., *supra* note 42, at *13 (rejecting the contention that state court no-fault collections actions were parallel to the insurer's federal court declaratory judgment claim, where the defendant healthcare provider's "actions in state court will not dispose of plaintiffs' RICO, common law fraud, unjust enrichment and declaratory judgment causes of action. Based on the distinct relief sought in the state and federal actions, the actions are not parallel."); but *see* Gov't Emples. Ins. Co. v. Five Boro Psychological Servs., P.C., 939 F. Supp. 2d 208, 216 (E.D.N.Y. 2013) (finding that a federal case regarding fraudulent insurance billing and state collection proceedings present an "example of parallel litigation in state and federal court").

[46] *See* Five Boro Psychological Servs., P.C., *supra* note 45.

[47] *See*, e.g., Colorado River, *supra* note 25, 424 U.S. at 818; Moses H. Cone Mem'l Hosp. v. Mercury Constr. Corp., 460 U.S. 1, 23 (1983); State Farm Mut. Auto. Ins. Co. v. Mallela, 175 F. Supp. 2d 401, 411 (E.D.N.Y. 2001).

[48] State Farm Mut. Auto. Ins. Co. v. Physicians Group of Sarasota, L.L.C., 9 F. Supp. 3d 1303, 1309 (M.D. Fla. 2014) (internal quotations and citation omitted).

result, the facial neutrality of any of the six factors is "a basis for the federal court to retain jurisdiction, not to yield it."[49]

When considering *Colorado River* abstention motions in no-fault anti-fraud cases, federal courts generally find that—even assuming the defendant can demonstrate parallelism—the six-factor balancing test militates against abstention. With respect to the first factor, neither an insurer's federal anti-fraud litigation nor the defendants' state court no-fault collections suits usually involve any res over which one of the courts has assumed jurisdiction. Considering that the facial neutrality of any of the six *Colorado River* factors weighs in favor of federal jurisdiction, the first *Colorado River* factor typically favors a plaintiff-insurer.

The second factor—the relative convenience of the federal and state forums—likewise usually weighs in favor of federal jurisdiction. In the majority of federal no-fault fraud cases, the federal district court will be located in the same area as the state courts in which the no-fault collections actions are pending. Thus, at best, the federal and state forums are equally convenient to the parties, which weighs in favor of federal jurisdiction.[50]

The third factor—avoidance of piecemeal litigation—usually weighs in favor of federal jurisdiction and against abstention. In the usual declaratory judgment claim, an insurer is seeking a declaration that it does not have to pay any of a healthcare provider's pending, fraudulent billing. Meanwhile, the healthcare provider is typically trying to collect on its pending billing through a multitude of individual state court collections lawsuits. Thus, if the insurer prevails in its declaratory judgment claim, it will resolve a multitude of individual state court collections lawsuits in a single, federal declaratory judgment action. As a result, *Colorado River* abstention in favor of a large number of state court no-fault collections lawsuits generally promotes piecemeal litigation, not prevents it. Accordingly, most federal courts that consider the issue in

---

[49] Woodford v. Community Action Agency of Greene County, 239 F.3d 517, 522 (2d Cir. 2001).

[50] *See*, e.g., Physicians Group of Sarasota, LLC., *supra* note 38, 9 F. Supp. 3d at 1309 (finding that the second Colorado River factor weighed against abstention, where all of the defendants' state court collections suits were pending in Florida, and the insurer's federal anti-fraud lawsuit also was pending in a federal district court in Tampa, Florida).

no-fault anti-fraud litigation have determined that the third factor weighs against abstention.[51]

In most no-fault anti-fraud cases, the fourth *Colorado River* factor will weigh mildly in favor of abstention, because the defendant healthcare provider will be in a position to say that it filed its state court collections lawsuits before the insurer commenced its federal anti-fraud lawsuit and asserted its declaratory judgment claim. However, as *Colorado River* and its progeny make clear, timing is far from the most important factor to consider, even assuming the parallelism of the state collections actions and the insurer's federal action.[52]

Similarly, in most federal no-fault anti-fraud cases, the fifth *Colorado River* factor will weigh slightly in favor of abstention, because state law rather than federal law will generally provide the rule of decision as to whether the defendant healthcare provider is or is not entitled to collect on its outstanding billing. However, "although the presence of federal issues strongly advises exercising federal jurisdiction, the absence of federal issues does not strongly advise dismissal, unless the state law issues are novel or particularly complex."[53] In this context, federal courts considering the fifth *Colorado River* factor have determined that the state law no-fault insurance issues are not especially novel or complex.[54] Thus, to the extent that the fifth factor favors abstention, it will usually be substantially outweighed by the balance of factors that weigh against abstention.

Finally, with respect to the sixth *Colorado River* factor, "if there is any substantial doubt as to [whether the state court litigation will provide an adequate resolution], it would be a serious abuse of discretion to grant the stay or dismissal at all."[55] In this context, an insurer

---

[51] *See*, e.g., Gov't Emples. Ins. Co. v. Li-Elle Serv., 2014 U.S. Dist. LEXIS 38855 at *14 to *15 (E.D.N.Y. 2014) (collecting cases).

[52] Moses H. Cone Mem'l Hosp., *supra* note 47, 460 U.S. at 21–22; *see also* Five Boro Psychological Servs., P.C., *supra* note 45, 939 F. Supp. 2d at 217 (holding that "[e]ven considering the advanced stage of some of" the defendant healthcare providers' state court no-fault collections actions, "in light of the heavy weight of factors in favor of the exercise of jurisdiction" the court would decline to invoke the "extraordinary and narrow exception" to its duty to adjudicate a controversy properly before it).

[53] State Farm Mut. Auto. Ins. Co. v. James M. Liguori, M.D., P.C., 589 F. Supp. 2d 221, 239–40 (E.D.N.Y. 2008).

[54] *Id*; *see also* Leica Supply, Inc., *supra* note 42, at *18 to *19.

[55] Moses H. Cone Mem'l Hosp., *supra* note 47, 460 U.S. at 28.

litigating a federal anti-fraud case will usually have solid arguments to the effect that state court no-fault collections lawsuits do not provide an adequate forum for protecting its rights.

For example, some state courts where no-fault collections suits commonly are pending—such as the New York City Civil Courts—have limited jurisdiction and cannot issue declaratory judgments. Even if state courts where collections suits are pending can issue declaratory judgments, it may as a practical matter be unwieldy for an insurer to have to counterclaim for individual declaratory judgments in hundreds, or even thousands, of discrete collections suits that are pending in disparate state courts. Thus, at worst, the sixth *Colorado River* factor usually will be neutral, which weighs against abstention.[56]

As a result, federal courts in no-fault anti-fraud cases will usually reject abstention pursuant to *Colorado River*.

2. Common Arbitrability Arguments and Counterarguments

As discussed above, some no-fault insurance states—such as New York, New Jersey, Minnesota, and Hawaii—either permit or require disputed no-fault insurance claims to be arbitrated. Similarly, many no-fault insurance policies permit arbitration of disputed claims at the option of either the claimant or the insurer. Oftentimes, these statutory or policy-based arbitration provisions are quite broad and can be read to require arbitration of virtually any material issue attendant to a no-fault claim. For example, New York's no-fault arbitration statute requires an insurer to "provide a claimant with the option of submitting any dispute involving the insurer's liability to pay" no-fault benefits to arbitration.[57] Likewise, New Jersey's arbitration statute makes virtually any dispute regarding payment of no-fault benefits subject to arbitration at the claimant's option.[58]

---

[56] Liguori, *supra* note 53, 589 F. Supp. 2d at 240 ("The last factor appears to be neutral. There is no reason to think that the state court would not adequately protect plaintiff's rights, but that in itself is not sufficient reason to abstain.").

[57] N.Y. Ins. Law § 5106(b).

[58] *See*, e.g., N.J. Stat. § 39:6A-5; State Farm Ins. Co. v. Sabato, 337 N.J. Super. 393 (N.J. App. Div. 2001) (holding that "the language of that statute should be read as broadly as the words themselves indicate, that statutory arbitrators are authorized to determine both factual and legal issues, and that coverage issues are to be decided by the arbitrator in the same manner as issues dealing with the extent of injury and the amount of recovery.").

Some defendants in no-fault insurance anti-fraud cases have argued for dismissal of insurers' declaratory judgment claims, contending that the declaratory judgment claims constitute an impermissible end-run around these types of compulsory no-fault arbitration statutes. Essentially, these defendants have contended that if a healthcare provider has an absolute right to arbitrate a disputed no-fault claim, then an insurer should not be permitted to dispute the claim (or a large collection of claims) in court through a declaratory judgment. Rather, whether or not a claim or collection of claims is fraudulent should be determined in the first instance by an arbitrator.

There have been occasional, outlying decisions in which courts have dismissed insurers' declaratory judgment claims in favor of arbitration—at least initially.[59] However, where an insurer can make a prima facie showing that some fraud is afoot, most courts will deny motions to dismiss declaratory judgment claims in no-fault fraud cases and will even stay and enjoin a healthcare provider's no-fault arbitration pending the disposition of the insurer's declaratory judgment claim.[60]

In general, these decisions rejecting the arbitrability of an insurer's declaratory judgment claim have been predicated on considerations

---

[59] *See*, e.g., Gov't Emples. Ins. Co. v. Tri-County Neurology & Rehab., LLC, 2015 U.S. Dist. LEXIS 162630 at *12 (D.N.J. 2015) and Gov't Emples. Ins. Co. v. Tri-Cnty. Neurology & Rehab., LLC, 2016 U.S. Dist. LEXIS 101494 (D.N.J. 2016) (dismissing a declaratory judgment claim in favor of no-fault arbitration on an abstention theory, but then—on reconsideration—reversing the initial decision and reinstating the declaratory judgment claim).

[60] *See*, e.g., Tri-Cnty. Neurology & Rehab., LLC, *supra* note 36, at *7 to *8 and fn. 4 (observing that New Jersey courts "routinely adjudicated declaratory judgment claims in cases involving fraud and payment of PIP benefits" and "routinely stay pending PIP arbitrations and enjoin parties from filing any new PIP arbitrations pending the disposition of an insurer's declaratory judgment . . . claims"); Liberty Mutual Insurance Company v. Advanced Medical Diagnostics of Queens, P.C., E.D.N.Y. Docket No. 1:13-cv-03758-ENV-LB, at Docket Entry 32, pp. 21–22 (denying motion to dismiss insurers' declaratory judgment claim in favor of arbitration and instead staying the alleged no-fault fraud ring's no-fault collections arbitration pending the disposition of the declaratory judgment claim); Allstate Ins. Co. v. Hisham Elzanaty, 929 F. Supp. 2d 199, 211–13, 216–22 (E.D.N.Y. 2013) (granting the motion to compel arbitration of pending billing, but then staying the arbitration pending the disposition of the plaintiff-insurers' declaratory judgment claim and collecting cases).

of judicial economy and a desire to avoid inconsistent decisions that could potentially make a mockery of the court's authority.[61] For instance, were a court to dismiss an insurer's declaratory judgment claim in favor of arbitration while retaining jurisdiction over the insurer's fraud-based claims, the insurer could be forced to defend hundreds of individual collections arbitrations—arising out of the same core facts as their fraud-based claims—that could be disposed of with far greater efficiency in the context of the declaratory judgment claim. The effect would be to waste the time and resources of both parties as well as the court and arbitrators.

Furthermore, considering the expedited nature of most no-fault arbitration proceedings, which generally permit little or no discovery and typically provide for expedited arbitral hearings lasting 15 minutes or less, most alleged no-fault fraud rings will be able to collect on some of their billing in arbitration, even when an insurer's fraud claims are very well founded. Thus, as a practical matter, if a court were to dismiss an insurer's declaratory judgment claim while retaining jurisdiction over its fraud-based claims, the result would be to invite the prospect of conflicting decisions. Some individual arbitrators might rule that an alleged no-fault fraud ring's billing

[61] *See*, e.g., Tri-Cnty. Neurology & Rehab., LLC, *supra* note 36, at fn. 7 (noting that it would be "illogical" for an insurer to sue an illegally organized healthcare provider and seek to recover the money it already paid to the healthcare provider, while being "without any remedy to prevent the healthcare provider from continuing its fraudulent scheme and collecting outstanding unpaid bills"); Hisham Elzanaty, *supra* note 60, 929 F. Supp 2d at 220 (observing that "It would severely threaten any judgment of this Court to have pending arbitrations or future arbitrations result in inconsistent rulings with regard to Uptown's eligibility for reimbursement of No-Fault insurance payments. The Court is fully aware that piecemeal litigation and inefficiency are at times unavoidable, especially in light of the FAA's strong mandate that contractual arbitration rights be respected. However, if these rights are delayed, rather than effectively terminated, the Court believes that a stay is the most appropriate solution here in order to avoid the large volume of arbitrations and inconsistent judgments that are gradually culminating in a procedural and substantive train wreck."); GEICO Ins. Co. v. Williams, 2011 NY Slip Op 30326U at *10 to *11 (Sup. Ct. Nassau Cty. 2011) (in an action seeking, among other things, a declaration that defendants were not entitled to recover no-fault benefits, the Court stayed all pending no-fault collections arbitrations pending the outcome of the declaratory judgment action "in the interests of judicial economy" and due to the possibility of "significantly varying outcomes" if the plaintiff-insurer was required to "litigat[e] each alleged fraudulent claim separately").

was totally legitimate, whereas—in time, with proper discovery—a court could reach the opposite conclusion. These are the concerns that have underpinned court decisions rejecting motions to dismiss insurers' declaratory judgment claims in favor of no-fault collections arbitration.

3. Mootness of Declaratory Judgment Claims

In some cases, a plaintiff-insurer will face arguments to the effect that since the filing of a declaratory judgment claim, subsequent events have arisen that render the declaratory judgment claim moot. For example, an insurer might assert a declaratory judgment claim based on a healthcare practice's fraudulent billing for a certain type of medically useless diagnostic test only to learn—at the close of discovery—that the healthcare practice stopped billing for that type of test immediately after the lawsuit was filed. Similarly, an insurer might contend in a declaratory judgment claim that a defendant healthcare practice falsely billed for lengthy and comprehensive patient examinations, only to find—on a motion for summary judgment or at trial—that once the lawsuit was filed the practice altered its billing practices to properly account for the length and nature of its examinations.

In these types of cases, where the activities that gave rise to the insurer's declaratory judgment claims are no longer occurring, the declaratory judgment claims will arguably be moot. For that reason, insurers and anti-fraud litigators should take care to avoid limiting the scope of their declaratory judgment claims to narrow, easily resolvable issues. Where possible, a declaratory judgment claim should be based on facts that demonstrate that some fundamental aspect of a defendant's practice is fraudulent or otherwise unlawful to an incurable degree. For instance, corporate structure issues, such as ownership of a healthcare practice by an unlicensed individual, will often not be curable during the course of an anti-fraud lawsuit, or at least not easily curable.

Along similar lines, where all, or substantially all, of a healthcare practice's revenues are derived from fraudulent billing—such as where a healthcare practice provides all of its treatments pursuant to a predetermined fraudulent treatment and billing protocol—it will be difficult for the practice to cure its fraudulent approach by making minor adjustments to it.

E. Other Common Arguments for Dismissal of No-Fault Anti-Fraud Lawsuits

There are a few other arguments for dismissal that commonly arise in the context of no-fault insurance anti-fraud litigation that merit some discussion.

1. Limitations Arguments

In a perfect world, an insurer would deploy its SIU investigators to maximum effect, detect every fraud in real time, and commence every lawsuit immediately after the underlying fraud was detected. More commonly, however, a fraudulent scheme will have been under way for years when it is first discovered by an insurer, and additional time will pass before the fraud can be fully comprehended, and before a complaint can be drafted and filed. As a result, insurers commonly face arguments that some or all of their claims are barred by the pertinent statutes of limitation.

As a result, it usually will be best practice for an anti-fraud litigator to plead some facts in the body of the complaint to demonstrate that the defendants acted to conceal their fraud in some manner. For example, in a complaint alleging that a medical practice illegally was owned and controlled by unlicensed non-physicians, an insurer usually will be in a position to allege that the practice nominally was owned on paper by a licensed physician, and that the corporate filings for the practice themselves falsely represented that a real doctor was in charge.

Along similar lines, in a complaint alleging that a healthcare provider's billing misrepresented the medical necessity of the underlying services, an insurer can allege that the billing and treatment notes for the services were organized in such a way as to create the illusion that the services were medically useful. These types of allegations—which sound in fraudulent concealment—usually will be sufficient to enable the insurer to raise an equitable tolling argument in opposition to a motion to dismiss based on the statute of limitations. While the granular specifics of equitable tolling doctrines may vary to some degree from state-to-state, all of them generally will toll a statute of limitations if a plaintiff—despite reasonable due diligence—could not have uncovered a defendant's fraud.

Where an insurer pleads some facts in its complaint to the effect that a defendant has acted to conceal its fraud, and raises an equitable tolling argument in opposition to a motion to dismiss based on the statute of limitations, courts usually will deny the motion to dismiss. Tolling arguments generally are fact-intensive, require discovery to adjudicate, and therefore are not properly resolved at the pleading stage unless an incontrovertible limitations defense appears on the face of the complaint.[62]

2. Res Judicata and Collateral Estoppel

By the time an insurer commences anti-fraud litigation against a group of defendants, it is reasonably likely that the insurer already has paid the defendants a substantial sum of money. It also is reasonably likely that—while some of this money was paid in reliance on the defendants' fraudulent billing—at least some of the money was paid pursuant to judgments in no-fault collections lawsuits, or pursuant to awards in no-fault collections arbitration. Against this backdrop, defendants in no-fault anti-fraud litigation have argued that res judicata should bar the insurer from recovering any money that it paid pursuant to judgments or arbitral awards.

They may have a point. Unless the insurer can make the difficult showing of extrinsic fraud or collusion that typically is necessary to reopen a judgment or arbitral award, any money that the insurer paid to a no-fault fraud ring pursuant to judgments or awards in collections

---

[62] *See*, e.g., State Farm Mut. Auto. Ins. Co. v. Warren Chiropractic & Rehab Clinic P.C., 2015 U.S. Dist. LEXIS 104332 at *49 to *52 (E.D. Mich. 2015) (rejecting the motion to dismiss on limitations grounds, where the insurer alleged that the defendants concealed their fraud); State Farm Mut. Auto. Ins. Co. v. Kugler, 2011 U.S. Dist. LEXIS 107005 at *43 (S.D. Fla. 2011) (rejecting a motion to dismiss the insurer's fraud complaint on limitations grounds, where the limitations periods were subject to equitable tolling, which the court found inappropriate for resolution on a motion to dismiss); State Farm Mut. Auto. Ins. Co. v. Accurate Med., P.C., 2007 U.S. Dist. LEXIS 74459 at *5 (E.D.N.Y. 2007) ("[T]he moving defendants' argument that plaintiff's claims regarding unnecessary medical treatment are barred by the statute of limitations necessarily assumes facts that are beyond the pleadings and that have yet to be developed. Indeed, the date by which plaintiff should have discovered the alleged fraud involves factual determinations that are unlikely to be resolved on a motion to dismiss.").

proceedings usually will be unrecoverable in subsequent anti-fraud litigation.[63] Therefore, when preparing a complaint, insurers and their counsel should avoid listing payments on judgments or arbitral awards among their alleged damages. Concomitantly, it is best practice to affirmatively allege, in the body of the complaint, that the alleged damages consist only of payments that the insurer voluntarily made in reliance on the defendants' fraudulent billing.

That said, if an insurer inadvertently includes among its damages a handful of payments made pursuant to collections arbitration or litigation, it generally will not provide any basis for dismissal of the insurer's entire complaint. Rather, the court usually will permit the action to proceed, with the potential damages reduced upon any judgment to account for any payments made pursuant to judgments or awards.[64]

In addition, some defendants in no-fault fraud cases have argued that, where an insurer fails to raise a fraud defense to a healthcare provider's no-fault collections lawsuits or arbitration, the insurer should be precluded from later asserting an affirmative fraud claim against that healthcare provider. These types of arguments typically will founder, because defendants will be hard-pressed to show that an insurer's fraud-based claims legitimately could have been resolved in the context of small-scale no-fault collections lawsuits or arbitration.[65]

In some cases, by the time an insurer commences an anti-fraud lawsuit, the defendants in the lawsuit will have prevailed in numerous

---

[63] *But see*, e.g., Allstate Ins. Co. v. Harvey Family Chiropractic, Physical Therapy & Acupuncture, PLLC, 2017 U.S. App. LEXIS 1474 at *4 to *5 (2d Cir. 2017) (suggesting, in dicta and without explication, that an insurer who was obligated to pay fraudulent claims in the context of no-fault collections arbitration or litigation, would be free to recover those payments if successful in a subsequent civil RICO case).

[64] *See*, e.g., Allstate Ins. Co. v. Elzanaty, 916 F. Supp. 2d 273, 298–99 (E.D.N.Y. 2013) (rejecting the motion to dismiss on res judicata grounds, where the defense was not set forth on the face of the complaint or in the public record and adjudication of the defense was therefore premature at the pleading stage); State Farm Mut. Auto. Ins. Co. v. Grafman, 655 F. Supp. 2d 212, 231 (E.D.N.Y. 2009) (same).

[65] *See*, e.g., Gov't Emples. Ins. Co. v. MLS Med. Group LLC, 2013 U.S. Dist. LEXIS 171983 at fn. 3 (D.N.J. 2013) (rejecting argument that insurer's fraud-based claims were barred because it did not raise them as defenses in no-fault collections arbitration, where arbitrators lacked jurisdiction to entertain insurer's fraud-based claims).

collections proceedings against the insurer. For example, an insurer may allege in an anti-fraud lawsuit that a healthcare provider routinely misrepresented the medical necessity of one type of service or another. However, the healthcare provider may be in a position to argue that it previously prevailed against the insurer in a large number of collections lawsuits or arbitral proceedings, and that—in the context of those lawsuits and proceedings—numerous judges and arbitrators held that the type of service at issue was, in fact, medically necessary. Under such circumstances, the healthcare provider may contend that the insurer's subsequent fraud claims are barred by collateral estoppel.

However, for collateral estoppel to bar relitigation of an issue—for instance the medical necessity of a healthcare service—the plaintiff must have had a full and fair opportunity to litigate the issue in the previous proceeding. Generally, plaintiff-insurers will be in a good position to argue that they did not have a full and fair opportunity to litigate the medical necessity of a healthcare service, or other types of misrepresentations, in the context of expedited no-fault collections litigation or arbitration.

For example, in order to prove that a healthcare provider billed for medically useless services, it often is necessary to look at the totality of the provider's billing and treatment records, in order to show that the provider purported to provide the same services to every insured, in the same manner, without regard for any insured's individual circumstances or presentment. Moreover, an insurer often will be in a position to argue that—given the lack of discovery that typically is available in collections lawsuits and arbitration—it never had a legitimate chance to fully and fairly litigate large-scale fraud occurring across hundreds of claims in the context of those types of proceedings. Overall, and as is the case with res judicata arguments—courts are unlikely to resolve collateral estoppel arguments at the pleading stage, unless the basis for the estoppel appears on the face of the complaint or is apparent from the public record.[66]

[66] *See*, e.g., Gov't Emples. Ins. Co. v. Tri-County Neurology & Rehab., LLC, 2015 U.S. Dist. LEXIS 162630 at *13 to *14 (D.N.J. 2015) (rejecting the argument that collateral estoppel barred relitigation of issues that supposedly could have been raised in no-fault collections arbitration, where basis for the estoppel did not appear on the face of the pleading and consideration of the argument required "a fact-intensive inquiry into the arbitration record on a claim-by-claim basis").

3. Implausibility Arguments

In what amounts to a "Hail Mary" argument, some alleged no-fault insurance fraud rings will argue that an insurer's anti-fraud complaint should be dismissed as implausible. For this proposition, they usually will seize on the Supreme Court's decision in *Bell Atlantic Corp. v. Twombly*, 550 U.S. 544, 555 (2007), which reconsidered the more liberal pleading standard enunciated in *Conley v. Gibson*, 355 U.S. 41, 45-46 (1957), to the effect that a motion to dismiss pursuant to Fed. R. Civ. P. 12(b)(6) should be granted only if it appears beyond doubt that the plaintiff can prove no set of facts in support of its claims that would entitle it to relief. Instead, under *Twombly*, a plaintiff must allege "enough facts to state a claim to relief that is plausible on its face."[67] Where a plaintiff has "not nudged [his] claims across the line from conceivable to plausible, [its] complaint must be dismissed."[68]

More recently, in *Ashcroft v. Iqbal*, 129 S. Ct. 1937 (2009), the Supreme Court provided further guidance, setting a two-pronged approach for courts considering a motion to dismiss. First, a court should identify the causes of action that are supported by factual allegations.[69] Second, "[w]hen there are well-pleaded factual allegations a court should assume their veracity and then determine whether they plausibly give rise to an entitlement to relief."[70] According to the Supreme Court, "[d]etermining whether a complaint states a plausible claim for relief [is] . . . a context-specific task that requires the reviewing court to draw on its judicial experience and common sense."[71] In this context, a claim has "facial plausibility when the plaintiff pleads factual content that allows the court to draw the reasonable inference that the defendant is liable for the misconduct alleged."[72]

While there is no end to the potential implausibility arguments that can be raised by defendants, in the context of no-fault anti-fraud cases they usually boil down to contentions that there is some evidence to rebut the plaintiff-insurer's claims. For example, a medical

---

[67] 550 U.S. at 570.

[68] *Id.*

[69] 129 S. Ct. at 1949–50, citing Twombly, 550 U.S. at 555.

[70] *Id.*

[71] *Id.* at 1950.

[72] *Id.* at 1949.

practice may argue that it could not possibly be illegally owned and controlled by laypeople because, after all, its corporate filings say that it is owned by a licensed physician. Of course, these defendants will not disclose that, although the corporate filings list a licensed physician as the owner of the medical practice, unlicensed individuals control the bank account for the practice and siphon off all of its revenues.

Or, to take another common example, a physician might argue that he could not have billed for medically unnecessary services, because the patient was referred to him by a chiropractor, who made a supposedly independent determination that the services were medically warranted. However, the physician may not reveal that the chiropractor is his brother-in-law, or that he kicked back a portion of the proceeds of his billing to the chiropractor in exchange for the referral.

Ultimately, when it comes to no-fault insurance anti-fraud litigation, most implausibility arguments will constitute improper attempts to conflate pleading with proof. At bottom, these arguments posit that, if there is evidence to rebut an insurer's fraud allegations, then the insurer has not proven its case at the pleading stage, and therefore the insurer has not stated a claim. Of course, this syllogism does not really stand up to scrutiny. An insurer—or, indeed, any plaintiff—is not required to prove its case at the pleading stage. Rather, on a motion to dismiss pursuant to Fed. R. Civ. P. 12(b)(6), the court is required to accept as true all factual statements alleged in the complaint and draw all reasonable inferences in favor of the nonmoving party.[73] In this context, the court's function is not to weigh the evidence that might be presented at a trial or on summary judgment, but merely to determine whether the complaint itself is legally sufficient.[74] Thus, arguments to the effect that an insurer's allegations are implausible because the insurer's complaint does not prove its case typically will come up short.

---

[73] *See*, e.g., Tal v. Hogan, 453 F.3d 1244, 1252 (10th Cir. 2006); Cleveland v. Caplaw Enters., 448 F.3d 518, 521 (2d Cir. 2006).

[74] *See*, e.g., Allstate Ins. Co. v. Tanella, 2012 U.S. Dist. LEXIS 186383 at *6 (E.D.N.Y. 2012); State Farm Mut. Auto. Ins. Co. v. CPT Medical Services, P.C., 375 F. Supp. 2d 141, 149 (E.D.N.Y. 2005).

8

Counterclaims in No-Fault Insurance Anti-Fraud Litigation

It takes a certain *sang froid* to submit a massive amount of fraudulent no-fault insurance billing to an automobile insurer. It is not a business for the faint of heart. The same brazen attitude that can lead a no-fault fraud ring to disregard the risk of anti-fraud lawsuits, professional disciplinary proceedings, or even criminal prosecution will often lead to a belief that the best defense to an insurer's anti-fraud complaint is a good offense, in the form of counterclaims.

This instinct is not entirely unfounded. No insurer wants to be on the receiving end of a no-fault fraud defendant's counterclaims, especially when—as often is the case—the counterclaims are couched in inflammatory language. Oftentimes, the counterclaims are worded to portray the insurer as a corporate behemoth intent on crushing small, "mom-and-pop" medical practices and avoiding payment on legitimate claims. In some cases, the counterclaims do not appear to be aimed at recovering damages from the insurer, but rather to exert an in terrorem effect and encourage the insurer to walk away from the litigation.

The potential universe of counterclaims that might possibly be asserted against an insurer in a no-fault anti-fraud case is limited only by the imagination of defense attorneys and will vary considerably from state to state. As a practical matter, it is impossible to anticipate every possible counterclaim that might arise. However, certain counterclaims tend to recur in no-fault anti-fraud litigation, and these common counterclaims merit discussion.

A. Contract-Based Counterclaims for Unpaid No-Fault Billing

The most obvious counterclaim—and one of the few that usually will withstand an insurer's motion to dismiss—is a contract-based counterclaim for unpaid no-fault insurance billing. Indeed, in federal no-fault anti-fraud cases, such counterclaims may be compulsory under Fed. R. Civ. P. 13(a).[1]

Of course, this is not to say that any contract-based counterclaim for unpaid no-fault insurance benefits will automatically be legally sufficient to withstand an insurer's motion to dismiss. For example, and as a general rule, a claim or counterclaim alleging breach of contract must—at a minimum—identify the contracts or provisions that have allegedly been breached.[2] By extension, where a counterclaim for breach of contract fails to adequately identify the contracts and contractual provisions at issue, the counterclaim will not satisfy even the basic notice pleading requirements of Fed. R. Civ. P. 8 and will be subject to dismissal.

---

[1] *See* Fed. R. Civ. P. 13(a) (generally requiring a responsive pleading to state as a counterclaim any claim that—at the time of its service—the pleader has against an opposing party if the claim (i) arises out of the transaction or occurrence that is the subject matter of the opposing party's claim and (ii) does not require adding another party over whom the court cannot acquire jurisdiction).

[2] *See*, e.g., Mowett v. JPMorgan Chase Bank, N.A., 2016 U.S. Dist. LEXIS 43204 at *9 (E.D. Mich. 2016) (dismissing a breach of contract claim where the plaintiff failed to identify the contractual provisions that were allegedly breached); Eprotec Pres., Inc. v. Engineered Materials, Inc., 2011 U.S. Dist. LEXIS 24231 at *22 (D.N.J. 2011) (noting that, under New Jersey law, "a complaint alleging breach of contract must, at a minimum, identify the contracts and provisions breached."); Kaplan v. Aspen Knolls Corp., 290 F. Supp. 2d 335, 337 (E.D.N.Y. 2003) ("A claim for breach of contract must allege, at a minimum, the terms of the contract, each element of the alleged breach and the resultant damages.").

Thus, where a defendant in a no-fault fraud case asserts a highly generalized, inchoate counterclaim for "all outstanding billing" or the like, the counterclaim will be legally insufficient and subject to dismissal.[3] Rather, to the extent that a defendant in a no-fault anti-fraud case seeks to assert a contract-based counterclaim for unpaid no-fault benefits, the counterclaim should set forth the specific charges at issue, as well as the specific insurance policies and policy provisions that ostensibly required the plaintiff-insurer to pay those charges.

Practice Points

Contract-Based Counterclaims

- ✓ Pursuant to Fed. R. Civ. P. 13 and some state rules of civil procedure, a defendant may be obligated to assert any claims it has against a plaintiff as compulsory counterclaims.
- ✓ This, in turn, may preclude a defendant in an anti-fraud case from pursuing collection on its fraudulent no-fault billing through small-scale collections lawsuits or arbitration, where discovery may be limited and the deck may be unfairly stacked against the insurer.
- ✓ Considering that the scope of discovery is likely to be broader in an anti-fraud lawsuit than in a small-scale no-fault collections proceeding, anti-fraud litigators should consider whether to move to stay or dismiss a defendant's no-fault collections lawsuits or arbitration so as to force the defendant to assert any collections claims it may have as compulsory counterclaims in the insurer's anti-fraud suit.

---

[3] *See*, e.g., Gov't Emples. Ins. Co. v. Korn, 2016 U.S. Dist. LEXIS 53210 at *9 to *11 (D.N.J. 2016) (dismissing contract-based counterclaims for unpaid no-fault insurance benefits, where the counterclaims failed "to identify the contracts, the insureds, the medical procedures, or the unpaid bills that would support their breach of contract claims"); McGee v. State Farm Mut. Auto. Ins. Co., 2011 U.S. Dist. LEXIS 128913 at *24 to *26 (E.D.N.Y. 2011) (dismissing healthcare provider's breach of contract claim, which was predicated on insurer's alleged nonpayment of no-fault benefits, where the healthcare provider failed "to tie any of the allegations to a specific provision of any agreement between" the insurer and any insured who assigned his or her policy to the healthcare provider).

B. Defamation-Based Counterclaims

To the extent that defendants in a no-fault anti-fraud case are inclined to assert counterclaims in the first place, they rarely limit themselves to contract claims for their outstanding billing. This is because the insurer is usually already facing potential liability on the outstanding billing in the form of a large number of pending no-fault collections lawsuits or arbitrations. As a result, a counterclaim for breach of contract will not expose the insurer to any liability other than what it was already facing, and the counterclaim will not have the desired in terrorem effect. Indeed, the insurer may welcome the opportunity to litigate all of the defendant's pending billing as a counterclaim in a single no-fault anti-fraud lawsuit rather than in a multitude of small-collections lawsuits or arbitral proceedings.

Because the true purpose of counterclaims in no-fault anti-fraud lawsuits is often to leverage possible extracontractual liability to persuade the insurer to discontinue its case, defendants in anti-fraud cases must look beyond breach of contract claims to achieve their objective. Toward that end, many alleged no-fault fraud rings counterclaim for defamation. In some cases, the alleged defamation is predicated on statements that allegedly were made by an insurer's SIU investigator or claims adjuster to an insured patient during the course of the insurer's investigation.

For instance, a healthcare provider may contend that an insurer committed defamation when its SIU investigator told one of the provider's patients that the provider was being investigated for suspected fraud. More commonly, however, the defamation counterclaim will be predicated on the allegations in the insurer's complaint. For example, the defendant will contend, in its counterclaim, that the insurer's fraud allegations themselves are defamatory.

Of course, SIU investigators and claims personnel should be, and generally are, trained to avoid making gratuitously defamatory statements regarding a suspicious healthcare provider. Statements made during a prelitigation investigation may not be privileged and could potentially subject an insurer to liability.[4] Nonetheless, defamation

[4] Nonetheless, a defendant may be hard-pressed to assert a viable defamation counterclaim based on an investigator's statement to the effect that the defendant is being investigated for suspected fraud because the statement would be true. *See*, e.g., Farmers Ins. Exch. v. First Choice Chiropractic & Rehab., 2015 U.S. Dist. LEXIS 96773

counterclaims that are based on statements made in a complaint itself or during the course of the resulting judicial proceedings will almost always be subject to dismissal. First, most states recognize a litigation privilege that protects litigants from liability for statements made in the context of litigation, including in complaints.[5] As a result, courts should dismiss defamation counterclaims against insurers, where the counterclaims are predicated on allegedly defamatory statements in the insurers' anti-fraud complaints.[6]

Second, statements made in the context of litigation—including allegations in anti-fraud complaints—will generally constitute protected petitioning activity. In this context, the Supreme Court has described the First Amendment right to petition as the right "to freely inform the government" of our wishes.[7] In order to safeguard the fundamental right to petition, the Supreme Court has developed an immunity for petitioning speech, now commonly referred to as

---

at *20 to *21 (D. Or. 2015) (granting summary judgment on the defendants' defamation counterclaim, where "the statements contained within [the insurer's] Reservation of Rights Letter, which generally informed individuals that their claims were under investigation and that [the insurer] was considering an array of evidence, were true, as investigations regarding some if not all of those files were concurrently occurring or occurred at some point with relation to this suit").

[5] *See*, e.g., Macedo v. LVNV Funding, LLC, 2016 U.S. Dist. LEXIS 70608 at *4 (M.D. Fla. 2016) ("Florida's litigation privilege affords absolute immunity for acts occurring during the course of judicial proceedings.") (Internal quotations and citation omitted); Malibu Media, LLC v. Doe, 2015 U.S. Dist. LEXIS 53784 at *12 (E.D. Mich. 2015) ("The allegations in Plaintiff's Complaint are not defamatory under Michigan law. Under the litigation privilege, Plaintiff's allegations are immune from a defamation claim by Defendant."); Marek v. Old Navy (Apparel) Inc., 348 F. Supp. 2d 275, 281 (S.D.N.Y. 2004) ("It is a well-established principle of New York law that statements made in judicial and quasi-judicial proceedings are privileged and may not be actionable so long as they are pertinent to the controversy."); Hawkins v. Harris, 661 A.2d 284, 289 (N.J. 1995) (New Jersey litigation privilege protects any statement "(1) made in judicial or quasi-judicial proceedings; (2) by litigants or other participants authorized by law; (3) to achieve the objects of the litigation; and (4) that have some connection or logical relation to the action.").

[6] *See*, e.g., Allstate Ins. Co. v. Tacoma Therapy, Inc., 2014 U.S. Dist. LEXIS 52934 at *11 to *13 (W.D. Wash. 2014) (dismissing a defamation counterclaim that alleged that allegations in the insurer's anti-fraud complaint were defamatory because "[s] tatements made during the course of and relevant to judicial proceeding are absolutely privileged.").

[7] E.R.R. Presidents' Conference v. Noerr Motor Freight, Inc., 365 U.S. 127, 137 (1961).

the Noerr-Pennington doctrine,[8] under which the federal courts recognize that, in general, claims stemming from a party's petition to the government—including complaints filed in civil actions—are immune from liability.[9] Moreover, although there is a "sham litigation" exception to the Noerr-Pennington doctrine, it will usually be inapplicable in no-fault insurance anti-fraud litigation. Specifically, the Supreme Court has promulgated a two-part test for sham litigation. First, the lawsuit must be objectively baseless in the sense that no reasonable litigant could reasonably expect success on the merits.[10] Only if the challenged litigation is objectively baseless will a court consider the litigant's subjective motivation.[11] The question then is "whether the baseless lawsuit conceals an attempt to interfere *directly* with the business relationships of a competitor . . . through the use [of] the governmental *process*—as opposed to the *outcome* of that process—as an anticompetitive weapon" (italics added for emphasis).[12] Few defendants in no-fault anti-fraud cases will be able to meet this stringent "sham litigation" exception to the Noerr-Pennington doctrine because they would have to demonstrate, in the first instance, that the insurer's complaint was filed in total bad faith and that the insurer's claims were totally baseless in fact and law.

To the limited extent that defendants in no-fault fraud cases attempt to support their defamation counterclaims with allegedly defamatory statements made outside the context of the litigation, such as statements by SIU investigators during the course of their investigations or statements made in the context of claims denials or explanations of benefits, the defamation counterclaims may nonetheless be defective as a matter of law. It is, for example, important to

[8] *See* Noerr, *supra* note 7; United Mine Workers v. Pennington, 381 U.S. 657 (1965).

[9] *See*, e.g., Ginx, Inc. v. Soho Alliance, 2010 U.S. Dist. LEXIS 64313 at *55 to *57 (S.D.N.Y. 2010) (Under the Noerr-Pennington doctrine, a "party's right to file a lawsuit without liability is unimpeachable unless the suit is a 'sham,' meaning 'objectively baseless.' Only if a lawsuit is so utterly devoid of merit as to qualify as 'objectively baseless' does the filing party's subjective motive for commencing the action become relevant."); DirecTV, Inc. v. Weikel, 2005 U.S. Dist. LEXIS 9902 at *18 (D. N.J. May 25, 2005), ("[t]he Noerr-Pennington doctrine immunizes litigation and other petitioning conduct from liability").

[10] *See*, e.g., Prof'l Real Estate Investors, Inc. v. Columbia Pictures Indus., 508 U.S. 49, 60 (1993).

[11] *Id.*

[12] *Id.*

remember that a viable defamation claim typically requires that the allegedly defamatory words be pleaded with some degree of particularity. As a result, defamation counterclaims that vaguely allege that an unspecified SIU investigator made some unparticularized defamatory statements on various indeterminate dates to several unnamed persons will usually not be legally sufficient to state a claim.

Nonetheless, insurers should be careful to avoid casting any aspersions on an actual or prospective fraud defendant outside of the context of litigation. Two of the most common areas where this can occur is in press releases announcing the filing of an anti-fraud case and in claims denials or explanations of benefits.

For example, some insurers—with good reason—may want to issue press releases regarding the commencement of an action against an alleged insurance fraud ring. Not only do such releases let the public know that the insurer is taking some action to combat fraud (and, by extension, the increased insurance premiums that often are associated with insurance fraud), but they also let those who are engaged in insurance fraud know that their activities will not be tolerated.

However, these types of press releases can give rise to a counterclaim or a separate action by a fraud defendant, because—arguably—the statements in a press release are not subject to any litigation privilege. Even the most anodyne statement in an insurer's press release—such as a straightforward and clearly truthful statement to the effect that the insurer has "commenced a lawsuit" against a defendant in which the defendant "is alleged to have engaged in fraud"—can mire the insurer in a recriminatory defamation or tortious interference counterclaim. Although, in the fullness of time such defamation or tortious interference claims might be dismissed for any number of reasons, the cost of litigating them might well outweigh any transient benefit attendant to the insurer's public announcement.[13]

Along similar lines, insurers should avoid including any language in their claims denials to a healthcare provider or in the explanations of benefits that they send to insureds that suggests that the underlying claim has been delayed or denied as the result of actual or suspected

[13] *See*, e.g., Rapuzzi Palumbo & Rosenberger, P.C. v. Gov't Emples. Ins. Co., 2011 N.Y. Misc. LEXIS 3193 at *26 to *28 (N.Y. Sup. Ct. 2011) (dismissing the lawyer and law firm's defamation-based counterclaims against the insurer, which allegedly had issued press releases announcing litigation against the lawyer and law firm for their alleged role in a racketeering conspiracy involving alleged no-fault fraud).

fraud or other misconduct. While, arguably, an insurer is within its rights to specify the precise reason why it is delaying or denying payment of a claim, the potential cost of casting aspersions on a healthcare provider in a claims denial or explanation of benefits generally will outweigh the prospective benefit. In most cases, it will be sufficient to say that the claim at issue is being delayed or denied pending review.

C. Tortious Interference Counterclaims

Like defamation counterclaims, tortious interference counterclaims are popular with defendants in no-fault fraud cases because they have the potential to expose the plaintiff-insurer to liability that goes beyond the value of the defendants' outstanding no-fault billing. However, like defamation counterclaims, many defendants in no-fault cases attempt to predicate their tortious interference counterclaims on the insurer's commencement and prosecution of the anti-fraud lawsuit. The typical allegation is that by filing a complaint that accused the defendants of no-fault insurance fraud, the insurer somehow tortiously interfered with the defendants' business. As a result, these types of tortious interference counterclaims will be barred by litigation privilege and by the Noerr-Pennington doctrine.

Even if a defendant can come up with some form of alleged tortious interference that goes beyond privileged litigation activity, the defendant will typically have a hard time meeting the tortious interference pleading standards. While tortious interference law varies to some extent from state to state, it generally requires that the defendant (or counterclaim-defendant) intentionally interfered with a contract or business relationship without justification through some unlawful or improper means, thereby causing damages.[14]

[14] *See*, e.g., Omni Healthcare Inc. v. Health First, Inc., 2016 U.S. Dist. LEXIS 107277 at *81 to *82 (M.D. Fla. 2016) (noting that, under Florida law, "[t]he elements of the tort of intentional interference with an advantageous business relationship are: 1) the existence of a business relationship, not necessarily evidenced by an enforceable contract; 2) knowledge of the relationship on the part of the

To the extent that a defendant in a no-fault case tries to predicate its tortious interference counterclaims on something other than the allegations in the insurer's complaint itself, the tortious interference counterclaim will usually be based on statements made by SIU personnel or other employees of the insurer during the course of the underlying anti-fraud investigation. Under such circumstances, the insurer should be able to secure dismissal of the counterclaim by pointing out that its investigation of the defendant was actually mandated by state law requiring insurers to conduct anti-fraud investigations and that the statements made during the course of the investigation constituted a legitimate and necessary part of the investigation.[15]

---

defendant; 3) an intentional and unjustified interference with that relationship by the defendant; and 4) damage to the plaintiff as a result of the breach of the relationship.") (Internal quotations and citation omitted); Lane v. Forever of PA, Inc., 2015 U.S. Dist. LEXIS 173755 at *37 to *38 (W.D. Pa. 2015) ("To state a claim for tortious interference with existing or prospective business relationships under Pennsylvania law, a plaintiff must allege: (i) an existing or prospective contractual relationship between the claimant and a third party; (ii) intent to harm the claimant by interfering with the existing relationship, or the intent to harm the claimant by preventing the relation from occurring; (iii) the absence of privilege or justification for such interference; and (iv) actual harm or damage to claimant as a result of such conduct."); Keene v. Rossi, 2015 U.S. Dist. LEXIS 176137 at *41 to *42 (E.D. Mich. 2015) ("The elements of a claim for tortious interference with contract under Michigan law are: (1) the existence of a contract; (2) breach of that contract; and (3) an unjustified instigation of the breach by the defendant. . . . Similarly, in order to prevail on a claim for tortious interference with a business advantage, the following must be proven: (1) a valid business relationship or expectancy; (2) knowledge of the relationship or expectancy on the part of the interferer; (3) an intentional interference inducing or causing a breach or termination of a relationship or expectancy; and (4) damages. . . . To prevail on either claim, a plaintiff must allege the intentional doing of a per se wrongful act, or the intentional doing of a lawful act with malice and unjustified in law, for the purpose of invading the contractual rights or business relationship of another.").

[15] *See*, e.g., Farmers Ins. Exch. v. First Choice Chiropractic & Rehab., 2015 U.S. Dist. LEXIS 96773 (D. Or. 2015), adopted by 2015 U.S. Dist. LEXIS 95898 at *21 to *22 (D. Or. 2015) (granting a summary judgment dismissing a healthcare provider's counterclaim for tortious interference with contract and intentional interference with economic relations, where alleged "tortious interference" was in the form of statements made by the insurer to insureds advising insureds of its investigation of healthcare provider's claims).

D. Malicious Prosecution

Malicious prosecution is not, strictly speaking, a proper counterclaim because a viable claim for malicious prosecution requires (i) that the defendant commenced a legal proceeding (ii) with malice and (iii) without probable cause and that (iv) the proceeding terminated in the plaintiff's favor.[16] Because malicious prosecution requires the termination of an action in favor of a plaintiff, it cannot be asserted as a counterclaim in an action that has not yet been terminated. Nevertheless, defendants in no-fault insurance fraud actions may try to assert malicious prosecution as a counterclaim because it allows them to posit that the insurer's lawsuit was actuated solely by malice rather than by large-scale fraudulent no-fault insurance billing.

To the extent that a defendant tries to assert malicious prosecution as a counterclaim, it will be subject to dismissal at the pleading stage. Even if the insurer's anti-fraud lawsuit is ultimately terminated in favor of a defendant and that defendant later commences a separate action against the insurer for malicious prosecution, the claim will be unlikely to result in any judgment against the insurer and, in most cases, will be subject to a pre-answer motion to dismiss. This is because—as the name implies—malicious prosecution claims require actual malice and a concomitant absence of probable cause.

Typically, where a claim for malicious prosecution alleges that a defendant acted to advance its own economic interests, no claim of actual malice will lie. As result, where a plaintiff alleges that an insurer commenced an anti-fraud suit to avoid paying a healthcare provider's no-fault insurance billing, the allegation will usually not support a malicious prosecution claim because the insurer's suit was motivated by its economic interests, not by malice.

More generally, it will be the rare case in which an insurer cannot make some colorable showing of probable cause for its anti-fraud lawsuit, even if the lawsuit ultimately terminated in favor of the

---

[16] These elements may vary somewhat from state to state, but *see*, e.g., Cardoso v. City of Brockton, 62 F. Supp. 3d 179, fn. 10 (D. Mass. 2014) (setting forth these elements as the elements of malicious prosecution under Massachusetts law); Bhd. Mut. Ins. Co. v. Salem Baptist Church, 985 F. Supp. 2d 624, fn. 6 (E.D. Pa. 2013) (setting forth these elements as the elements of malicious prosecution under Pennsylvania law); Bello v. Johnson, 2010 U.S. Dist. LEXIS 109073 at *8 (S.D. Fla. 2010) (setting forth these elements as the elements of malicious prosecution under Florida law).

defendant. Considering that a malicious prosecution claim requires not only malice, but also a lack of probable cause for the underlying suit, malicious prosecution claims by former defendants in anti-fraud cases will usually be doomed to failure.

E. Other Common Counterclaims

While counterclaims for defamation, tortious interference, and breach of contract are the most prevalent in no-fault insurance anti-fraud litigation, defendants in no-fault fraud cases have—at times—tried different approaches. For example, some defendants have attempted to state claims against insurers for fraud. These types of counterclaims are usually based on the notion that the insurer somehow colluded with the physicians they retained to perform peer reviews or independent medical examinations of suspect claims in order to fraudulently deny those claims. However, courts have dismissed these types of fraud-based claims and counterclaims because the alleged "fraud" does not posit a breach of any duty that is separate and independent from the insurer's contractual obligations to pay no-fault claims.[17]

Defendants in no-fault insurance fraud cases have also attempted to assert counterclaims against insurers based on alleged violations of state consumer protection laws. These types of counterclaims typically

---

[17] *See*, e.g., State Farm Mut. Auto. Ins. Co. v. Radden, 2016 U.S. Dist. LEXIS 20717 at *4 to *5 (E.D. Mich. 2016) (where the healthcare provider alleged that the plaintiff-insurer "engaged in a fraudulent scheme with doctors who perform independent medical exams and other (unidentified) co-conspirators to deny, delay and diminish payment on claims"; the fraud counterclaim was dismissed because the healthcare provider did "not allege a breach of duty that is separate and distinct from [the insurer's] contractual obligations."); McGee v. Allstate Ins. Co., 2011 U.S. Dist. LEXIS 89081 at *12 (E.D.N.Y. 2011) (dismissing the healthcare provider's fraud claim where the claim was based on allegations that the insurer "fraudulently induced him to provide treatment" to its insureds "with no intention of providing payment for that medical treatment," because "at most, a claim in contract might lie on such allegations."); but *see* MedCity Rehab. Servs., LLC v. State Farm Mut. Auto. Ins. Co., 2013 U.S. Dist. LEXIS 45142 at *14 to *18 (E.D. Mich. 2013) (denying the insurer's motion to dismiss healthcare provider's fraud claims that were predicated on allegations that the insurer falsely represented that it was investigating the provider's claims, when in fact it already had decided not to pay any of the provider's claims, and the provider relied on the representation to his detriment by continuing to provide services to the insurer's insureds).

allege that the insurer's failure to pay a healthcare provider's no-fault billing has some deleterious effect on consumers at large, for instance by driving small healthcare providers out of the market. While state consumer protection laws may vary considerably in their scope, courts are likely to find that the kind of private disputes between an insurer and a healthcare provider regarding payment of no-fault benefits is not sufficiently consumer oriented to support a counterclaim under state consumer protection laws.[18]

What is more, in alleging a consumer protection counterclaim that is based on an insurer's nonpayment of no-fault insurance benefits, a healthcare provider will be hard-pressed to show any wrongful conduct that goes beyond mere breach of contract. As a result, courts are likely to dismiss the consumer protection counterclaims as duplicative of the contract counterclaims that the healthcare provider simultaneously asserted, or should have asserted.

In some instances, a defendant in a no-fault fraud case will attempt to assert what is essentially a bad faith counterclaim against the plaintiff-insurer. These types of counterclaims typically invoke either the implied covenant of good faith and fair dealing, state unfair trade practices laws that require insurers to handle insurance claims in good faith, or both. While the specific allegations will naturally differ somewhat from case to case, bad faith counterclaims are usually based on the notion that the insurer has refused to promptly and fairly process claims that it knows to be valid and has taken an unfairly aggressive stance toward the healthcare provider simply because the provider treats a high volume of patients with no-fault insurance.

Bad faith counterclaims of this type are typically defective and subject to dismissal because they are redundant of the breach of contract counterclaims that the healthcare providers either are, or should be, asserting to recover on their outstanding no-fault claims.[19]

---

[18] *See*, e.g., Gov't Emples. Ins. Co. v. Hazel, 2014 U.S. Dist. LEXIS 133870 at *35 to *43 (E.D.N.Y. 2014), adopted by 2014 U.S. Dist. LEXIS 129594 (E.D.N.Y. 2014) (rejecting the proposed counterclaim under New York consumer protection law where the defendant did not sufficiently allege that the insurer's conduct was directed at consumers).

[19] *See*, e.g., McGee v. State Farm Mut. Auto. Ins. Co., 2011 U.S. Dist. LEXIS 128913 at *26 to *28 (E.D.N.Y. 2011) (dismissing the healthcare provider's claim for breach of the implied duty of good faith and fair dealing, where the healthcare provider alleged, in substance, that the insurer breached the duty of good faith and fair dealing

Relatedly, bad faith counterclaims may also be precluded by state law, making mandatory arbitration the only remedy for recovery of unpaid no-fault benefits.

For example, in New Jersey, multiple courts have held that bad faith claims are impermissible in the no-fault context and must be dismissed in deference to mandatory no-fault arbitration.[20] In Minnesota, as previously noted, state law mandates that healthcare providers must submit any disputed claim against an insurer for less than $10,000 in no-fault insurance benefits to mandatory arbitration.[21] Considering that courts lack subject matter jurisdiction over no-fault claims of $10,000 or less that are subject to the mandatory arbitration requirement, that most individual no-fault insurance claims will amount to less than $10,000, and that individual no-fault claims may not be aggregated for purposes of avoiding the mandatory arbitration requirement, most Minnesota healthcare providers would be unable to proceed on a bad faith claim.[22]

---

when it breached its insurance contracts by unfairly denying the provider's no-fault claims).

[20] *See*, e.g., Pain & Surgery Ambulatory Surgical Ctr. v. Liberty Mut. Ins. Co., 2007 U.S. Dist. LEXIS 45122 at *10 (D.N.J. 2007) ("[A] bad faith claim for wrongful withholding of PIP benefits cannot be sustained in New Jersey, and Defendant's motion to dismiss Count Three of Plaintiff's complaint is GRANTED"); Endo Surgical Center, P.C. v. Liberty Mut. Ins. Co., 391 N.J. Super. 588–95 (App. Div. 2007) (reversing the denial of an insurer's motion to dismiss a common law "bad faith" claim and holding that "if an insured (or an insured's assignee) were allowed to pursue a common law claim for an alleged bad faith denial of PIP benefits under which there would be an entitlement to a jury trial, this would open the door to circumvention of the statutorily mandated alternative dispute resolution procedure provided by N.J.S.A. 39:6A-5.1").

[21] *See* Minn. Stat. § 65B.525, subdivision 1 ("The Supreme Court and the several courts of general trial jurisdiction of this state shall by rules of court or other constitutionally allowable device, provide for the mandatory submission to binding arbitration of all cases at issue where the claim at the commencement of arbitration is in an amount of $ 10,000 or less against any insured's reparation obligor for no-fault benefits or comprehensive or collision damage coverage.").

[22] *See*, e.g., Alpine Glass, Inc. v. State Farm Fire & Cas. Co., 2013 U.S. Dist. LEXIS 78225 at *11 to *14 (D. Minn. 2013) (the courts lack subject matter jurisdiction over no-fault claims of $10,000 or less, and small claims cannot be aggregated to exceed $10,000 and avoid mandatory arbitration).

9

Discovery in No-Fault Insurance Anti-Fraud Litigation

Some no-fault anti-fraud cases will settle at or around the pleading stage in advance of any meaningful discovery. In the best-case scenario, the plaintiff-insurer's SIU investigators will assemble a damning dossier on a no-fault insurance fraud ring, the results of the investigation will appear powerfully on the face of the complaint, and the defendants will hasten to make a deal that the insurer will find acceptable. In most cases, however, the alleged fraud ring will elect to brazen it out—at least for a while—and the case will proceed into discovery.

In federal court, discovery cannot proceed immediately upon the filing of a complaint or even upon the defendants' filing of an answer or other response to the complaint. Instead, pursuant to Fed. R. Civ. P. 26(d) and 16(b), discovery generally does not start until the parties have met and conferred to discuss a proposed discovery plan and until the court has set a discovery schedule. While all of this is supposed to occur within the earlier of 90 days after any defendant has been served with the complaint, or 60 days after any defendant has appeared,[1] sometimes a scheduling order is not issued for months after

[1] *See* Fed. R. Civ. P. 16(b)(2).

a complaint has been filed and the defendants have appeared. More commonly, however, discovery will commence within a few months after the complaint is filed and served.

State court discovery procedures vary considerably and often permit service of discovery immediately upon joinder of issue. Nonetheless, as a practical matter, discovery often will not commence in earnest until the court holds a conference with the parties' counsel and sets a discovery schedule, similar to what occurs in federal court.

A. Initiating a Litigation Hold

Once a party reasonably expects that litigation may ensue, that party is obligated to preserve records and information—including electronically stored information—that may be relevant to the subject matter of the litigation. This is called a "litigation hold."[2] It is best practice for attorneys to advise their clients to institute the requisite hold once it appears that litigation may occur and to ensure that their clients have an adequate process for instituting a litigation hold.

In the context of no-fault anti-fraud litigation, a litigation hold should be instituted immediately once the case moves out of the SIU investigative stage and is in the hands of an attorney, even if there is not yet absolute certainty that a lawsuit will ever be filed. The attorney should provide her client with notice of the need for the hold in writing and should specify (i) the subject matter of the potential litigation, (ii) the types of material—including electronically stored material—that must be preserved, (iii) the pertinent time frame applicable to the materials that must be preserved, (iv) the potential consequences—including spoliation sanctions—that could obtain if the materials subject to the hold are not preserved, and (v) a reminder that the hold will remain in place until further notice. Though the attorney can draft the litigation hold notice, it should be distributed by someone with authority within the client's organization to

[2] *See*, e.g., HM Elecs., Inc. v. R.F. Techs., Inc., 2015 U.S. Dist. LEXIS 104100 (S.D. Cal. 2015) ("Attorneys have a duty to effectively communicate a 'litigation hold' that is tailored to the client and the particular lawsuit, so the client will understand exactly what actions to take or forebear, and so that the client will actually take the steps necessary to preserve evidence.").

everyone within the organization who is likely to have discoverable material to better ensure compliance.

The client should be advised to appoint an individual or individuals as "information custodians" to serve as the designated point of collection and protection for all potentially relevant material. This information custodian should be required to take responsibility for identification and sequestration of all potentially relevant information, documents, and data (in their native format), as well as to periodically ascertain compliance with the hold. For an insurer considering an anti-fraud case, the best information custodians will oftentimes be senior SIU personnel working in tandem with designated information technology staff. It is best to avoid appointing more junior staff as information custodians because information custodians are likely to be deposed as litigation proceeds, and more senior personnel are likely to have a higher level of judgment and poise. Outside counsel likewise has a duty to oversee compliance with a litigation hold.[3]

B. Motions to Stay Discovery

Oftentimes, rather than engage in the discovery process at all, a defendant in a no-fault insurance fraud case will seek a stay of discovery shortly after the action is commenced. The typical scenario in which this occurs is one in which the defendant has filed a motion to dismiss some or all of the insurer's claims rather than an answer to the complaint. The defendant may argue that the motion to dismiss might eliminate some or all of the insurer's discrete causes of action, thereby limiting the scope of discovery or eliminating the need for discovery altogether. The defendant will go on to argue that he should not be required to engage in expensive and time-consuming discovery until it is clear whether or not the case will proceed or what claims will remain in the case if the case does proceed.

These types of arguments can have considerable surface appeal. After all, judges are aware that discovery can be expensive and are

---

[3] *See*, e.g., Zubulake v. UBS Warburg LLC, 229 F.R.D. 422 (S.D.N.Y. 2004) ("A party's discovery obligations do not end with the implementation of a 'litigation hold'—to the contrary, that's only the beginning. Counsel must oversee compliance with the litigation hold, monitoring the party's efforts to retain and produce the relevant documents.").

sensitive to undue burden arguments. What could be more unduly burdensome than forcing a defendant to engage in expensive discovery in a case that is on the cusp of dismissal? Even so, stays of discovery are generally disfavored, and courts have considerable discretion to balance the burden on a defendant against a plaintiff's right to expeditiously prosecute its case and vindicate its rights. In the exercise of this discretion, courts require litigants to show good cause for a stay of discovery, with the burden on the movant.[4]

Although the standards that are applied in determining good cause for a stay of discovery vary somewhat from jurisdiction to jurisdiction, the pendency of a dispositive motion such as a pre-answer motion to dismiss—standing alone—will usually not be sufficient.[5] Rather, in determining whether to stay discovery during the pendency of a motion to dismiss, courts will generally look at the briefing on the motion and make a preliminary determination as to whether the motion is likely to result in the dismissal of all, or some substantial part, of the case.[6]

Courts also weigh the risk of unfair prejudice to the party opposing the proposed stay when determining whether a stay is appropriate.[7] To the extent that a motion to dismiss seems likely to dispose of a case, either in whole or in some substantial part, courts will often grant motions to stay discovery until the motion is decided. On the

---

[4] *See*, e.g., State Farm Mut. Auto. Ins. Co. v. Accurate Med., P.C., 2007 U.S. Dist. LEXIS 74459 at *3 (E.D.N.Y. 2007) ("A party seeking a stay of discovery pursuant to Fed. R. Civ. P. 26(c) bears the burden of showing good cause."); Gerald Chamales Corp. v. Oki Data Americas, Inc., 247 F.R.D. 453, 454 (D.N.J. 2007) ("A protective order pursuant to Fed. R. Civ. P. 26(c) may only be issued if 'good cause' is shown.").

[5] *See*, e.g., Porter v. Five Star Quality Care-MI, LLC, 2014 U.S. Dist. LEXIS 26487 at *8 to *9 (E.D. Mich. 2014) ("It is not the usual practice of this Court . . . to order a stay of discovery solely on the ground that a defendant has filed a motion to dismiss."); Accurate Med., P.C., *supra* note 4 ("The pendency of a dispositive motion is not, in itself, an automatic ground for a stay. . . . Rather, a court determining whether to grant a stay of discovery pending a motion must look to the particular circumstances and posture of each case."); Maher Terminals, LLC v. Port Auth., 2013 U.S. Dist. LEXIS 72719 at *5 (D.N.J. 2013) ("It is well settled that the mere filing of a dispositive motion does not constitute 'good cause' for the issuance of a discovery stay.") (Internal quotations and citations omitted).

[6] *See*, e.g., Maher Terminals, LLC, *supra* note 5, at *9; Porter, *supra* note 5, at *9 to *10; Accurate Med., P.C., *supra*, note 4.

[7] *See*, e.g., Accurate Med., P.C., *supra*, note 4.

other hand, if a motion to dismiss seems unlikely to dispose of a significant part of a case, motions to stay discovery will typically be denied.

As a result, when opposing a motion to stay discovery, anti-fraud litigators should make sure to muster and present all of the evidence supporting the allegations in their complaint. This will not only help demonstrate to the court why a pending motion to dismiss is unlikely to result in the complete dismissal of the action and why a stay of discovery would therefore be inappropriate, but will also provide a valuable opportunity to remind the court of any defects in the defendants' arguments for dismissal of the complaint.

Anti-fraud litigators also should collect and present to the court any evidence that the defendants intend to use any stay of an action as an opportunity to continue their fraudulent scheme, to secrete or dissipate their assets, or to otherwise act to the plaintiff-insurer's prejudice. For example, is there evidence that the defendants are actively pursuing collection on their outstanding, fraudulent billing? Is it likely that the defendants will continue to collect on their fraudulent billing during the pendency of any stay of discovery in the anti-fraud action? If so, then these facts can be used to demonstrate that a stay of discovery in the anti-fraud case would cause the plaintiff-insurer to be prejudiced.

Along similar lines, is there any evidence to suggest that the defendants have secreted or dissipated their assets, are about to do so, or have few ties to the community and can decamp to some other country with the proceeds of the fraudulent scheme? Oftentimes, this sort of evidence will be contained within the defendants' bank records and will not be available to the insurer in advance of discovery. However, sometimes the insurer will have this information at the pleading stage and will be in a position to present it to the court.

In addition, insurers will often be in a position to demonstrate that they will be prejudiced by a stay if they can show that there is some real prospect that evidence will be lost or spoliated during the pendency of the stay or that important witnesses will be unavailable or forgetful by the time the stay is lifted. If, for instance, a participant in or a witness to a no-fault fraud scheme is elderly or in poor health, an insurer may be able to demonstrate that it would be prejudiced by a stay. Likewise, where a healthcare practice operates on an itinerant basis with no single fixed office or has evaded disclosure in other forums such as its own no-fault collections proceedings, the insurer may be in a position to contend that critical evidence could be lost if discovery is stayed.

C. Relevance and Its Limits

Assuming that a defendant does not seek a stay of discovery or if a stay is denied or ultimately lifted, anti-fraud litigators must begin to frame their discovery requests. This requires consideration of relevance and its limits.

Pursuant to Fed. R. Civ. P. 26(b)(1), parties generally

> may obtain discovery regarding any nonprivileged matter that is relevant to any party's claim or defense and proportional to the needs of the case, considering the importance of the issues at stake in the action, the amount in controversy, the parties' relative access to relevant information, the parties' resources, the importance of the discovery in resolving the issues, and whether the burden or expense of the proposed discovery outweighs its likely benefit. Information within this scope of discovery need not be admissible in evidence to be discoverable.

Though relevance assessments may vary from state to state, in both federal and state law the general presumption is that evidence is to be deemed relevant where there is any possibility that it will make a fact of consequence to the determination more or less likely than it would be without the evidence.

Although "relevance" has been construed broadly for discovery purposes, the 2015 amendments to the Federal Rules of Civil Procedure place a renewed emphasis on "proportionality." As set forth above, even where evidence is otherwise relevant, it need not be produced in discovery unless it is "proportional to the needs of the case," taking into account a variety of considerations aimed at ensuring that the scope of permissible discovery actually bears some legitimate relationship to the issues that actually need to be resolved in the case.

Though much of the case law regarding relevance in no-fault insurance anti-fraud litigation predates the 2015 amendments to the Federal Rules, the 2015 amendments simply emphasize a proportionality requirement that already was inherent in Rule 26.[8] As a result, the pre-2015 discovery rulings in no-fault insurance anti-fraud litigation should continue to be persuasive in future cases.

With that in mind, it is worthwhile to discuss the general categories of discovery that are sought by insurers in typical no-fault insurance anti-fraud cases and the kinds of relevance rulings that courts have issued with respect to those categories of discovery.

In a case involving a healthcare provider that is alleged to have an illegal corporate structure, most insurers will be interested in reviewing the healthcare provider's bank records, tax returns, general ledgers, payroll records, and other financial records. Insurers also will be interested in reviewing a healthcare practice's leases, vendor agreements, and related materials to the extent that the healthcare provider is alleged to be unlawfully controlled by unlicensed individuals and entities, who often use exorbitant leases and vendor agreements as vehicles to exert their illegal ownership and control over a practice. These materials will enable the insurer to "follow the money" and—by extension—to demonstrate that the practice is unlawfully owned or controlled by unlicensed nonprofessionals.

Along similar lines, a healthcare provider's business and financial records, including lease agreements with its referral sources, may be used to prove that the provider pays illegal kickbacks in exchange for patient referrals, however well those kickbacks may be disguised. As a general rule, where an insurer has well-pleaded allegations to the effect that a healthcare provider is illegally organized or engages in some other type of financial impropriety that affects its entitlement to bill for or to collect no-fault insurance benefits, courts have determined that the healthcare provider's financial and business records are relevant and subject to disclosure.[9]

---

[8] *See* Notes of Advisory Committee on 2015 amendments, stating that "[r]estoring the proportionality calculation to Rule 26(b)(1) does not change the existing responsibilities of the court and the parties to consider proportionality. . . ."

[9] *See*, e.g., Gov't Emples. Ins. Co. v. Specialty Medical Services, LLC, D.N.J. Case No. 2:14-cv-08015-KSH-CLW, at Docket No. 60 (denying a motion to quash plaintiff-insurers' subpoena seeking corporate bank records for healthcare practices, where the plaintiff-insurers had alleged that the healthcare practices unlawfully were owned and controlled by non-physicians); State Farm Mut. Auto. Ins. Co. v. Physiomatrix, Inc., 2013 U.S. Dist. LEXIS 189646 at *8 to *12 (E.D. Mich. 2013) (in a no-fault fraud case, denying a motion to quash bank subpoenas where the subpoenaed bank records were relevant to "help establish ownership and control over the

A healthcare provider's financial and business records may be relevant and discoverable even in cases that do not involve allegations of an illegal corporate structure or other, overt financial impropriety. For example, if an insurer has alleged a RICO conspiracy claim under 18 U.S.C. § 1962(d), a healthcare practice's financial records may be relevant to demonstrate the scope of the alleged conspiracy.[10] Similarly, a practice's financial records can be relevant to demonstrate that the practice derives the substantial majority of its revenues from fraudulent no-fault insurance billing. This, in turn, can be used to demonstrate that the practice's business primarily or inherently is unlawful for purposes of establishing a threat of continued criminal activity and the pattern of racketeering activity necessary to support a civil RICO claim.

While courts adjudicating no-fault fraud cases will commonly order disclosure of a corporate defendant's business and financial

---

various entities, will establish the structure of the enterprise (namely the connections between and among the named parties and various nonparties who were also alleged to be part of the underlying conspiracy), will measure the scope of the fraud, will reveal additional potential parties and witnesses, will show motive for the alleged conspiracy, and will help prove damages"); MedCity Rehab. Servs., LLC v. State Farm Mut. Auto. Ins. Co., 2013 U.S. Dist. LEXIS 64670 at *22 (E.D. Mich. 2013) (in a no-fault fraud case, the professional corporation's financial records were relevant to establishing the financial relationships among the physician-owner, the professional corporation, and the other purported participants in the scheme, and were discoverable); State Farm Mut. Auto. Ins. Co. v. Tabakman, 2008 U.S. Dist. LEXIS 77784 at *6 to *7 (E.D.N.Y. 2008) (declining to quash bank subpoenas in a no-fault fraud case where the plaintiff-insurer sought evidence of kickbacks); State Farm Mut. Auto. Ins. Co. v. CPT Medical Services, P.C., 375 F. Supp. 2d 141, 155–56 (E.D.N.Y. 2005) (finding "financial records, including tax returns of the defendants relating to transactions which generated cash" to be discoverable to demonstrate the extent to which defendants profited from alleged fraudulent billing scheme).

[10] *See*, e.g., Gov't Employees Ins. Co. v. Five Boro Psychological Servs. PC., E.D.N.Y. Case No. 12-cv-02448, at May 24, 2013 Docket Entry (declining to quash bank subpoenas in a no-fault fraud case where subpoenaed bank records were, among other things, relevant to demonstrate the scope of the alleged racketeering conspiracies and the pattern of racketeering activity); Physiomatrix, Inc., *supra* note 9; Allstate Ins. Co. v. Elzanaty, 2012 U.S. Dist. LEXIS 171962 at *4 to *5 (E.D.N.Y. 2012) (denying a motion to quash bank subpoenas in a no-fault fraud case where accounts at issue were "depositories for monies from the alleged RICO corporations" and where the plaintiffs had "reason to believe that the accounts at issue [were] integrally connected to the alleged conspiracy").

records, they often shy away from ordering disclosure of a noncorporate defendant's personal financial records—at least at first.

For instance, where an insurer is suing a medical professional corporation through which a large amount of fraudulent billing was submitted, together with its owners and employees, courts will typically require the professional corporation to disclose its financial records, but will not, in the first instance, require the natural person defendants to disclose their financial records. This is because the corporate financial records for the pertinent professional entity will often be sufficient to enable the insurer to prove its case. If the professional corporation is unlawfully organized or is being used to engage in some other type of illegal financial activity such as a kickback scheme, the corporate finances usually will tell the tale.

In addition, courts recognize that personal financial records will often contain sensitive or confidential information that has no conceivable bearing on any fact of consequence to the determination of a case. While most financial records of a corporate medical practice will have some relevance to an insurer's fraud allegations, the opposite is true with respect to an individual defendant's personal financial records.

None of this is to say that, in a proper case, a court will deny an insurer discovery with respect to an individual defendant's personal finances. Some fraudulent healthcare providers submit their billing through unincorporated sole proprietorships and use personal bank accounts as depositories for the proceeds of the fraudulent scheme. In other cases, the proceeds of a fraudulent scheme may initially be deposited into a corporate bank account, but the corporate bank records will show that the money was immediately transferred out into a defendant's personal account. In such instances, courts are likely to determine that a defendant's individual financial records are subject to disclosure.

Even so, insurers should expect that—where a fraud was carried out through an entity—the courts will require them to look at the corporate bank records first and will order disclosure of a defendant's personal financial records only to the extent that the corporate bank records do not tell the complete story.

The second general category of discovery that is sought by insurers in no-fault anti-fraud cases is documents and other records pertaining to a defendant's treatment and billing practices. These documents typically include patient files maintained by a defendant healthcare provider, as well as bills and related correspondence between the provider and the insurer. This category of materials will manifestly be relevant to an insurer's claims in virtually every no-fault insurance anti-fraud case. To the extent that the insurer has alleged that the healthcare provider routinely billed inflated amounts for medically unnecessary or illusory services, the provider's treatment and billing records will make the fact of the treatment and billing fraud more or less likely than it would be without the evidence. For instance, the records can be used to show that the healthcare provider purported to render the same treatment to virtually every patient in the same manner without regard for the patients' individual symptoms or circumstances. The records can also be used to show a pattern of unlawfully upcoded or unbundled charges.

What is more, a healthcare provider's treatment and billing records can be relevant even in cases that are premised exclusively on illegal corporate structure issues and that are not predicated directly on allegations to the effect that the provider billed for healthcare services that were medically useless or illusory. For example, if a healthcare provider routinely bills for medically unnecessary services or provides services in a manner that is below the pertinent standard of care, it is good circumstantial evidence that the healthcare provider is truly owned and controlled by a licensed practitioner.

Because a defendant healthcare practice's treatment and billing records are so obviously relevant to most kinds of no-fault anti-fraud claims, defendants rarely raise a relevance challenge to requests for such records. Rather, to the extent that a defendant raises any objection at all to the production of such records, the objection is usually couched as a proportionality challenge. In substance, a defendant may contend that she has treated a large number of the insurer's insureds, that the underlying patient records run to tens or hundreds of thousands of pages, and that the production of such a large volume of records would pose an undue burden and be disproportionate to the needs of the case. While many modern healthcare practices maintain their patient and billing records electronically—which would tend to obviate any burden of production—defendants in no-fault insurance fraud cases tend to do things the old-fashioned way and keep their records in paper files, to the extent that they keep them at all. This makes it easier to destroy or otherwise spoliate the records when it starts to appear as if the game is up.

As a result, defendants in no-fault fraud cases may be able to muster a colorable undue burden argument in response to a demand for all of their patient and billing files. Nonetheless, courts typically order such records to be produced because their relevance to the underlying case outweighs the burden of production. To the extent that courts impose any limitations on the production of patient treatment and billing records, the most common limitation is to require the parties to randomly select a statistically significant sample of the treatment and billing records at issue and to require the production of the records included within the random sample.

Of course, anti-fraud litigators must not only consider the relevance of the discovery requests that they propound on behalf of their plaintiff-insurer-clients, but also the relevance of the discovery requests that typically are served by defendants in no-fault fraud cases. In this context, while plaintiff-insurers can, in theory, challenge the proportionality of a defendant's discovery requests, a plaintiff in most cases will receive less of a sympathetic hearing than a defendant on a proportionality objection. After all, the plaintiff made the decision to commence the litigation in the first place. What is more, where the plaintiff is a large and well-resourced corporation—as is the case with virtually every plaintiff-insurer—the court may be inclined to discount any undue burden arguments.

Nonetheless, defendants in no-fault insurance anti-fraud cases commonly overreach in their discovery requests and seek documents and information with no conceivable relevance to the claims or defenses in the case. While it is impossible to recount the litany of overbroad and irrelevant discovery requests that have been served by defendants in no-fault fraud cases, some of the more common categories of overbroad requests include (i) requests for documents or information regarding every lawsuit the plaintiff-insurer has ever filed, against any defendant, anywhere, in the past; (ii) requests for documents or information regarding every instance in which the insurer has disputed or paid a charge under a given CPT code, regardless of the context in which the charge was submitted and regardless of whether it was submitted by the defendants in the case; (iii) requests for documents and information regarding employees of the plaintiff-insurer who were not in any way involved in the handling or investigation of the defendants' no-fault claims; and (iv) requests for documents and information concerning all of the insurer's internal policies and procedures regardless of whether the policies and procedures played any role in the handling or investigation of the defendants' no-fault claims.

In most cases, defendants propound radically overbroad and irrelevant discovery requests in the hope that they will persuade the insurer that the scope of the case will be far greater than anticipated and that the cost of litigating the case will outweigh any prospective benefit the insurer might receive from the litigation. Ordinarily, if the insurer objects to the overbroad discovery requests, the defendants will make no real effort to pursue them because the court is likely to sustain the insurer's irrelevance and overbreadth objections if the defendants make a motion to compel and because the cost of any motion to compel therefore would exceed the benefit.

While the universe of documents and information that are discoverable from an insurer in a no-fault anti-fraud action will necessarily vary depending on the allegations in a discrete case, some categories of documents and information will be relevant and discoverable in almost any anti-fraud suit. For instance, an insurer's claims files with respect to the no-fault claims it has received from a defendant healthcare provider will virtually always be relevant and will have to be produced, subject to any applicable attorney-client, work product, or other applicable privilege. To the extent that the insurer has alleged that a healthcare provider submitted inflated billing for medically unnecessary services, the information in the claims files—including police reports, hospital records, the defendant healthcare provider's treatment records, and the treatment records for other healthcare providers who contemporaneously purported to treat the insured patients at issue—will certainly make the fact of the inflated billing and medically unnecessary services more or less likely than it would be without the evidence. The claims files will typically be relevant and discoverable even in a corporate structure fraud case that does not involve any stand-alone allegations regarding inflated billing or medically unnecessary services.

For example, the defendant healthcare provider will be in a position to argue that the claims files are relevant to show that its services were medically warranted and that the putative legitimacy of the services makes it more likely that the provider was, in fact, lawfully owned by a licensed professional. More generally, the claims files are reasonably likely to contain information that would support or rebut an insurer's claim that it justifiably relied on a defendant's fraudulent misrepresentations and that the insurer was damaged by such reliance.

Similarly, an insurer's investigative files with respect to a defendant will generally be discoverable—again, subject to any attorney-client, work product, or other privileges that may legitimately apply to specific documents or information within the files.[11] Not only will SIU and other investigative files tend to demonstrate whether, to what extent, and when an insurer justifiably was relying on allegedly fraudulent claims submissions, but the files often will contain information that bears directly on the gravamen of the insurer's fraud claims—such as witness statements and the like. Although an insurer may contend that the materials in its investigative files constitute work product, or material prepared in anticipation of litigation, the defendant healthcare provider will often be able to show that the investigative materials were compiled before litigation actually was anticipated. Even those investigative materials that were genuinely prepared in anticipation of litigation may be subject to disclosure if the defendant can demonstrate a substantial need for the materials and that it is unable to obtain the substantial equivalent of the materials through other means.[12]

An insurer's internal training manuals—including claims-handling manuals and SIU training manuals—will also typically be discoverable to the extent that they guided the insurer's investigation of a defendant or handling of the defendant's claims. While these types of materials will usually not have any legitimate bearing on the claims or defenses in an anti-fraud case, defendants will be well-positioned to argue that they are likely to contain detailed procedures for the review of suspect claims and therefore are relevant to the insurer's justifiable reliance and the accrual of the pertinent statutes of limitation.

In this context, it is important to note that not every training manual promulgated by an insurer will be relevant to a no-fault anti-fraud case. For example, many insurers create different training manuals for different parts of the country and periodically revise or update their training manuals. Thus, a request for training manuals without

[11] *See*, e.g., State Farm Mut. Auto. Ins. Co. v. Eastern Med., P.C., 2008 U.S. Dist. LEXIS 59891 at *17 to *19 (E.D.N.Y. 2008) (ordering production of the plaintiff-insurer's SIU files in an anti-fraud case, with the exception of information regarding the insurer's fraud detection plan and materials protected by the attorney-client or work product privileges).

[12] *See*, e.g., Fed. R. Civ. P. 26(b)(3).

an appropriate temporal or geographic limitation would be overbroad and subject to a valid objection that would probably be sustained by the court. To the extent that a defendant requests an insurer's internal training manuals, the insurer should resist the production of any manuals other than those that directly guided the handling and investigation of the defendant's claims.

Often, where an insurer's anti-fraud complaint alleges that a healthcare provider billed for medically useless or illusory services, it will be clear to the defendants that—in preparing the complaint—the insurer used the services of a consulting expert in the pertinent discipline. As a result, defendants in no-fault fraud cases commonly demand the production of documents or information generated by these consulting experts, including correspondence, written reports, draft reports, and the like. However, and as noted above, Fed. R. Civ. P. 26(b)(4)(D) and its state law equivalents generally protect consulting expert opinions from disclosure, unless and until it appears as if the consulting expert is going to testify at trial. While there are some relatively narrow exceptions to this rule—for instance, where a defendant has a substantial need for the consulting expert materials to prepare its case and cannot, without undue hardship, obtain their substantial equivalent by other means—it will be a rare case in which such materials will have to be produced by an insurer in discovery.

Other than claims files, investigative files, and—where applicable—training manuals, there will usually be few other materials in the insurer's possession, custody, or control that are relevant to the claims and defenses in a no-fault anti-fraud case and are therefore discoverable.

D. Discovery Confidentiality Orders

Of course, even materials that are otherwise relevant and discoverable can contain sensitive or confidential commercial information. An insurer's claims files, SIU files, and training manuals may not only contain confidential commercial information, but the manner in which they are compiled and maintained may, upon analysis, disclose information regarding the insurer's internal processes that the insurer may prefer not to disseminate. For their part, the defendants in a no-fault anti-fraud case may not want their patient files or financial records to be disclosed outside of the context of the litigation.

As a result, it is usually best practice for the parties to anti-fraud litigation to seek a discovery confidentiality order from the court before exchanging any discovery, despite the fact that either a plaintiff-insurer or a defendant in a no-fault fraud case may have some tactical reason for not seeking a confidentiality order. For example, the insurer may believe that if it publicly files evidence of a defendant's fraud with the court and exposes the evidence to the scrutiny of regulatory authorities, law enforcement, or other insurers that also may have received suspicious claims from the defendant, the defendant may elect to settle early to cut off the risks attendant to further public disclosure. Similarly, the defendant may feel that if it disseminates documents and information regarding the insurer's claims-handling and investigative practices in public court filings, the insurer may be motivated to walk away from the case in order to prevent further revelations. This type of tactical gamesmanship rarely has the desired result, inasmuch as—instead of generating a quick settlement—it usually simply drives the parties to stipulate to the entry of a confidentiality order to which they should have stipulated at the outset. It also tends to harden the parties in their positions and aggravate the court.

With that in mind, in the best-case scenario, the parties will meet and confer in good faith at the outset of discovery to develop a proposed order and then submit it to the court for review and entry. In the event that a defendant refuses to confer in good faith to develop an appropriate discovery confidentiality order, the plaintiff-insurer can submit a proposed order to the court individually, note that the defendant has unreasonably refused to consent to it, and ask the court to enter it over any objections that the defendant may have. Courts are usually very receptive to such confidentiality orders, often make form confidentiality orders available on their websites for the use of parties and their counsel, and look askance at parties that unreasonably refuse to consent to such orders.

While the parties to a no-fault anti-fraud suit may want to tailor their proposed confidentiality order to the discrete issues in their case, any confidentiality order should—at a minimum—contain the following, material provisions:

i. The parties to the litigation, and any third parties that may produce any discovery in the context of the litigation, shall have the ability to designate as "confidential" any information, document, or thing, or portion of any document or thing (a) that contains trade secrets, competitively sensitive technical, marketing, financial, sales or other confidential business information; (b) that contains private or confidential personal information; (c) that contains information received in confidence from third parties; or (d) which the producing party otherwise believes in good faith to be entitled to protection.

ii. All material designated as "confidential" shall be used by the receiving party solely for purposes of the prosecution or defense of the action; shall not be used by the receiving party for any business, commercial, competitive, personal, or other purpose; and shall not be disclosed by the receiving party to anyone other than (a) counsel to the parties; (b) experts or consultants retained by the parties, provided that those experts or consultants execute non-disclosure agreements; (c) secretarial, paralegal, clerical, coping, and data-processing personnel of the parties, their counsel, their experts, and their consultants; (d) the court and court personnel; (e) witnesses, provided that it appears that the witness authored or received a copy of the material, was involved in the subject matter described therein, or is employed by the party who produced the material; (f) vendors retained by or for the parties to assist in preparing for pretrial discovery, trial, and/or hearings, including, but not limited to, court reporters, litigation support personnel, jury consultants, and individuals to prepare demonstrative and audiovisual aids for use in the courtroom or in depositions or mock jury sessions, as well as their staff, stenographic, and clerical employees whose duties and responsibilities require access to such materials; and (g) the parties, the officers and directors of the parties, and employees of the parties, provided that their employment requires that they participate in the litigation.

iii. With respect to any depositions that involve a disclosure of material designated as "confidential," a party shall have until 30 days after receipt of the deposition transcript within which to inform all other parties that portions of the transcript are to be designated confidential.

iv. Any party shall have the ability to challenge the designation of any material as "confidential" and to seek an appropriate ruling from the court.

v. To the extent consistent with applicable law, the inadvertent or unintentional disclosure of "confidential" material that should have been designated as such, regardless of whether the information, document, or thing was so designated at the time of disclosure, shall not be deemed a waiver in whole or in part of a party's claim of confidentiality, either as to the specific information, document, or thing disclosed or as to any other material or information concerning the same or related subject matter. Such inadvertent or unintentional disclosure may be rectified by notifying in writing counsel for all parties to whom the material was disclosed that the material should have been designated "confidential" within a reasonable time after disclosure. Such notice shall constitute a designation of the information, document or thing as "confidential."

vi. No information that is in the public domain, which is already known by the receiving party through proper means, or which is or becomes available to a party from a source other than the party asserting confidentiality, rightfully in possession of such information on a nonconfidential basis, shall be deemed or considered to be "confidential" material.

In addition, either the defendants in an anti-fraud case or the plaintiff-insurer may contemplate including provisions in discovery confidentiality orders that require the destruction of certain documents or other materials at the conclusion of the case. In this context, anti-fraud litigators and their insurer clients should be aware of state laws that may require the preservation of insurer claims or investigative files for delineated periods.[13] This, in turn, can present insurers with a difficult choice—either comply with state record retention laws or comply with the discovery confidentiality order—and can be the subject of unnecessary litigation. Nonetheless, there is a work-around that can avoid situations of this type: To the extent that a document

[13] *See*, e.g., 11 N.Y.C.R.R. § 243.2 (setting forth various record retention rules for insurers in New York).

destruction provision is included in a proposed discovery confidentiality order, it should require—at most—only that each party must destroy documents it received in discovery rather than documents that it both received and produced.

E. The Use of Interrogatories in No-Fault Anti-Fraud Cases

Every litigator will have a general familiarity with the preparation and service of interrogatories, responses to interrogatories, and—in particular—the types of objections that can be interposed in response to interrogatories. It is, however, worthwhile to discuss the best way to make effective use of interrogatories in the specific context of no-fault insurance anti-fraud litigation.

Initially, it is important to emphasize that anti-fraud litigators should avoid any attempt to substitute pages and pages of interrogatories for deposition testimony. While it may be tempting to burden an adversary with the task of providing written responses to hundreds of particularized inquiries regarding their practice structure, the medical necessity of their services, and the like, courts often will strike excessive interrogatories—even interrogatories that seek otherwise relevant information—as unduly burdensome and will require the pertinent inquires to be made at depositions instead.

Indeed, Fed. R. Civ. P. 33 generally limits the number of interrogatories that a party may serve to no more than 25, including all subparts, unless the parties stipulate to a different amount or the court orders a different amount. While state rules of civil procedure may not explicitly limit the permissible number of interrogatories, state court judges—as a practical matter—will be receptive to complaints if it appears that a party has served a vexatious number of inquiries.

With that in mind, it will usually be a good idea to refrain from serving the maximum permissible number of interrogatories at once and, instead, to hold some interrogatories in reserve for future use. That way, it will be possible—in advance of depositions—to follow up on any new lines of inquiry that are opened by a defendant's responses to the initial interrogatories.

As a general rule, in no-fault anti-fraud cases, interrogatories will be one of the least effective discovery devices because defendants usually understand the theory of the insurer's case. As a result, their responses to an insurer's interrogatories will be small masterpieces of dissembling and evasion, with a heavy dollop of recrimination and self-justification.

For example, an inquiry into the standards applied by a healthcare provider when determining the need for a diagnostic test may be met with a response to the effect that "all decisions at my practice are based on my independent medical judgment as to what is in the best interest of the patient." Similarly, when an insurer has alleged that a healthcare provider is secretly controlled by unlicensed nonprofessionals and the insurer inquires into the amounts that the unlicensed parties charge the practice for "management" services, the practice might respond with "fair market value." While these types of evasive responses might not withstand a motion to compel, they tend to make interrogatories a less efficient way to obtain information than depositions, where an anti-fraud litigator is free to pose follow-up questions in real time.

1. Representative Interrogatories in Corporate Structure Fraud Cases

In a corporate structure fraud case—for instance, a case involving a healthcare practice that is illegally owned and controlled by an unlicensed non-physician—a defendant will rarely provide a straightforward answer to interrogatories asking whether the practice is solely owned by licensed professionals or whether unlicensed parties share in the revenues of the practice. Even so, a plaintiff-insurer can use interrogatories to obtain evidence of an unlicensed party's concealed, illegal ownership interest in or control over a healthcare practice.

Toward this end, in a corporate structure fraud case, a plaintiff-insurer's interrogatories should—at a minimum—request that the defendants

i. identify all bank accounts into which or from which the revenues of the healthcare practice have been deposited or disbursed;
ii. identify each person or entity that was authorized to sign checks, make withdrawals, or transfer funds on behalf of the healthcare practice;
iii. identify each person or entity that is in possession of the healthcare practice's (a) tax returns, (b) general ledgers, (c)

bank statements and cancelled checks, and (d) patient files, as well as the current location of those documents;

iv. identify the persons or entities that were responsible for providing the healthcare practice with (a) billing and collection services, (b) marketing services, (c) management services, (d) consulting services of any type, and/or (e) tax preparation services;

v. identify the persons or entities that were members, officers, directors, or partners in the healthcare practice or that had a financial interest in the practice and the time period in which the interests in the practice were held;

vi. identify every physical location from which the healthcare practice operated, whether the locations were owned or leased, and—if leased—identify the lessor;

vii. identify each post office box used in relation to the operation and management of the healthcare practice's business, the name of the person and/or entity in whose name the post office box was registered, each person who had keys and/or access to the box;

viii. identify each piece of equipment used in relation to the operation and management of the healthcare practice's business, whether the equipment was owned or leased, and—if leased—identify the lessor;

ix. identify each person who was employed by the healthcare practice or associated with the practice as an independent contractor, their respective duties and job descriptions, and the time period in which they were associated with the practice; and

x. identify each person or entity that was involved in the creation or submission of the healthcare practice's bills and treatment reports.

These categories of inquiry are useful in corporate structure fraud cases because they leave little room for evasion. Note that they do not ask the ultimate questions in the case—for instance, there is no request that the defendants set forth "every unlicensed individual with an interest in the healthcare practice" or even "every unlicensed individual with authority to sign checks on behalf of the practice." Because the interrogatories request basic facts, there is little room for a defendant to spin its responses. While the interrogatory responses might not prove the insurer's case on their own, they open up other avenues of inquiry that can be pursued via document requests, subpoenas, or at depositions, where the ability to ask follow-up questions will make it hard for defendants to avoid providing information.

2. Representative Interrogatories in Medical Necessity Cases

In a case alleging that a healthcare provider misrepresented the medical necessity of its services, or that they actually were provided in the first instance, interrogatories should focus on the circumstances under which the services were recommended, the manner in which the services were performed, and the impact of the services on the insured patient's overall treatment plan. Again, the primary purpose of the interrogatories will be to identify and open up prospective lines of inquiry, not to obtain admissions that go to the ultimate issues in the case.

It usually will be a waste of time to ask, for example, that a healthcare provider "identify every instance in which a service was billed but not provided" or to "identify every diagnostic test that played no legitimate role in the treatment of the patient." It is better to ask a healthcare provider to explain how a patient's treatment plan was changed as the result of a diagnostic test or to set forth its training and experience in the performance of a given procedure.

For example, in a medical necessity case, a plaintiff-insurer's interrogatories should, as a starting point, request that the defendants

i. identify each person who was involved in the performance of the healthcare services at issue, as well as their respective training and education in the performance of the services at issue and the time period in which they performed the services at issue;
ii. identify each piece of equipment used in the performance of the healthcare services at issue and the training and education that each person involved in the performance of the services had in the use of the equipment;
iii. identify all research of which the defendants are aware that supports the performance of the healthcare services in question in the manner in which they were performed;

iv. identify all of the insurer's insureds whose treatment plans were changed, in whole or in part, based on the results of the services provided by the defendants; and
v. identify every person or entity that referred more than 10 percent of the healthcare provider's patients to the healthcare provider.

As with the sample interrogatories in corporate structure cases, these sample medical necessity interrogatories request basic facts in order to provide a starting point for additional questions that can be posed at depositions. They do not necessarily go to the ultimate questions in the case and do not provide much of an opportunity for evasive responses.

In addition to these sample interrogatories in corporate structure and medical necessity cases, there are a few types of interrogatories that will generally be applicable to any kind of no-fault insurance fraud litigation. For example, insurers should generally ask no-fault fraud defendants to identify any criminal, administrative, or professional disciplinary proceedings in which they have been named as defendants or respondents. Records from these types of proceedings often contain information that an insurer can use to prosecute or provide support for its anti-fraud case. While, in some cases, records from these types of proceedings may be publicly available via a simple Internet search, oftentimes an insurer will need to know the venue of the proceeding in order to obtain the records.

Similarly, insurers should request that defendants in no-fault fraud cases identify every proceeding in which they provided sworn testimony, either in the course of an examination under oath, during a deposition, or at trial. In most cases, by the time an insurer commences anti-fraud litigation, the defendants will have submitted a large amount of fraudulent billing and will have actively pursued collection on their billing. By extension, the defendants in many cases will have commenced lawsuits or arbitration to collect on their billing and will have provided sworn testimony in the context of those proceedings or as part of the insurer's statutory right to take their examinations under oath as part of the claims verification process. This sort of testimony—which almost never is publicly available—can also be used to support a subsequent anti-fraud lawsuit.

F. The Use of Document Requests in No-Fault Anti-Fraud Cases

As with interrogatories, every litigator will generally be familiar with the use of document requests. While neither the Federal Rules of Civil Procedure nor their state law equivalents put any limits on the number of document requests that may be served, anti-fraud litigators should do their best to serve a reasonable number of requests, tailored to the discrete issues in the case. This will help avoid the appearance that their discovery requests are aimed to vex and harass a defendant rather than to obtain relevant documents from a defendant.

Though the nature of a plaintiff-insurer's document requests will necessarily vary from case to case, it is possible—as with interrogatories—to identify certain categories of documents that will usually be relevant to, and should be requested in, the common types of no-fault insurance anti-fraud cases.

1. Representative Document Requests in Corporate Structure Fraud Cases

In a typical corporate structure fraud case, the plaintiff-insurer will want to request all documents that tend to disclose—or that could potentially lead to documents that disclose—the ownership structure of the healthcare practice in question and the identity of the individuals or entities that effectively control the practice. Toward that end, the document requests should—at a minimum—call for the production of the following material:

i. the healthcare practice's federal, state, and local tax returns, including all schedules and attachments, for the pertinent period;
ii. the healthcare practice's quarterly payroll tax returns, including all schedules and attachments, for the pertinent period;
iii. the healthcare practice's general ledgers for the pertinent period;
iv. the healthcare practice's bank records, including all statements, cancelled checks, and signature cards, for the pertinent period;

v. all documents relating to or reflecting corporate formalities followed by the practice, including corporate filings, resolutions, and minutes;
vi. all documents relating to any billing or collection agreements to which the healthcare practice was a party during the pertinent period;
vii. all documents relating to any management agreements to which the healthcare practice was a party during the pertinent period;
viii. all documents relating to any marketing agreements to which the healthcare practice was a party during the pertinent period;
ix. all documents relating to any consulting agreements of any type to which the healthcare practice was a party during the pertinent period;
x. all documents relating to any lease agreements to which the healthcare practice was a party during the pertinent period, including but not limited to facility and equipment lease agreements;
xi. all documents relating to the individual healthcare providers who purported to provide services on behalf of the healthcare practice, including their personnel files and documents reflecting certification, training, education, licensure, experience, résumé, and/or curriculum vitae;
xii. all documents relating to the selection of the CPT codes that were billed to the plaintiff-insurer on behalf of the healthcare practice;
xiii. all marketing materials relating to the healthcare practice;
xiv. all documents relating to or reflecting communications between and among the healthcare practice and its referral sources;
xv. all documents relating to or reflecting any authorization to sign documents for or on behalf of the healthcare practice or any of its personnel; and
xvi. all documents relating to or reflecting the creation or revision of bills and treatment reports on behalf of the healthcare practice or any of its personnel.

These sample document requests are not intended to be exhaustive and will necessarily vary somewhat from case to case. However, the categories of documents identified in these requests—standing alone—should provide a plaintiff-insurer with a fairly clear picture of the true ownership interests in and control over a healthcare practice. For instance, even if—as almost always is the case—an illegally organized healthcare practice does not list unlicensed individuals as shareholders or members in its corporate filings, the bank records and tax returns may show substantial suspicious financial transfers to or for the benefit of such unlicensed parties. Likewise, exorbitant billing, collections, management, or lease agreements—which require payments far in excess of the fair market value of the underlying services or leaseholds—can provide strong evidence that the vendors and landlords have an illegal stake in the professional practice.

2. Representative Document Requests in Medical Fraud Cases

Where the defendants are alleged to have billed for medically unnecessary or illusory services, an insurer's document requests—like its interrogatories—will focus on the circumstances under which the services were recommended, the manner in which the services were performed, and the impact of the services on the insured patient's overall treatment plan. In particular, an insurer will, as a starting point, want to request the following categories of documents:

i. all documents pertaining to the specific healthcare services that the healthcare practice provided to the insurer's insureds, including but not limited to the complete patient file for each insured who treated with the practice;
ii. all documents pertaining to any machine, equipment, or device used by the healthcare practice to provide healthcare services to the insurer's insureds, including but not limited to documents relating to the type, quality or utility of the machine, equipment or device, published studies, instruction manuals, warranty documents, brochures, promotional materials, and purchase orders;
iii. all documents pertaining to any research studies or publications that support the performance of the healthcare services at issue;
iv. all documents pertaining to any protocols that were followed in the performance of the healthcare services at issue;

v. all documents pertaining to any quality assurance program that was followed in connection with the healthcare services in question;

vi. all documents concerning the qualifications and licensure of any person who performed the healthcare services at issue;

vii. all documents concerning the selection of the CPT codes that were used to bill for the healthcare services at issue;

viii. all documents referring to or evidencing referrals to the healthcare practice for the performance of the healthcare services in question;

ix. all documents pertaining to any communications regarding the performance of the healthcare services at issue;

x. all documents reflecting any changes to the treatment plan of any of the insurer's insureds based on the performance of the healthcare services at issue;

xi. all documents pertaining to or reflecting any criminal, administrative, professional disciplinary, or malpractice proceedings against any healthcare provider responsible for providing any of the healthcare services at issue; and

xii. all documents pertaining to or reflecting any attempt to collect on any charges for the healthcare services at issue.

Aside from these sample document requests, there are some additional categories of document requests that will be relevant in almost any sort of no-fault anti-fraud litigation. For instance, insurers always should ask for copies of transcripts of sworn testimony provided by or on behalf of the defendants in any examinations under oath, depositions, or trials to the extent that such testimony pertains to the healthcare practices or treatments at issue in an anti-fraud case. Similarly, insurers should request copies of any documents referenced in a defendant's interrogatory responses and all documents that a defendant reviewed or consulted in preparing its responses to the insurer's interrogatories.

Depending on the venue of the anti-fraud litigation, insurers also may be able to make an early demand for copies of any documents relating to any expert with whom a defendant has consulted regarding the issues in the case and/or copies of all documents—to the extent that they are not covered by some other demand—that a defendant may seek to introduce into evidence at trial. However, to the extent that the anti-fraud case is proceeding in federal court, a defendant will typically not be required to produce these documents until later in the case, if at all. As discussed previously, Fed. R. Civ. P. 26(b)(4)(D), the opinions of consulting experts are generally shielded from disclosure unless and until it appears that the consulting expert will be called as a witness at trial. Pursuant to Fed. R. Civ. P. 26(a)(3)(B), pretrial disclosures—including the disclosure of documents that a party intends to use at trial—usually do not have to be made until at least 30 days before the trial.

G. The Use of Third-Party Subpoenas in No-Fault Anti-Fraud Cases

In the typical no-fault anti-fraud case, a plaintiff-insurer not only will require documents and information from the defendants in the case, but also will require various categories of information and material from third parties. For example, in a case involving corporate structure fraud, the insurer should not have to rely on the defendants to make full and complete production of their financial records such as bank statements, tax returns, and the like. Indeed, it would be foolhardy to depend on a defendant who is accused of large-scale fraud to make a clean breast of the documents and information that would enable an insurer to prove its case.

Similarly, in a case involving fraudulent billing for medically unnecessary services, critical records may be in the hands of state regulators or other insurers that may have received similar fraudulent billing from the defendants. For example, state regulators may have investigative files regarding a healthcare provider that are not shielded by any applicable law or privilege and that could help an insurer prove that the provider is not in compliance with the law and therefore is ineligible to collect no-fault benefits. Along similar lines, discovery obtained by one insurer in a prior case may be subject to production to a different insurer for use in a subsequent case.

With that in mind, in addition to serving discovery requests on the defendants in a no-fault anti-fraud case, insurers should prepare and serve third-party subpoenas on any third parties that are likely to have discoverable information regarding a defendant's fraudulent scheme. While the pertinent third parties and discoverable information will necessarily vary from case to case, in a typical corporate structure fraud case, the plaintiff should serve subpoenas on the banks used by the defendants as depositories for the proceeds of the fraudulent scheme. These subpoenas should seek all of the defendants' bank records during the pertinent period, which will be relevant to demonstrate the true ownership of the corporate defendants, the legality or illegality of their corporate structure, and the scope of the defendants' conspiracy.

For similar reasons, in a corporate structure case, it will usually be wise to subpoena the defendants' accountants for any tax returns, schedules, or work papers that may be germane to the corporate structure of a suspicious healthcare practice.

More generally, insurers may consider serving subpoenas on the collections attorneys who represent an alleged no-fault fraud ring in collections matters, seeking their retainer or engagement agreements with the defendants. Retainer agreements usually are not privileged, and if someone other than a licensed professional has entered into a retainer agreement with a collections attorney on behalf of a professional healthcare practice, it can be good circumstantial evidence that the practice is not owned by the professional who purports to be the owner.

In addition, it almost always is a good idea for an anti-fraud litigator to check court dockets and other public records to determine whether a defendant has been named in any professional disciplinary or licensing proceedings or in any previous anti-fraud or related litigation. If so, then it may be worthwhile to subpoena the pertinent regulatory authorities and plaintiffs for any investigative or litigation materials—such as transcripts of testimony or discovery responses—that are not privileged or subject to an effective protective or confidentiality order. While, in many cases, these types of subpoenas will be met with stiff resistance, a plaintiff-insurer will often be able to show on a motion to compel that the subpoenaed documents or information are relevant and discoverable and must be produced over any objections.

H. The Use of Depositions in No-Fault Anti-Fraud Cases

As a general rule, discovery devices can be used in any sequence,[14] and so—in theory—it is possible to take depositions of parties and nonparties before document production is complete, responses to

[14] *See*, e.g., Fed. R. Civ. P. 26(d).

interrogatories are served, and so forth. However, as a practical matter, most litigants in no-fault anti-fraud cases—plaintiffs and defendants alike—will prefer to wait until document discovery is substantially complete before noticing party depositions or serving subpoenas for third-party depositions. Indeed, it can be so difficult to effectively take or defend a deposition without document discovery that a litigant should consider seeking a protective order if an adversary seeks depositions before document discovery is substantially complete.

While depositions should ordinarily wait until document discovery is largely completed, that is not to say that a plaintiff-insurer should wait until document discovery is complete before serving its deposition notices. Rather, it usually is a good idea to serve deposition notices early in the case, soon after discovery commences. While the notices should specify that the depositions will be held at some fixed date after the substantial conclusion of document discovery or on some mutually agreeable date and time after the conclusion of document discovery, the early service of deposition notices helps to preserve a party's claim to priority of depositions. While a court may, upon a party's motion, intervene to determine the priority of depositions, the party that served its deposition notices first often will have a compelling argument to the effect that it should be entitled to conduct its depositions first, especially if that party is the plaintiff.

1. Representative Deponents and Lines of Inquiry in Corporate Structure Fraud Cases

The deposition witnesses in a no-fault anti-fraud suit will necessarily vary considerably from case to case. However, there are certain witnesses and lines of inquiry that usually should be pursued in the most common types of cases. For example, in a case involving a healthcare practice that is alleged to have an illegal corporate structure, a plaintiff-insurer almost always will want to take the depositions of the licensed healthcare providers who purport to own the practice, the unlicensed laypersons who are alleged to secretly and unlawfully own and control the practice behind the scenes, and other key insiders at the practice, including the employees or independent contractors who purport to provide healthcare, billing, management, bookkeeping, or other critical services for or on behalf of the practice. In addition, the insurer should depose the healthcare practice itself through a corporate witness who is prepared by the practice to testify on its behalf.[15]

Like the witnesses themselves, the lines of inquiry in a corporate structure fraud will be different in every case. Even so, there are certain subjects that should be explored in almost every corporate structure fraud suit, particularly

i. the deponent's background, including her educational history, professional qualifications and licensing, employment history, criminal history, and professional disciplinary history;
ii. the deponent's work schedule during the period giving rise to the litigation;
iii. the history of the professional practice through which the allegedly fraudulent billing was submitted, including the date on which it was formed, its officers and directors over time, the locations from which it operated, the identities and roles of its respective employees and independent contractors, their respective hours, and the circumstances surrounding any changes in the practice's ownership or personnel; and
iv. the identities and roles of all significant outside services providers for the professional practice, including management, consulting, billing, banking, and accounting providers, as well as landlords, and the terms of the practice's agreements with each.

Obviously, these topics are just a starting point, but they are a starting point that is likely to lead to many other related, relevant

[15] *See*, e.g., Fed. R. Civ. P. 30(b)(6) ("In its notice or subpoena, a party may name as the deponent a public or private corporation, a partnership, an association, a governmental agency, or other entity and must describe with reasonable particularity the matters for examination. The named organization must then designate one or more officers, directors, or managing agents, or designate other persons who consent to testify on its behalf; and it may set out the matters on which each person designated will testify. A subpoena must advise a nonparty organization of its duty to make this designation. The persons designated must testify about information known or reasonably available to the organization. This paragraph (6) does not preclude a deposition by any other procedure allowed by these rules.").

lines of questioning. For instance, once a defendant identifies the bank used by the subject healthcare practice, a plaintiff-insurer will want to know who opened the account, who had the authority to sign checks on the account, whether a signature stamp was used to sign the checks, who applied any signature stamp to the checks, and so forth.

Similarly, if the deponent is a licensed professional and purports to own a healthcare practice but testifies that he is working several jobs at once, a plaintiff-insurer will want to know more about whether the professional's schedule would actually permit him to operate the healthcare practice at issue in the case. If the witness testifies that the practice uses a management company, the insurer will want to know how much the management company is paid in relation to the gross revenues of the practice, what services the practice receives in return, and whether the management company has effective, day-to-day control over the practice's finances. If it should seem that the healthcare practice is paying rent at several locations, which could indicate a concealed kickback or illegal referral-fee arrangement, the plaintiff-insurer will want to know what other healthcare providers operate from those locations, whether the defendant receives referrals from the other providers at those locations, the amount of rent that is paid by the healthcare practice at those locations, and whether the healthcare practice operates from those locations on a consistent basis or only occasionally or sporadically.

2. Representative Deponents and Lines of Inquiry in Medical Fraud Cases

Where the focus of a case is on medical fraud—for instance, where a defendant is alleged to have billed for medically unnecessary or illusory services—the plaintiff-insurer also will want to depose the owners of the practice, as well as any persons or entities who were involved in the performance of the pertinent services or the submission of billing for the services. As in a corporate structure fraud case, the insurer should also depose the healthcare practice itself through a corporate witness.

While, again, the avenues of inquiry necessarily will vary from case to case, there are certain subjects that provide a good starting point for most medical fraud depositions, specifically,

i. the deponent's background, including her educational history, professional qualifications and licensing, employment history, criminal history, and professional disciplinary history;
ii. the background—including educational history, professional qualifications and licensing, employment history, criminal history, professional disciplinary history—for any person who performed services that were billed through the professional practice to the plaintiff-insurer, as well as their work schedules at the practice in question;
iii. the source of the referrals, if any, that resulted in the performance of the services that were billed to the insurer and the history and nature of the relationships between the referral sources and the recipient of the referrals; and
iv. an explanation of the medical necessity for the services that were billed to the insurer and the standard of care for the performance of the services that were billed to the insurer.

Again, these topics are just points of departure that are likely to open up many related lines of questioning. For example, if the witness billed for lengthy and extensive patient examinations and testifies that the examinations were warranted by the severity of the patients' presenting problems, the plaintiff-insurer may want to confront the witness with evidence, such as police reports, hospital records, accident photographs, and the like, that indicates that the patients could not have suffered from any serious injuries in their accidents. If the witness testifies that she received all of her patient referrals from a small group of chiropractors, the plaintiff may want to explore the nature of the witness's relationship with her referral sources, including whether she operated from the offices of her referral sources, paid them rent, and whether the amount of the rent suggests that the putative rent payments in actuality were disguised kickbacks. If the witness testifies that all of the services that were billed to the insurer through his healthcare practice were performed by three employee-physicians, the insurer will want to know the work schedules for the physicians, whether they simultaneously worked for other practices, and whether the physicians' schedules would have reasonably permitted them to perform the services in question.

3. Preparing Individual and Corporate Witnesses and Defending Depositions

Of course, anti-fraud litigators not only must take depositions; they must also prepare their own witnesses and defend depositions. In theory, a defendant in a no-fault insurance anti-fraud case may seek the depositions of a broad range of the insurer's personnel and associates, including claims adjusters, SIU investigators, outside claims handling vendors, and executives from various levels of the organization.

However, as a practical matter, depositions are expensive. What is more, a plaintiff-insurer usually will be able to raise good undue burden and proportionality arguments to limit the number of depositions to the extent that court rules or orders do not already limit the number of available depositions, which they usually do. As a result, it is more common for defendants in anti-fraud cases to seek a corporate deposition of the plaintiff-insurer pursuant to Fed. R. Civ. P. 30(b)(6) or its state law equivalents, as well as a limited series of additional depositions of the SIU and claims personnel that most directly were involved in the case.

Every attorney has their own preferred ways to prepare witnesses for depositions and will adjust their methods based on the facts of the underlying case and the capacity of the witness at hand. Nevertheless, there are certain steps that should always be followed in preparing witnesses to testify for a plaintiff-insurer in a no-fault anti-fraud case.

For example, an anti-fraud litigator should ensure that the witness has read the pleadings, any dispositive and discovery motions that have been filed in the case, and any significant discovery that has been produced in the case. The complaint, together with the facts set forth in any dispositive or discovery motions, will help to ground the witness in the narrative of the case and can help ensure that the witness' testimony stays "on message."

In addition to the pleadings and any substantive motion papers that have been filed in the case, it usually will be worthwhile to have the witness review the materials that are referenced in the complaint, such as claims files relating to the fraudulent claims at issue in the case, evidence indicating that the healthcare practice at issue in the case has an illegal corporate structure, and so forth. If the materials referenced in the complaint are voluminous—such as large numbers of claims files, containing thousands of pages apiece—then the witness can review a representative sample of the materials, so long as they illustrate the allegations in the complaint.

Other than the pleadings, materials referenced in the pleadings, significant discovery production, and any papers filed in the litigation that might supplement the narrative in the complaint, there should not be much other material for the witness to review. In particular, the attorney should remember that anything the witness might review to prepare for the deposition will be discoverable and should caution the witness not to review any material that is privileged or otherwise immune from discovery.

After the witness has taken some time to get up to speed on the case (to the extent that he is not already closely familiar with the facts), it will usually be a good idea for the insurer's counsel to conduct one or more preparatory meetings with the witness. During these meetings, the witness should be familiarized or reacquainted with the deposition process, including the significance of testimony under oath, the manner in which the testimony may be used, and the general ground rules for depositions. In particular, and though this will be remedial for most litigators, it is important to emphasize to the witness that he or she should respond as succinctly as possible to the deposition questions and should refrain from volunteering any information, much less any information that goes beyond the question that was asked. To ensure that the witness is fully prepared to respond to the likely inquiries, it almost always will be worthwhile to conduct a mock deposition using a list of anticipated questions and to work with the witness to refine his or her responses either in real time or upon a review of a videotape of the mock deposition.

Mock depositions and an emphasis on succinct testimony are especially important because once the deposition actually occurs, there usually will be little opportunity for the defending attorney to interject himself into the process. Most civil procedure rules place stringent limits on speaking objections, and an attorney who objects to some question or line of inquiry in a suggestive or argumentative manner can find herself on the receiving end of a sanctions motion. Unless a question inquiries into matters that are privileged, there usually will be no legitimate basis for an attorney to instruct her client not to answer.[16]

---

[16] *See*, e.g., FED. R. CIV. P. 30(c)(2) ("An objection at the time of the examination—whether to evidence, to a party's conduct, to the officer's qualifications, to the manner of taking the deposition, or to any other aspect of the deposition—must be noted on the record, but the examination still proceeds; the testimony is taken subject to

Of course, if a defendant's attorney is conducting a deposition vexatiously, or in bad faith, the proper remedy usually will be to stop the deposition to seek the court's intervention to limit or terminate the deposition.[17] While this sort of thing does occur—not least in cases involving large-scale fraud allegations, which can get heated—it is relatively rare, given the general professionalism of the bar.

I. Responding and Objecting to Attempts to Increase Discovery Burdens in No-Fault Anti-Fraud Cases

As discussed previously, aside from claims files, investigative files, and—in some cases—training manuals, there usually will be few other materials in the insurer's possession that are relevant to the claims and defenses in a no-fault anti-fraud case and therefore discoverable from the insurer. Any subcategory of discoverable material, such as treatment records, police reports, photographs of accident scenes, correspondence between and among the parties and their counsel, peer-review reports, independent medical examination reports, investigative reports, and so on, will almost always be contained within the claims files and investigative files. No insurer or anti-fraud litigator should ever commence anti-fraud litigation without the expectation that these categories of files will have to be produced, at least once they are redacted to exclude any privileged documents or communications.

While insurers should generally expect to produce relevant claims files and SIU files in an anti-fraud case, many alleged no-fault insurance fraud rings will seek to dramatically expand the scope of discovery in an anti-fraud suit to encompass matters with no colorable

---

any objection. An objection must be stated concisely in a nonargumentative and nonsuggestive manner. A person may instruct a deponent not to answer only when necessary to preserve a privilege, to enforce a limitation ordered by the court, or to present a motion under Rule 30(d)(3)."); *see also* Fed. R. Civ. P. 30(d)(3) (stating, among other things, that "[a]t any time during a deposition, the deponent or a party may move to terminate or limit it on the ground that it is being conducted in bad faith or in a manner that unreasonably annoys, embarrasses, or oppresses the deponent or party. The motion may be filed in the court where the action is pending or the deposition is being taken. If the objecting deponent or party so demands, the deposition must be suspended for the time necessary to obtain an order.").

[17] *See*, e.g., Fed. R. Civ. P. 30(d)(3).

relationship to the claims or defenses in the case. In some cases, this is an attempt to fish for a counterclaim, whereas in others it is simply an attempt to make the insurer's cost of the litigation exceed the prospective benefit.

For example, a defendant may request production not only of the claims files that relate to the insureds who they themselves purported to treat, but also the claims files for every claim that the insurer received in the state during the time period at issue. Similarly, a defendant in a no-fault fraud case not only may request the claims-handling policy manuals that governed the processing of their own claims, but also all of the insurers' claims handling policy manuals from every state whether or not the manuals had any colorable relationship to the handling of the particular claims at issue. One discovery demand commonly advanced by no-fault insurance fraud rings is a demand for a copy of all of the pleadings, motion papers, and other filed documents from every lawsuit in which the insurer has been a plaintiff or a defendant—a demand that, if complied with, would require the insurer to produce tens of millions of pages of documents, at enormous expense.

While a defendant may be able to make some tangential relevance arguments with respect to these types of demands—for instance, a claim that the insurer's nationwide or statewide claims-handling practices are relevant to show that the insurer could not have justifiably relied on the defendants' misrepresentations—courts will usually reject them. Most defendants' counsel are aware that a motion to compel production of broad swathes of material with only the most attenuated connection to the litigation is likely to fail, especially considering the proportionality requirements that are front and center in Fed. R. Civ. P. 26 and that are also applied by state courts. As a result, in the face of an insurer's irrelevance, overbreadth, and undue burden objections, defendants will typically abandon their demands for claims or litigation records that are unconnected to the claims and healthcare providers at issue in an anti-fraud case.

Should a defendant elect to expend its resources in what usually will be a quixotic motion to compel production of these types of impertinent materials, the plaintiff-insurer should cross-move for a protective order pursuant to Fed. R. Civ. P. 26(c) or its state law equivalent. In any such motion, the insurer should ask that—to the extent that the court orders production of the sought-after material—the defendants who are demanding the production be required to pay all or part of the cost of production.

Another common way that defendants in no-fault anti-fraud cases try to increase an insurer's discovery burdens is through the use of onerous contention interrogatories. Broadly speaking, contention interrogatories are interrogatories that ask for an opinion or contention regarding a fact or an application of law to fact.[18] For example, a defendant healthcare provider may propound an interrogatory to an insurer that asks the insurer to "set forth every act that allegedly committed by the defendant that the insurer contends constituted common law fraud" or that asks the insurer to "set forth every way in which the defendant participated in the operation and management of an enterprise in a manner sufficient to impose civil RICO liability." It can take hours, or even days, to prepare particularized and extensive responses to these types of contention interrogatories, a process that can be redundant considering that information that is responsive to contention interrogatories is often already set forth in the body of a well-pleaded, particularized fraud complaint or can be elicited with far greater efficiency in depositions.

As a result, while Fed. R. Civ. P. 33 permits contention interrogatories and while some courts will order a plaintiff-insurer to respond to contention interrogatories, the more common practice is for a court to defer responses to contention interrogatories until the close of discovery. By that point, many typical contention interrogatories that are served in no-fault anti-fraud litigation will have been mooted by deposition testimony or document production that furnishes the same information sought through the contention interrogatories.

PRACTICE POINTS

Responding to Interrogatories

✓ Defendants in no-fault insurance anti-fraud litigation commonly pose contention or other interrogatories asking the plaintiff-insurer to set forth the basis for its claims or to identify every document that supports one or another of its claims.

[18] *See* FED. R. CIV. P.33(a)(2) ("An interrogatory is not objectionable merely because it asks for an opinion or contention that relates to fact or the application of law to fact, but the court may order that the interrogatory need not be answered until designated discovery is complete, or until a pretrial conference or some other time.").

- ✓ Pursuant to Fed. R. Civ. P. 33 and some of its state civil procedure equivalents, if the answer to an interrogatory can be discerned from a party's business records and the burden of deriving the answer will be substantially the same for either party, the responding party can answer the interrogatory by specifying the records to be reviewed and making the records reasonably available to review.
- ✓ Thus, anti-fraud litigators should consider whether these types of interrogatories can be answered by simply referring the defendant to the pertinent portions of the insurer's claims files and SIU files and by making the claims files and SIU files available for review.

J. Motions to Compel

Defendants in no-fault insurance anti-fraud litigation often fail to meet their discovery obligations. In some cases, this failure takes the form of a refusal to engage in the discovery process at all, while in others it amounts to dilatory or incomplete responses to an insurer's discovery requests.

Regardless of the form that it takes, a defendant's failure to meet its discovery obligations in a no-fault fraud case is usually motivated by a desire to delay the insurer's case long enough to secrete and dissipate the proceeds of the underlying scheme or the defendant's other assets. Less frequently, though it does occur, a defendant's dilatory or inadequate response to a discovery request is driven by some genuine objection to the request—for instance, a contention that a given request is unduly burdensome, that it is seeking information that is not relevant to the claims or defenses in the action, and so forth. However, the scope of discovery in the typical anti-fraud case is fairly broad, and as long as a plaintiff-insurer does not propound discovery requests with no legitimate connection to the issues in the case, a defendant in such a case will typically have difficulty advancing any colorable relevance, overbreadth, or undue burden objections.

When confronted with a recalcitrant defendant that is failing or refusing to engage in the discovery process, a plaintiff-insurer will want to make a motion to compel the defendant to produce the pertinent discovery.

In federal court, motions to compel typically follow a streamlined process that is overseen by a magistrate judge. While the exact procedures vary from court to court and generally are set by the local civil rules that are promulgated by the individual district courts, they usually are designed to minimize paper filings and expedite resolution of the underlying discovery disputes. For example, Fed. R. Civ. P. 37(a)(1), federal court local civil rules, and state court rules typically require the parties to a discovery dispute to meet and confer regarding the dispute in good faith before bringing the dispute to the attention of the court. Then, to the extent that the parties are unable to resolve the dispute, the movant must typically raise the dispute to the court in a brief letter (often three or four pages or less), at which point the opposing party will have a short period in which to respond with its own brief letter. Once it receives the parties' respective letters, the court will generally convene a teleconference or in-person conference with the parties, entertain some brief argument on the motion, and issue a ruling.

State court procedures on motions to compel are often more extensive and time-consuming due to the absence of magistrate judges who are specifically tasked with overseeing discovery and the absence of local civil rules aimed at expediting discovery motion practice. In contrast to many federal courts, state courts often entertain formal discovery motion practice, complete with notices of motion, extended briefing, lengthy briefing schedules, and lengthy time to resolution.

As a result, discovery motions in state court often take far longer to resolve than discovery motions in federal court. This is a significant issue, because discovery—or, more commonly, the threat that an insurer is poised to obtain damning discovery via a motion to compel—is often a catalyst for settlement of an anti-fraud case. Thus, where discovery motions take a long time to resolve, it often can cause meaningful delays to the ultimate resolution of the case. This is one of the reasons why some anti-fraud litigators prefer to file their cases in federal court, to the extent that they have a viable claim to diversity or federal question jurisdiction.

1. Laying the Groundwork for a Motion to Compel

Regardless of whether an anti-fraud case is pending in state or federal court, the first step when confronted with a defendant that is refusing to meet its discovery obligations is to lay the proper groundwork for a motion to compel. This usually requires the plaintiff-insurer to engage in—and document—good-faith attempts to obtain the sought-after discovery without resorting to motion practice. As noted above, federal courts, as well as some state courts, require the parties to a discovery dispute to meet and confer in good faith to try and resolve any discovery disputes before bringing them to the attention of the court.

The first step in any good-faith effort to resolve a discovery dispute without resort to motion practice should be a letter to opposing counsel (or a pro se defendant) setting forth the defendant's failure to produce the pertinent discovery, explaining why the discovery is relevant to the claims and defenses in the case, and demanding the discovery by a certain date. The letter should permit a reasonable time for compliance, taking into account when the request for the discovery first was promulgated and the amount of time that has elapsed since the discovery was due to be produced. Because the letter will likely have to be attached as an exhibit to any subsequent submission to the court, it should have an even keel and avoid a hectoring or strident tone. In this context, it is important to note that in some federal and state courts, judges will hold that a failure to timely respond to a discovery request or to raise any objections to the discovery request constitutes a waiver of any objections that the defendant otherwise might have had to the request.[19] Thus, to the extent that a defendant has failed to timely object to a given discovery request, the letter should contend that the defendant has waived any objection to the request.

Many courts require—as a component of any good-faith attempt to resolve a discovery dispute in advance of motion practice—that the parties go beyond correspondence and actually confer in person or by telephone. Thus, it usually will be best practice to immediately follow up on any "good-faith" letter with a telephone call to opposing counsel or to a pro se defendant.

If the initial correspondence and telephone call do not produce the desired result, an anti-fraud litigator should not immediately seek

---

[19] *See*, e.g., State Farm Mut. Auto. Ins. Co. v. Warren Chiropractic & Rehab Clinic P.C., 2015 U.S. Dist. LEXIS 87661 at *4 to *9 (E.D. Mich. 2015) (untimely responses to discovery requests can constitute waiver of objections to those requests); Labarbera v. Absolute Trucking, Inc., 2009 U.S. Dist. LEXIS 70901 at *3 (E.D.N.Y. 2009) ("It is well established that by failing to respond or object to a discovery request in a timely manner, a party waives any objection which may have been available.").

the court's intervention. Rather, it will usually be best to send at least one, and often several, follow-up letters and to make follow-up telephone calls in a continued attempt to resolve the dispute without involving the court. Each letter should be preserved and each telephone call should be documented, as further evidence of the prospective discovery movant's good faith, and submitted to the court as exhibits to any subsequent discovery motion. It often is worthwhile to include, in each letter to opposing counsel, a brief précis of the allegations in the case, the factual support for the allegations, and the reason why the additional discovery sought from the defendant plainly is relevant to the case. The inclusion of such synopses in the letters to opposing counsel will make the prospective discovery movant's good faith manifest to the court when and if the court reviews the letter as an exhibit to any future discovery motion.

2. Motions to Compel in No-Fault Anti-Fraud Litigation

To the extent that a defendant in a no-fault fraud case fails to respond to good-faith efforts to secure relevant and discoverable material or information, a motion to compel will be necessary. As discussed above, if the case is pending in federal court, the motion will in most cases be addressed to the magistrate judge and will likely follow a relatively expedited procedure to resolution. State court procedures will vary to a greater degree and may involve a more formal and extended process. Wherever the venue, the key considerations will be whether the sought-after evidence is relevant and whether the burden of production is in line with the actual needs of the case.[20]

Against this backdrop, courts adjudicating no-fault insurance anti-fraud cases have repeatedly addressed the most common discovery disputes that arise in such actions. While the decisions may vary somewhat based on the strength of the plaintiff-insurer's presentation

---

[20] *See, e.g.*, Fed. R. Civ. P. 26(b)(1) ("Unless otherwise limited by court order, the scope of discovery is as follows: Parties may obtain discovery regarding any nonprivileged matter that is relevant to any party's claim or defense and proportional to the needs of the case, considering the importance of the issues at stake in the action, the amount in controversy, the parties' relative access to relevant information, the parties' resources, the importance of the discovery in resolving the issues, and whether the burden or expense of the proposed discovery outweighs its likely benefit. Information within this scope of discovery need not be admissible in evidence to be discoverable.").

and the general facts of each case, anti-fraud litigators have substantial precedent to support motions to compel production of the discovery that is usually necessary to prove the typical no-fault insurance fraud claims.

For example, courts have repeatedly found that the financial records of a healthcare provider and the defendants associated with that healthcare provider, including bank records, corporate tax returns, and the like, are relevant to plaintiff-insurers' no-fault fraud claims and are therefore discoverable.[21] While, in some of these cases,

[21] *See*, e.g., Gov't Emples. Ins. Co. v. Specialty Medical Services, LLC, D.N.J. Case No. 2:14-cv-08015-KSH-CLW, at Docket No. 60 (denying a motion to quash plaintiff-insurers' subpoena seeking corporate bank records for healthcare practices where the plaintiff-insurers had alleged that the healthcare practices were unlawfully owned and controlled by non-physicians); *see also* Gov't Employees Ins. Co. v. Five Boro Psychological Servs. PC, E.D.N.Y. Case No. 12-cv-02448, at May 24, 2013 Docket Entry (declining to quash bank subpoenas in a no-fault fraud case where the subpoenaed bank records were, among other things, relevant to demonstrate the scope of the alleged racketeering conspiracies and the pattern of racketeering activity); State Farm Mut. Auto. Ins. Co. v. Physiomatrix, Inc., 2013 U.S. Dist. LEXIS 189646 at *8 to *12 (E.D. Mich. 2013) (in a no-fault fraud case, denying a motion to quash bank subpoenas where the subpoenaed bank records were relevant to "help establish ownership and control over the various entities, will establish the structure of the enterprise (namely the connections between and among the named parties and various nonparties who were also alleged to be part of the underlying conspiracy), will measure the scope of the fraud, will reveal additional potential parties and witnesses, will show motive for the alleged conspiracy, and will help prove damages"); MedCity Rehab. Servs., LLC v. State Farm Mut. Auto. Ins. Co., 2013 U.S. Dist. LEXIS 64670 at *22 (E.D. Mich. 2013) (in a no-fault fraud case, a professional corporation's financial records were relevant to establishing the financial relationships among the physician-owner, the professional corporation, and the other purported participants in the scheme, and were discoverable); State Farm Mut. Auto. Ins. Co. v. McGee, 2012 U.S. Dist. Lexis 188346 (E.D.N.Y. 2012) (granting financial disclosures to the plaintiff-insurer in a no-fault fraud case); Allstate Ins. Co. v. Elzanaty, 2012 U.S. Dist. LEXIS 171962 at *4 to *5 (E.D.N.Y. 2012) (denying a motion to quash bank subpoenas in a no-fault fraud case where the accounts at issue were "depositories for monies from the alleged RICO corporations" and where the plaintiffs had "reason to believe that the accounts at issue [were] integrally connected to the alleged conspiracy"); State Farm Mut. Auto. Ins. Co. v. Tabakman, 2008 U.S. Dist. LEXIS 77784 at *6 to *7 (E.D.N.Y. 2008) (declining to quash bank subpoenas in no-fault fraud case where the plaintiff-insurer sought evidence of kickbacks); State Farm Mut. Auto. Ins. Co. v. Accurate Med., P.C., 2007 U.S. Dist. LEXIS 75336 at *3 to *4 (E.D.N.Y. 2007) (in a no-fault fraud case involving allegations that healthcare providers were unlawfully organized, agreeing with the plaintiff-insurer that the scope of subpoenas was appropriate for ascertaining the financial relationship of the moving defendants

the financial discovery was relevant to prove the plaintiff-insurers' allegations that a healthcare practice had an illegal corporate structure, courts also have found financial discovery in no-fault cases relevant to prove the connections between the defendants, the patterns of racketeering activity, and the scope of the alleged conspiracies.[22]

Of course, a healthcare provider's patient records relating to a plaintiff-insurer's insureds will virtually always be relevant and discoverable in a case alleging that the healthcare provider billed for medically unnecessary or illusory services.[23] Very few defendants in no-fault anti-fraud cases will actually take the position that their patient records ought not be produced because they are not relevant to the claims or defenses in a case. More commonly, if a no-fault fraud defendant intends to resist disclosure of patient records, he will either not respond to the discovery requests at all—in which case he will likely waive any overbreadth, undue burden, or relevance objections—or he will make a timely objection to the effect that the pertinent records already are in the plaintiff-insurer's possession, and that the burden of production of a large number of patient records therefore outweighs the value of the production to the discovery process.

Although a plaintiff-insurer should prevail on a motion to compel production of patient records regarding services that resulted in fraudulent no-fault billing, anti-fraud litigators should avoid any appearance of vexatious or harassing litigation tactics. Toward that end, a plaintiff-insurer should evince a willingness to compromise on the production of patient records before moving to compel their production by a defendant. For instance, the insurer might agree, in the first instance, to review a sample of a defendant's patient records to ascertain whether the defendant's records are actually identical to the

---

and nonparties); State Farm Mut. Auto. Ins. Co. v. CPT Medical Services, P.C., 375 F. Supp. 2d 141, 155–56 (E.D.N.Y. 2005) (finding "financial records, including tax returns of the defendants relating to transactions which generated cash" to be discoverable to demonstrate the extent to which the defendants profited from alleged fraudulent billing scheme).

[22] *See*, e.g., Five Boro Psychological Servs. PC., *supra* note 10; Physiomatrix, Inc., *supra* note 9.

[23] Indeed, patient records also can be relevant in a case alleging that a healthcare provider has an illegal corporate structure. For instance, if the patient records for a healthcare practice disclose a pattern of substandard, medically unnecessary, or illusory treatment, it can be evidence that the practice secretly and unlawfully is owned and controlled by unlicensed nonprofessionals.

records it already possesses. Or, if the insurer is sufficiently satisfied that the defendant's misrepresentations were pervasive across all of its records, it might agree to the production of a statistically significant sample of records and to try the case based on the sample rather than on the whole.

As a general rule, a plaintiff-insurer should avoid seeking discovery sanctions in its first motion to compel. While some judges can be very stern in announcing at the outset of the discovery process that a refusal to provide discovery will result in sanctions, these types of pronouncements are often honored in the breach. Courts frequently grant second, third, or even fourth chances to recalcitrant defendants, and a strident demand for sanctions based on an early failure to produce discovery can look like an unreasonable overreach and prejudice the movant as much as the respondent.

Nonetheless, if a defendant's failure to produce relevant and discoverable information recurs throughout a case or is in defiance of court orders, a sanctions request will be appropriate. Like any underlying motion to compel, a related motion for sanctions should take an even tone, recite at length the movant's good-faith efforts to secure compliance, include any pertinent correspondence as exhibits to document those good-faith efforts, and generally appear apologetic at having to involve the court in the dispute in the first instance. Requests for discovery sanctions should escalate progressively. While sanctions statutes generally vest the court with considerable discretion to impose a sanction of its choosing, up to and including entry of default judgment, it rarely will be a good idea to demand a default judgment, a large financial sanction, or some similarly severe penalty on an initial sanctions request. For a first request, it generally will be appropriate to request the costs and attorneys' fees on the underlying motion to compel and to reserve more onerous sanctions in the event that the defendant's discovery misconduct persists.

K. Expert Witnesses and Expert Disclosures

In many no-fault insurance fraud cases, especially cases involving misrepresentations regarding technical medical issues, plaintiff-insurers will seek expert opinions at the pleading stage when they begin drafting their complaints. For example, without an expert opinion as to the validity of a diagnostic test, it may be difficult for an insurer to sufficiently allege that a healthcare provider billed for medically unnecessary diagnostic tests. Even where a given type of healthcare service is medically unnecessary or illusory on its face, it usually is best practice to work with an expert in preparing the complaint because the expert's input can add significant color to the allegations.

Federal and state courts differ somewhat in when and to what extent a consulting expert's opinion must be disclosed. However, as a general matter, the opinion of a consulting expert does not usually need to be disclosed unless the plaintiff-insurer intends to present that consulting expert as a witness at trial or unless the party seeking the disclosure can show exceptional circumstances, such as the unavailability of critical information through other means.[24]

Thus, if a plaintiff-insurer in a no-fault fraud case uses the services of a consulting expert to frame its complaint and does not intend to present that expert as a witness at trial, the insurer usually will never need to disclose the opinions of that consulting expert or even the consulting expert's identity. To the extent that a defendant demands—as they often do—that the insurer identify its consulting experts and disclose their opinions before that consulting expert has been identified as a trial witness, the proper response is to object to the demand and seek a protective order if the defendant persists in the demand or moves to compel.

While a plaintiff-insurer generally need not disclose the opinions of its consulting experts, it almost always will need to present expert testimony at trial. For example, in a case involving misrepresentations as to the medical necessity of healthcare services, a plaintiff-insurer will usually need an expert in the pertinent discipline to testify as to the applicable standards of care and how the services at issue failed to meet those standards of care. Similarly, in a case involving a healthcare practice with an illegal corporate structure, an insurer may need to present the testimony of a forensic accountant to demonstrate how an unlicensed individual or entity exercised an unlawful level of control over the practice and its revenues.

Identifying and retaining an appropriate expert witness can be one of the biggest challenges for a plaintiff-insurer in a no-fault anti-fraud

---

[24] *See, e.g.*, Fed. R. Civ. P. 26(b)(4)(D); Fla. R. Civ. P. 1.280(b)(5)(B); MCR 2.302(b)(4)(B); Minn. R. Civ. P. 26.02(e)(2) (all generally providing that facts known or opinions held by consulting experts are not discoverable unless the expert will be a witness at trial or on a showing of exceptional circumstances).

case. Many of the most distinguished experts in healthcare disciplines have busy professional and academic schedules and are not available to participate in the time-consuming expert witness process. Even if they have the time to spare, some prospective healthcare experts are reluctant to testify against a colleague, either out of professional courtesy, fear of reprisal, or both. Financial experts, such as forensic accountants, who may be called upon to testify in corporate structure fraud cases, pose a different set of problems: Because many of them specialize in litigation-related work, they are open to claims that they are "professional witnesses" who will say anything for the party that is paying their fee.

Although identifying and retaining an expert witness can be difficult, there are certain rules of thumb that, if observed, will usually lead to a productive result. First, avoid retaining any expert witness who has an ongoing financial or business relationship with the plaintiff. For example, many plaintiff-insurers will have various physicians or other healthcare providers who conduct peer reviews of claims or who conduct independent medical examinations of insured patients as part of the claims review process. These types of experts often have a surface appeal because they may be intimately familiar with a defendant healthcare provider's claims from the claims review process and therefore may require less time to get up to speed on the anti-fraud litigation. Even so, they usually are unsuitable for service as expert witnesses in a major anti-fraud lawsuit because their ongoing business relationships with a plaintiff-insurer may be used to call their objectivity into question.

Second, choose a local expert where possible. While, in some cases it may be worthwhile to bring in a nationally recognized expert from out of state to testify regarding some arcane and highly specialized procedure, the types of healthcare services that are billed to no-fault insurers are usually rather prosaic, and virtually every state should have a pool of experts who are more than qualified to testify about the services at issue. At the same time, judges or juries may respond better to testimony from an expert who lives and practices among them.

Third, ensure that nothing in the expert's background conflicts with the testimony they are going to give. If, for example, a plaintiff-insurer's complaint alleges that a chiropractor billed for a medically useless diagnostic test, the plaintiff-insurer's expert witness should not routinely order that test herself. Along similar lines, if a plaintiff-insurer intends to present a forensic accountant to testify that a healthcare provider's corporate structure is illegal, the accountant should not have previously offered testimony in an earlier case to the effect that a similar corporate structure was lawful.

Finally, and most generally, the expert should not only be well credentialed, but also well spoken and presentable. While it is wonderful to have an expert witness who is at the pinnacle of her field, the medium can be as important as the message, and inept communications skills can ruin what otherwise might be powerful testimony.

Once an expert witness is identified and retained, the Federal Rules of Civil Procedure and state rules of civil procedure impose somewhat different processes for expert disclosures. In federal court, the rules generally require a party to disclose the identities of any experts it intends to present at trial at least 90 days before the trial.[25] Rebuttal experts must generally be identified within 30 days after disclosure of the expert who is to be rebutted.[26] In practice, however, most federal courts in no-fault anti-fraud cases will set a different schedule for expert disclosures and will require them to be made within a month or two after the close of fact discovery.

The Federal Rules of Civil Procedure require that the expert disclosures be accompanied by a written report, prepared and signed by the expert witness, setting forth (i) a complete statement of all opinions the witness will express and the basis and reasons for them; (ii) the facts or data considered by the witness in forming them; (iii) any exhibits that will be used to summarize or support them; (iv) the witness's qualifications, including a list of all publications authored in the previous 10 years; (v) a list of all other cases from the previous 4 years in which the witness testified as an expert at trial or by deposition; and (vi) a statement of the compensation to be paid for the study and testimony in the case.[27]

By contrast, state civil procedures rules tend to impose a less formal process for expert disclosures. These rules generally do not set any fixed time frame for expert disclosures and instead usually require

---

[25] *See* Fed. R. Civ. P. 26(a)(2)(D).

[26] *Id.*

[27] *See* Fed. R. Civ. P. 26(a)(2)(B).

them to be made in response to an opposing party's interrogatories.[28] What is more, state court rules do not usually require the production of a formal report setting forth the expert's opinion, although they do require that the expert disclosure set forth the substance of the expert's opinion and—in some cases—the expert's qualifications.[29]

These differences in state and federal court expert disclosure procedures are largely cosmetic. In practice, expert disclosures in no-fault anti-fraud cases will almost always be made within a month or two after the close of fact discovery, with rebuttal expert disclosures within a month or two after the initial expert disclosures and depositions of the respective expert witnesses within a month or two thereafter. These time frames take into account the fact that most parties to an anti-fraud suit will not be in a position to identify their expert witnesses until after fact discovery is complete because some issues may fall out of the case or be added to the case as discovery proceeds.

Whether the pertinent civil procedure rules require the production of a formal expert report or more abbreviated expert disclosures in interrogatory responses, anti-fraud litigators should work closely with the expert witnesses in preparing any written summary of the expert's opinions. While, of course, the ultimate product should reflect the expert's views rather than the attorney's aspirations, the attorney can play an important role in ensuring that the expert's opinion is completely relevant to the issues in the case, avoids any impertinent digressions, and is presented as powerfully as possible. This is especially important because a well-crafted expert report—or summary of

---

[28] *See*, e.g., MINN. R. CIV. P. 26.02(e)(1) ("A party may through interrogatories require any other party to identify each person whom the other party expects to call as an expert witness at trial, to state the subject matter on which the expert is expected to testify, and to state the substance of the facts and opinions to which the expert is expected to testify and a summary of the grounds for each opinion. . . . Upon motion, the court may order further discovery by other means, subject to such restrictions as to scope and such provisions, . . . concerning fees and expenses, as the court may deem appropriate."); ALM R. CIV. P. Rule 26(b)(4)(A) (same); MCR 2.302(B)(4)(a)(i) ("A party may through interrogatories require another party to identify each person whom the other party expects to call as an expert witness at trial, to state the subject matter about which the expert is expected to testify, and to state the substance of the facts and opinions to which the expert is expected to testify and a summary of the grounds for each opinion.").

[29] *Id.*

the opinions an expert will present at trial—can focus a defendant's mind on the futility of his position, lead to a settlement in advance of trial, and obviate the need for the expert to testify at all.

In this context, drafts of expert reports or disclosures and communications between counsel and experts are generally shielded from disclosure by the work product doctrine.[30] Nevertheless, the usual extraordinary circumstances exceptions apply, and attorneys and expert witnesses should avoid the creation of draft reports that deviate materially from one to the other. Rather, it almost always will be best practice for the attorney and expert to have an extended discussion of the contents of the expert disclosures before putting pen to paper to ensure that the expert's fundamental opinion is consistent in every draft report.

Once the parties exchange their expert disclosures, including any rebuttal disclosures, it will be time to take expert depositions. As noted previously, the expert depositions will usually be conducted a month or two after the disclosures are made to permit the parties to prepare for the depositions in light of the contents of the disclosures. In most cases, the plaintiff-insurer will have served its expert disclosures first, and the plaintiff's expert will be the first to be deposed. The usual guidelines for deposition preparation apply. The plaintiff's expert should review the pleadings and other substantive motion papers that were filed in the case, any materials that were referenced in the pleadings or motion papers, and any pertinent discovery that was exchanged in the case. The expert should, of course, refamiliarize herself with the facts giving rise to her opinion, including the contents of any claims files or financial records that support her opinion. The attorney should provide the expert with the general guidelines for deposition testimony, including the need to be as succinct as possible and avoid digression.

As with any witness, it will usually be worthwhile for the attorney and expert to engage in a mock deposition and for the attorney to question the witness with respect to any information that might tend to undermine or contradict her opinion. If the witness has given testimony in a large number of cases, has previously given conflicting testimony, is receiving a large fee for her testimony, or is subject to impeachment for some other reason, it is best to cover those

---

[30] *See*, e.g., Fed. R. Civ. P. 26(b)(4).

issues during the mock deposition (or, better yet, before the expert is retained) to ensure that the witness is prepared to address them.

Where a plaintiff-insurer has a well-founded anti-fraud case, it can be very difficult for a defendant to muster colorable expert testimony on its behalf. While, for instance, different physicians may have different views on the standard of care for patients with soft-tissue injuries, there is a general consensus on what is appropriate treatment and what is not. As a result, it can be challenging to find an expert who is prepared to defend treatment patterns that fall outside of the mainstream, let alone treatment patterns that fall far outside the mainstream.

Similarly, while a healthcare practice that pays 90 percent of its gross revenues in "management" fees to unlicensed nonprofessionals might argue that those payments represented fair market value for management services, most business and financial experts would probably disagree. As a result, expert witnesses presented by defendants in no-fault anti-fraud cases tend to be marked by a lack of professional distinction, personal or business relationships with the defendant, long histories as professional witnesses, or all of the above.

While the lines of inquiry during an expert deposition will naturally vary from case to case, the thrust of the questions should be aimed at demonstrating that the expert's testimony fails to meet the standards enunciated by the Supreme Court in *Daubert v. Merrell Dow Pharms.*, 509 U.S. 579 (1993) and in Daubert's progeny, in particular

i. whether the expert's theory or technique can be, and has been, tested;
ii. whether the theory or technique has been subjected to peer review or publication;
iii. the known or potential rate of error and the existence and maintenance of standards controlling the theory or technique's operation;
iv. general acceptance of the theory or technique in the scientific community;
v. the relationship of the theory or technique to methods that have been established to be reliable;
vi. the qualifications of the expert witness;
vii. the nonjudicial uses to which the expert's method has been put;

viii. whether the expert is proposing to testify about matters growing naturally and directly out of research they have conducted independent of the litigation or whether they have developed their opinions expressly for the purposes of testifying;
ix. whether the expert has unjustly extrapolated from an accepted premise to an unfounded conclusion;
x. whether the expert adequately has accounted for obvious alternative explanations;
xi. whether the expert is being as careful as he would be in his regular professional work outside his paid litigation consulting; and
xii. whether the field of expertise claimed by the expert is known to reach reliable results for the type of opinion the expert would give.[31]

When questioned along these lines, defense experts in no-fault anti-fraud cases will often have difficulty justifying their conclusions. For example, there often will be few peer-reviewed publications supporting aggressive and expensive interventional pain management treatment for patients whose underlying accidents were manifestly minor. To the extent that some outlying peer-reviewed publications support some form of aggressive treatment, they usually will be contravened by the general consensus against such treatment in the medical community. What is more, where a defendant proffers an expert to support some arcane or unusual treatment, the expert will often have to admit that he does not typically render such treatments to his own patients in his own practice.

Along similar lines, defense experts in corporate structure or kickback cases may encounter considerable difficulty presenting colorable explanations for suspicious payments from a healthcare practice to its "managers" or referral sources. For instance, if a healthcare practice pays 80 or 90 percent of its gross revenues to unlicensed "managers" or "consultants," can the expert present any objective support for the notion that such exorbitant payments represent fair market value for the services rendered? Can the expert point to any legitimate research

[31] *See, e.g.*, Daubert v. Merrell Dow Pharms., 509 U.S. 579, 593–94 (1993); Fed. R. Evid. 702, Advisory Committee Notes: 2000 Amendments.

showing that such payments are customary amongst legitimate healthcare practices? Probably not.

Of course, the *Daubert* standards work both ways. Just as anti-fraud litigators should seek to expose a defense expert's junk science, they should prepare their own expert witnesses to provide colorable, objective scientific support for their opinions. In this context, many experts—especially licensed healthcare providers with long clinical experience—will "know" whether a given healthcare service is or is not generally accepted within their field, but they may not be able to cite to the latest peer-reviewed literature that supports the consensus view. Similarly, a financial expert such as a forensic accountant may "know" from experience that there is something problematic with a healthcare practice that pays 90 percent of its revenues to unlicensed parties but may not be prepared to point to specific studies or data to support their conclusion. Anti-fraud litigators should use mock depositions of their expert witnesses to ensure that the witnesses can not only state their conclusions, but are also prepared to point to objective, reputable scientific support for their conclusions.

10

Provisional Remedies in No-Fault Insurance Anti-Fraud Litigation

While in theory a plaintiff-insurer might seek any number of provisional remedies in a no-fault anti-fraud case, the most common provisional remedies that are sought are a stay of a defendant's attempts to collect on his outstanding, allegedly fraudulent billing pending the disposition of the case, an injunction against the commencement of any new collections proceedings during the pendency of the case, and an order of pre-judgment attachment against a defendant's assets. We will discuss each of these remedies in turn.

A. Stays of Collections Proceedings and Injunctions Against the Commencement of New Collections Proceedings

As discussed previously, by the time that an insurer commences an anti-fraud lawsuit, it has usually paid a substantial sum to the defendants in reliance on their fraudulent billing. In the typical case, the plaintiff-insurer will seek to recover this money through common law fraud, unjust enrichment, civil RICO, or state law anti-fraud claims. At the same time, the defendants will usually have submitted a significant amount of billing that remains outstanding and unpaid, and the defendants will actively be trying to collect on this billing through a large number of small-collections lawsuits or arbitrations. As a result, in addition to their other claims, most insurers will assert a declaratory judgment claim, seeking a declaration to the effect that they are not liable to pay any of the defendants' pending billing because it is fraudulent and unreimbursable.

This can lead to an untoward spectacle. For example, an insurer may have stated a very colorable claim for a declaratory judgment to the effect that all of a defendant's billing is fraudulent and unreimbursable. However, even as the insurer's declaratory judgment claim is pending in one forum, the defendant may be trying to recover in other forums on that same fraudulent and unreimbursable billing through a myriad of small-collections lawsuits and arbitrations. What is more, the defendant may well be succeeding in its collections efforts, considering the general lack of discovery in no-fault collections arbitration and the stacked deck that insurers often face in small-scale collections lawsuits.

The overall result can be a lack of economy and risk of inconsistent results as dozens or hundreds of individual collections arbitrations or lawsuits proceed, with varying outcomes, despite the fact that the plaintiff-insurer has asserted a declaratory judgment claim that could dispose of all of the defendant's pending billing at one fell swoop. Moreover, to the extent that a defendant is able to collect on its outstanding billing during the pendency of the insurer's anti-fraud suit, the defendant will be in a position to use the proceeds of the billing to fund its defense and prolong the anti-fraud litigation. On the other hand, if a defendant is prevented from funding its defense with the ongoing proceeds of its fraudulent scheme, it can promote an early settlement.

For these reasons—and to the extent possible—it will usually be worthwhile for a plaintiff-insurer to seek a stay of a defendant's collections activity and an injunction against the commencement of any new collections proceedings during the pendency of the insurer's anti-fraud lawsuit.

Initially, it is important to note that pursuant to the federal Anti-Injunction Act and in the interests of federal-state comity, federal courts are generally powerless to stay state court proceedings.[1] As

[1] *See* 28 U.S.C. § 2283 ("A court of the United States may not grant an injunction to stay proceedings in a State court except as expressly authorized by Act of Congress, or

a result, where an insurer's anti-fraud case is pending in federal court and the defendants are attempting to collect on their outstanding billing in state court, the insurer will be unable to obtain a stay of the state court collections cases from the federal court where the anti-fraud case is pending. This is not to say that the insurer is without a remedy—rather, the remedy simply will be more onerous to obtain. In particular, the insurer will have to commence a separate action in state court or seek consolidation of the pending state court collections actions and then move the state court for a stay of the state court collections cases.

The Anti-Injunction Act will only make it difficult for the insurer to obtain a stay of a defendant's collections activity if the insurer's anti-fraud case is pending in federal court and the defendant's collections efforts are proceeding in state court. If the defendant is seeking to collect on its outstanding billing through arbitration—as is required in some no-fault states—the Anti-Injunction Act will present no bar to a stay. Similarly, if the plaintiff-insurer has elected to litigate its anti-fraud case in state court, the Anti-Injunction Act—which applies only to federal courts—will have no effect.

While different courts may apply somewhat different standards in determining whether to stay or enjoin no-fault collections proceedings, the case law indicates that courts generally look to (i) whether a stay and injunction would be in the interests of economy, (ii) whether a stay and injunction would prevent inconsistent decisions, and (iii) whether the plaintiff-insurer can meet the standards for issuance of injunctive relief.[2] In most anti-fraud cases, insurers will have compelling arguments to meet these standards.

---

where necessary in aid of its jurisdiction, or to protect or effectuate its judgments."); *see also* Pelfresne v. Williams Bay, 917 F.2d 1017, 1019 (7th Cir. 1990) ("The main purpose of the Anti-Injunction Act is to avoid the affront to comity (the mutual respect of sovereigns) that would be entailed if a court of one sovereign, namely a federal court, attempted to enjoin proceedings in the court of another sovereign, namely a state court.").

[2] *See*, e.g., Allstate Ins. Co. v. Hisham Elzanaty, 929 F. Supp. 2d 199, 220–22 (E.D.N.Y. 2013) (staying and enjoining defendants' no-fault collections arbitration pending the disposition of insurer's anti-fraud suit, where the insurer met the requirements for injunctive relief, the stay and injunction were in the interests of economy, and the stay and injunction would reduce the risk of arbitral decisions that could be inconsistent with the outcome of the anti-fraud suit); Allstate Ins. Co. v. Lopez, 311 N.J. Super. 660, 675–80 (N.J. Law Div. 1998) (same).

First, it almost always will be most economical to stay no-fault collections lawsuits or arbitrations during the pendency of an insurer's declaratory judgment claim if the declaratory judgment claim could dispose of all of the collections proceedings on a wholesale basis. This is especially true if there is some overarching issue with a defendant's billing that makes all of it fraudulent for substantially the same reasons. For instance, in a case involving a healthcare practice with an illegal corporate structure, all of that practice's billing will have misrepresented the practice's corporate legitimacy and eligibility to collect no-fault insurance benefits in the first instance. As a result, there is little point in permitting the practice's collections proceedings to proceed individually or for the merits of each proceeding to be determined individually. Rather, because the determination of a single issue—the practice's corporate structure—can be made in the context of the insurer's anti-fraud lawsuit, where it potentially could resolve a large number of the defendant's pending collections proceedings, a stay of the collections proceedings during the pendency of the insurer's anti-fraud suit makes sound economic sense.

Similarly, where a defendant has provided substantially similar, medically unnecessary treatment to a large cohort of patients without regard for the patients' individual circumstances or presentment, the determination of a single issue—whether the defendant renders treatment pursuant to a predetermined, fraudulent protocol—could potentially resolve a large number of the defendant's pending collections proceedings. Again, in such a case, a stay of the collections proceedings until the disposition of the insurer's anti-fraud case would be most economical.

What is more, oftentimes arbitrators, or judges in state courts of limited jurisdiction where no-fault collections suits are typically filed, lack the ability or the authority to adjudicate large-scale insurance fraud claims. For example, no-fault arbitrators and courts of limited jurisdiction typically cannot award treble damages to an insurer on a civil RICO or state law anti-fraud claim.

Moreover, the limited discovery that is available in most no-fault collections proceedings effectively prevents insurers from proving large-scale fraud schemes in the context of such proceedings.

Therefore, in the unlikely event that an insurer was able to present the full contours of a defendant's fraudulent scheme as a defense or counterclaim in the context of a collections proceeding, it would be unable to obtain complete relief in such a proceeding. This tends to underscore how the interests of economy can be served by a stay of no-fault collections proceedings pending the disposition of an insurer's anti-fraud case.

Second, courts tend to give considerable weight to whether a stay of no-fault collections proceedings during the pendency of an insurer's anti-fraud case will reduce the risk of inconsistent decisions. These concerns are usually driven by a desire to preserve the integrity of the court's ultimate judgment in the anti-fraud case.[3] On a motion to stay and enjoin a defendant's no-fault collections proceedings, an insurer should be in a good position to argue that there is a clear and present danger of inconsistent results if the collections proceedings go forward pending the disposition of an anti-fraud suit. After all, the insurer will have the benefit of full and complete discovery in the anti-fraud suit and will be able to present evidence regarding long-term patterns of fraudulent conduct. By contrast, collections proceedings typically focus on individual claims with limited discovery and no real way for an insurer to prove patterns of fraudulent conduct that only may be discerned upon review of a large number of claims.

Third, although the standards for injunctive relief may vary to some limited extent from court to court, the general requirements should be familiar to any litigator: (i) a likelihood of success on the merits, (ii) irreparable harm to the movant absent the requested injunctive relief, and (iii) a balance of the equities tipping in the movant's favor.

To demonstrate a likelihood of success on the merits, a plaintiff-insurer should not need to show that it definitely will prevail on its anti-fraud claims. Rather, it will be sufficient for the insurer to make a prima facie showing that it has a reasonable probability of success on the merits. While this can be difficult at the pleading stage, a well-pleaded, detailed fraud complaint, coupled with some evidence to support the allegations in the complaint—if not to prove them—should be enough.[4]

---

[3] *See*, e.g., Elzanaty, *supra* note 2, 929 F. Supp. 2d at 220 (noting that it would "severely threaten any judgment of this Court to have pending arbitrations or future arbitrations result in inconsistent rulings with regard to [the defendant's] eligibility for reimbursement of No-Fault insurance payments.").

[4] *See*, e.g., Elzanaty, *supra* note 2, 929 F. Supp. 2d at 222 (plaintiff-insurer demonstrated sufficiently serious questions going to the merits of its case, and obtained a stay and injunction of defendant's collections proceedings, where they "adequately

Irreparable harm can present a thornier problem. As every law student learns, injuries that can be addressed through financial restitution do not constitute irreparable harm for purposes of obtaining a preliminary injunction. Thus, a defendant in a no-fault insurance fraud case may be in a position to argue that any injuries the insurer might suffer as the result of the continuation of collections proceedings adequately could be redressed through money damages when and if the insurer prevails in the anti-fraud case. Nonetheless, courts in no-fault anti-fraud cases have found a showing of irreparable harm to be sufficient to support a stay of collections proceedings where (i) there is a potential for piecemeal resolution of collections proceedings, coupled with the risk of inconsistent decisions,[5] and (ii) the insurer could be subject to millions of dollars in fraudulently obtained judgments and would be required to present duplicative testimony in multitudinous collections proceedings and where piecemeal resolution of the collections proceedings would make it difficult for the insurer to effectively present its defenses in the context of those proceedings.[6] Because these same considerations will be present in most no-fault anti-fraud cases, insurers should have compelling arguments to the effect that, absent a stay, they will suffer some cognizable, irreparable injury.

Similarly, insurers often will be able to present colorable arguments to demonstrate that the balance of equities tips in their favor and militates for a stay of a defendant's collections proceedings pending the resolution of the insurer's anti-fraud case. As discussed above, state no-fault laws typically provide for interest—and often high rates of interest—on overdue no-fault claims. As a result, defendants in

---

detailed a complicated scheme of alleged fraudulent activity and the Court has already denied the Defendants' motion to dismiss for failure to state a claim."); Wave Form Sys. v. AMS Sales Corp., 73 F. Supp. 3d 1052, 1059 (D. Minn. 2014) ("To demonstrate a likelihood of success on the merits, as required for preliminary injunction, movant must show that it has a fair chance of prevailing on its claims."); Grimes v. Corr. Med. Servs., 2011`U.S. Dist. LEXIS 25923 at *6 to *7 (D.N.J. 2011) (to demonstrate a "reasonable probability of success on the merits," "[i]t is not necessary that the moving party's right to a final decision after trial be wholly without doubt; rather, the burden is on the party seeking relief to make a prima facie case showing a reasonable probability that it will prevail on the merits . . . .") (Internal quotations and citation omitted).

[5] *See* Elzanaty, *supra* note 2, 929 F. Supp. 2d at 222.

[6] *See* Allstate Ins. Co. v. Lopez, 311 N.J. Super. 660, 670–71 (N.J. Law Div. 1998).

no-fault fraud cases may find themselves hard-pressed to argue that they will suffer any cognizable prejudice if their collections activities are delayed.

For example, if a defendant's collections proceedings are stayed and the plaintiff-insurer ultimately prevails in its anti-fraud case and obtains a declaratory judgment to the effect that the defendant is not liable to collect on its pending billing, then the defendant cannot legitimately argue that he was prejudiced by the stay. To the contrary, he never was entitled to collect on his pending billing in the first instance. On the other hand, if the plaintiff-insurer does not prevail on its declaratory judgment claim, then the defendant healthcare provider will be entitled to interest on its outstanding claims, thereby obviating any prejudice.[7]

B. Orders of Pre-Judgment Attachment

Orders of pre-judgment attachment are rare and difficult to obtain considering that they effectively permit a plaintiff to freeze a defendant's assets before the defendant's liability to the plaintiff has been adjudicated. Moreover, pre-judgment attachment standards vary considerably from state to state, and federal courts apply the law of the forum state in determining whether pre-judgment attachment is available.[8] Most states do not permit pre-judgment attachments at all or else limit the remedy to such an extent that it is practically unavailable in the context of no-fault insurance anti-fraud litigation.

Even so, some no-fault states, like New York and Minnesota, have relatively liberal pre-judgment attachment statutes and generally permit orders of pre-judgment attachment where it appears that

---

[7] *See*, e.g., Elzanaty, *supra* note 2, 929 F. Supp. 2d at 222 (finding that there would be no prejudice to defendant if its PIP arbitrations were stayed, considering that "if it ultimately prevails in this matter" it would "be entitled to the collection of interest at a rate of two percent every month that the No-Fault payments are overdue."); Lopez, *supra* note 2, 311 N.J. Super at 670 (holding that "A stay will not prejudice the defendants. Rather, a stay will maintain the status quo while the coverage issues are litigated. Any hardship to the defendants is minimal and is more than outweighed by the irreparable harm Allstate will otherwise suffer if a stay is not granted.").

[8] *See* Fed. R. Civ. P. 64 (providing, in pertinent part, that "every remedy is available that, under the law of the state where the court is located, provides for seizing a person or property to secure satisfaction of the potential judgment . . . .").

the plaintiff has a probability of success on the merits and can show that the defendant is secreting or dissipating his assets to frustrate the enforcement of any judgment that might be rendered in the plaintiff's favor.[9] By contrast, New Jersey's pre-judgment attachment statute is more restrictive and—in the usual no-fault fraud case—will generally not permit pre-judgment attachment unless the defendant is a non-resident or is about to abscond from the state.[10]

To the extent that the remedy is available at all, a plaintiff-insurer in a no-fault anti-fraud case usually will not know whether it has grounds to seek a pre-judgment attachment until some discovery has occurred. Oftentimes, financial discovery, in particular, will reveal evidence that a defendant is squirreling away its assets through suspicious transfers. For instance, the bank records for a defendant healthcare practice may indicate that the owner of the practice, who also is a defendant in the case, began to withdraw large sums of money from the practice's bank accounts in untraceable cash shortly after being served with the plaintiff-insurer's complaint. Along similar lines, a defendant's bank records may reveal that he issued multiple checks each day for a few thousand dollars apiece to a close personal relation for no apparent purpose. Under these types of circumstances, courts—especially the courts in New York—have granted insurers' motions for pre-judgment attachment in no-fault anti-fraud cases.[11]

Typically, a motion for an order of pre-judgment attachment should be brought on via an order to show cause to limit the defendant's ability to accelerate the secretion or dissipation of assets during the pendency of a motion on notice. As part of the proposed order to show cause, the plaintiff-insurer should request an ex parte temporary restraining order to prevent any further dissipation of the defendant's assets pending the disposition of the underlying motion. In addition, as part of the motion, the plaintiff-insurer should request an order directing the defendant at issue to disclose all of her substantive

[9] *See*, e.g., N.Y. C.P.L.R. § 6201; MINN. STAT. § 570.01, *et seq*.

[10] *See* N.J.S.A. 2A:26-2; N.J.S.A. 2A:15-41.

[11] *See*, e.g., Government Employees Ins. Co. v. Akpinar, E.D.N.Y. Case No. 11-cv-4667, Order (September 28, 2012); Allstate Insurance Company v. Alexander Rozenberg, E.D.N.Y. Docket No. 08-cv-0565, Order (January 26, 2009) (granting motions for pre-judgment attachment where it appeared that the defendants were acting to secrete or dissipate their assets).

assets. This will ensure—to the extent possible—that the insurer is aware of all assets that should be subject to the attachment order.

While motions for orders of pre-judgment attachment rarely are granted, when they are granted they usually will bring an anti-fraud case to a rapid conclusion. If a motion for pre-judgment attachment is granted, it is a strong indication that the court views the defendant with a jaundiced eye and that future rulings in the case will be unfavorable for that defendant. Moreover, a defendant may find it difficult to pay for ordinary personal expenses with a pre-judgment attachment order in place, much less any luxuries to which they have become accustomed.

11

Settlements, Summary Judgment, and Trial in No-Fault Insurance Anti-Fraud Litigation

The vast majority of no-fault insurance anti-fraud litigation settles in advance of summary judgment or trial. Relatively few cases even proceed beyond the opening stages of discovery, because—if an insurer is able to meet the fraud pleading requirements, and allege prima facie fraud-based claims in detail—most no-fault insurance fraud rings realize that their activities will not withstand any further inspection.

At the same time, except in the most egregious cases, most plaintiff-insurers are prepared to settle on relatively reasonable terms and will not let a great settlement be the enemy of a good settlement. There are several reasons why this is the case, including a desire to avoid the expense of protracted litigation, the inherent uncertainly of litigation, and the intrinsic appeal of a bird in hand.

What is more, and for better or for worse, no-fault insurance fraud rings usually have some settlement leverage, even in cases where the evidence against them is particularly damning. For instance, at the time when a no-fault anti-fraud suit is commenced, the insurer has usually paid a substantial amount of the defendants' fraudulent billing, but the defendants typically have a great deal of additional fraudulent billing that remains outstanding and unpaid. Sometimes, the amount of outstanding and unpaid billing is greater than the amount of billing that the insurer already has paid, and the defendants actively are pursuing recovery on their outstanding billing through a multitude of individual, small-scale collections lawsuits and arbitrations. As discussed above, the deck often is stacked against insurers in these collections proceedings because the proceedings cover individual claims, discovery is limited, and insurers therefore lack the ability to prove large-scale patterns of fraud occurring across multiple claims over time. Although an insurer might seek a stay of these collections proceedings in its anti-fraud case, there usually is no guarantee that a stay will be granted, the stay might take time to obtain, and in the interim the collections lawsuits and arbitrations will proceed apace. These collections lawsuits and arbitrations cost insurers money even if the insurers ultimately prevail in them, and, considering the stacked deck, they often lose.

Even in cases where a defendant has no outstanding collectable billing or is losing in its attempts to collect on its billing, the defendant nonetheless may have some settlement leverage. For example, courts usually are willing to indulge a defendant who stands accused of fraud and to entertain even obviously futile motions and arguments in the interests of giving the defendant the fairest possible hearing. This, in turn, can make the threat of protracted and expensive litigation manifest. Where it appears to an insurer that it might become embroiled in a prolonged war of attrition, it is a small wonder that many insurers are prepared to settle cases early for substantially less than they might obtain on summary judgment or at trial, after months or even years of litigation.

A. Common Settlement Parameters in No-Fault Anti-Fraud Litigation

Although there usually are strong incentives for every party to an anti-fraud case to settle as early as possible, most insurers will prefer to proceed with a relatively strong case unless at least three settlement parameters are met: (i) a release by the defendant of all of its outstanding and unpaid billing, (ii) payment by the defendant of at least some amount of restitution, and (iii) some kind of restrictions on future billing by the defendant.

1. Releases of Outstanding and Unpaid Billing

A defendant's release of outstanding and unpaid billing often is an insurer's threshold requirement for settlement. Were an insurer to accept restitution from a defendant without receiving a concomitant release of that defendant's outstanding billing, the defendant could simply fund the restitution out of the proceeds of its outstanding billing. Moreover, and as noted above, at the time when an anti-fraud lawsuit is commenced, the amount of a defendant's outstanding billing will usually be high and will sometimes exceed the amount that the plaintiff-insurer already has paid to the defendant on its prior fraudulent billing. Thus, a release of a defendant's outstanding billing will usually be a—and sometimes the—primary value driver of the litigation.

While most insurers will demand a complete release of all pending billing as a necessary condition of any settlement, in some cases they may accept something short of a complete release. Depending on the relative strength of an insurer's case, the insurer might accept a release of claims within a certain date range or a release of claims related to certain discrete healthcare services but not others. For example, an insurer may have compelling proof that a defendant billed for medically useless diagnostic tests but is unable to point to any specific fraud with respect to the other services the defendant provided. Under such circumstances, the insurer might be willing to consider a release of the defendant's billing for the diagnostic tests without demanding a release of the defendant's billing for its other services. Similarly, an insurer may be in a position to prove that a defendant submitted fraudulent billing during a specific time period but be unable to demonstrate that the defendant's billing was fraudulent outside of that time period. In such as a case, the insurer might entertain a release of the billing during the period when the fraud occurred but not during other periods.

Regardless of the scope of the ultimate release, plaintiff-insurers should take care to include certain language in the release provisions. First, to the extent that the defendant releasing the pending billing is an entity, such as a healthcare practice, the plaintiff-insurer should require the individual executing the release to represent and warrant that she has the authority to execute the release on behalf of the entity. This is especially important in cases involving corporate structure fraud, where true ownership of a healthcare practice may be in doubt.

Second, the plaintiff-insurer should ensure that the release provisions not only release the pending billing, but also obligate the defendant to effectuate the dismissal of any pending collections lawsuits and arbitrations by a date certain. Otherwise, the insurer might itself have to use the release to secure the dismissal of pending collections proceedings, a time-consuming and expensive process that can chip away at the value of the underlying release.

Third, the defendant should promise not to submit any future billing with dates of service on or before the date of the release. This will ensure that the release covers not only any outstanding billing that the defendant submitted as of the date of the release, but also any billing that the defendant could have submitted as of the date of the release.

Fourth, the release should include a provision requiring the defendant to indemnify the insurer for any violation of the release following a reasonable cure period. The inclusion of such a provision will provide the defendant with an incentive to rein in any collections lawyers who might not be aware of the release and might continue to prosecute collections proceedings on behalf of the defendant in violation of the release.

2. Payment of Restitution

The amount of restitution demanded by an insurer will obviously vary depending on the circumstances of the individual case. Sometimes, and especially where a defendant is walking away from a massive amount of outstanding billing pursuant to a release, an insurer might be willing to accept a relatively low amount of restitution. Conversely, where a defendant does not have a great deal of outstanding billing and the value of a release is more limited, an insurer usually will want to see more in restitution.

The restitution provisions of any settlement agreement should include certain clauses aimed at ensuring that the restitution actually is paid in accordance with the agreement. First, and most obviously, the provisions should require the restitution payment to be made by a date certain. If the defendant is going to pay the restitution in installments over time, the dates for all of the respective payments should be identified, and the insurer may want to insist on interest provisions. The agreement should require the restitution payments to be made via a certified or attorney's escrow check made payable to the insurer to obviate any need to deal with returned checks. Finally, the restitution clauses should include meaningful consequences for non-compliance, such as a provision permitting the insurer to immediately enter judgment against the defendant for liquidated damages over and above the restitution amount in the event that the restitution is not timely paid. In addition, to the extent that the defendant fails to pay the restitution, any release from the insurer to the defendant should be rendered void ab initio.

3. Restrictions on Future Billing

In a limited set of cases, where the evidence against a defendant is extremely conclusive and damning and the defendant is highly motivated to settle at almost any cost, the plaintiff-insurer may be in a position to demand that the defendant never again submit any no-fault insurance billing. More commonly, however, the best an insurer will be able to achieve will be reasonable future billing restrictions aimed at preventing a defendant from enacting the same kind of fraudulent scheme in the future as it did in the past.

Because insurers should, as a rule, avoid appearing as if they are interfering with the professional judgment of a healthcare provider—even a manifestly fraudulent healthcare provider—these types of restrictions always should be phrased as restrictions on billing, rather than restrictions on treatment. In other words, pursuant to the terms of the restrictions, the defendant should remain free to treat her patients however she chooses except that the defendant will be precluded from billing the insurer for certain types of services in certain ways.

The future billing restriction provisions of any settlement agreement not only should provide that the insurer has no obligation to pay the defendant for the services in question, but that the defendant shall not even attempt to bill the insurer for the pertinent services.

For example, a billing restriction provision limiting future billing for initial examinations to billing under CPT code 99202 (i.e., the second-lowest level of initial examination) might provide, in substance, that "The defendants shall not bill the insurer for, the insurer shall not be obligated to pay the defendants for, and the defendants shall not collect from the insurer for, initial examinations at any rate higher than the rate applicable to CPT code 99202."

Similarly, a billing restriction provision limiting the number of NCV tests that may be billed in the future to the insurer might state that "The defendants shall not bill the insurer for, the insurer shall not be obligated to pay the defendants for, and the defendants shall not collect from the insurer for, NCV tests conducted on more than eight (8) nerves on any individual insured."

It is important to place limitations not only on the insurer's obligations to pay a defendant for certain services, but also on the defendant's act of billing itself to reduce the likelihood of inadvertent payments by the insurer on billing that violates the billing restriction agreement.

In addition, to eliminate any potential misunderstandings, any billing restriction agreement should specify that the insurer reserves its right to challenge or defend against even those charges that might be submitted in the future in accordance with the billing restriction agreement. In other words, even if a defendant complies with its agreement to limit all future billing for initial examinations to CPT code 99202 or to limit future billing for NCV tests to eight nerves per insured patient, the insurer should retain the right to resist payment on those charges if the underlying services were medically unnecessary, provided in violation of the law, or otherwise unreimbursable.

It also is critical to ensure that the billing restriction provisions in a settlement agreement with a defendant apply not only to that defendant, individually, but also to any entities, regardless of form, that are owned or controlled by that defendant. Were it otherwise, then a defendant could circumvent the billing restrictions and render them ineffective by simply incorporating a new healthcare practice and submitting its future billing in the name of the new healthcare practice rather than in his own name.

While these are the most material provisions that should appear in any settlement of a no-fault insurance anti-fraud case, there are other provisions that are commonly included in such agreements. The most significant additional term that is usually included in an agreement settling a no-fault anti-fraud case is a confidentiality provision. For example, most defendants will want to include a confidentiality provision in their settlement agreements out of concern that disclosure of the facts of a case or the terms of the settlement could draw lawsuits from other insurers or attention from state regulatory authorities or law enforcement. Except in the limited circumstances where the outcome of a case reflects poorly on an insurer or where an insurer was forced to enter into an unfavorable settlement, most insurers will have little interest in confidentiality. To the contrary, if an insurer succeeds in wresting a favorable settlement from a defendant, the insurer may want to broadly disseminate the terms of the settlement as a cautionary tale for other no-fault fraud rings.

Insurers should be aware that such confidentiality provisions can have unintended consequences. For example, a confidentiality provision limiting the insurer's ability to disclose any facts regarding its investigation of a defendant in any circumstances might preclude the insurer from using its investigative findings in a subsequent case against that defendant in the event that the defendant turns out to be a recidivist. This situation arises more than one might think. Oftentimes, a defendant will have engaged in one type of fraud—say, billing for medically useless diagnostic tests—and, following an anti-fraud lawsuit by an insurer, might enter into a settlement with the insurer that restricts its billing for those diagnostic tests. Thereafter, the defendant might stop billing for the diagnostic tests and begin to submit fraudulent billing for medically unnecessary pain management injections. If the insurer then commences a second lawsuit against the defendant based on its fraudulent billing for the pain management injections, the insurer will likely want to plead the facts of its previous investigation of the defendant into its second complaint. However, if the settlement in the first case contains confidentiality provisions that limit the insurer's ability to disclose the results of the investigation that led to the first case, the insurer will be precluded from pleading the facts of its first case into its second complaint.

Thus, to the extent that a plaintiff-insurer agrees to any confidentiality provisions in settling a case on favorable terms, it should try to limit the confidentiality provisions to the terms of the settlement agreement itself. At the same time, the insurer should avoid making the confidentiality provisions of a settlement agreement applicable to its investigation and all of the facts giving rise to the litigation.

In addition, plaintiff-insurers and anti-fraud litigations should consider including the following additional terms in their settlements of no-fault anti-fraud cases:

i. a provision specifying that the parties represent and warrant that each had the benefit of representation by independent legal counsel and understand and agree to be bound by the terms set forth in the settlement and that the settlement shall not be construed against any party—which can be important to head off any subsequent argument by a defendant that he was "taken advantage of" by the insurer in the context of the settlement negotiations;

ii. a provision specifying that the court where the action is pending will retain jurisdiction to enforce the terms of the settlement and that the law of the forum state shall govern the interpretation of the agreement—to ensure that the court that is familiar with the case is the court responsible to resolve any disputes under the settlement;

iii. a provision requiring the parties to execute such other documents and take such other action as may reasonably be necessary to further the purposes of the settlement;

iv. provisions prohibiting assignment or modification of rights or obligations under the settlement agreement without the express written consent of all parties to the agreement; and

v. a fee-shifting provision, entitling the prevailing party in any dispute under the settlement agreement to recover its attorneys' fees and costs.

B. Summary Judgment Motions in No-Fault Anti-Fraud Litigation

Most no-fault insurance fraud cases settle, except in a relatively rare instances in which a plaintiff-insurer's claims are discussed with prejudice. As a result, motions for summary judgment or trials are quite rare in no-fault anti-fraud litigation, and reported decisions discussing summary judgment motions, much less trials, are few and far between. Even so, it is worthwhile to briefly discuss some of the common procedural and substantive issues that may arise in the unusual instance where an anti-fraud case proceeds to summary judgment.

While state and federal summary judgment procedures may differ to some extent, the general requirements for summary judgment are the same across the board and should be familiar to any litigator. In particular, to obtain summary judgment, a movant must generally demonstrate that there is no genuine dispute as to any material fact and that the movant is entitled to judgment as a matter of law.[1] The moving party bears the initial burden of pointing to evidence in the record—such as depositions, documents, affidavits, and so on—that it believes demonstrates the absence of any genuine issue of material fact.[2] In the alternative, the movant may support a contention that there is no dispute as to any material fact by showing that the opposing party cannot produce any admissible evidence to demonstrate any legitimate dispute as to a material fact.[3] Assuming that the moving party can meet this burden, the burden shifts to the nonmoving party to identify "specific facts showing that there is a genuine issue for trial."[4]

In this context, not every factual dispute will be "genuine." Rather, a dispute is genuine only where the evidence is such that a reasonable factfinder could return a verdict for the nonmoving party.[5] Given that summary judgment is a harsh remedy, courts are required to view the evidence in the light most favorable to the nonmoving party and to draw all permissible inferences in favor of the nonmoving party.[6]

Against this backdrop, it is not hard to see why it can be difficult for a plaintiff-insurer to obtain summary judgment in a no-fault anti-fraud case. For instance, in a case involving fraudulent billing for medically unnecessary services, a defendant healthcare provider

---

[1] *See, e.g.*, Fed. R. Civ. P. 56(a) (providing that "The court shall grant summary judgment if the movant shows that there is no genuine dispute as to any material fact and the movant is entitled to judgment as a matter of law."); Brill v. Guardian Life Ins. Co. of Am. 142 N.J. 520, 528–29 (N.J. 1995) ("[A] court should grant summary judgment when 'the pleadings, depositions, answers to interrogatories and admissions on file, together with the affidavits, if any, show that there is no genuine issue as to any material fact challenged and that the moving party is entitled to a judgment or order as a matter of law.'"); Fabio v. Bellomo, 504 N.W.2d 758 (Minn. 1993) ("A motion for summary judgment shall be granted when the pleadings, depositions, answers to interrogatories, and admissions on file, together with the affidavits, if any, show that there is no genuine issue of material fact and that either party is entitled to a judgment as a matter of law.").

[2] *See, e.g.*, Fed. R. Civ. P. 56(c); Celotex Corp. v. Catrett, 477 U.S. 317, 323 (1986).

[3] *Id.*

[4] Anderson v. Liberty Lobby, Inc., 477 U.S. 242, 248 (1986).

[5] *Id.*

[6] *See, e.g.*, Anderson, *supra* note 4, 477 U.S. at 255.

almost always will be in a position to submit some evidence to raise a dispute as to medical necessity. While a bare, self-serving affidavit may not be sufficient to defeat a summary judgment motion, a defendant in a no-fault fraud case will usually be able to muster supporting affidavits from others involved in the scheme, a smattering of questionable research studies, and the opinions of paid expert witnesses. Courts would view this sort of evidence in a favorable light on any summary judgment motion, and where a defendant stands accused of serious frauds, a court is likely to be even more indulgent than usual.

Cases involving corporate structure fraud can present a closer question, and it is in these types of cases—rather than medical necessity cases—where a plaintiff-insurer may stand at least a fighting chance of obtaining summary judgment. For example, it may be challenging for a defendant to contend that a healthcare practice is legitimately owned and controlled by licensed professionals when the bank records and tax returns for that practice show that unlicensed individuals and entities are receiving the lion's share of its gross revenues. However, insurers will have a heavy lift on summary judgment even in corporate structure fraud cases. For example, the defendants in such cases will usually be able to present some outside expert opinion—however implausible—to the effect that the healthcare practice's transfers of exorbitant sums to unlicensed individuals and entities represented fair market value for the services that those individuals and entities supposedly provided to the practice. Again, in the discrete context of a summary judgment motion, a court will give these types of submissions more weight than they otherwise might carry at trial, especially where the defendant is being accused of a serious fraud.

Overall, in no-fault anti-fraud cases, motions for summary judgment will usually be a waste of time and resources, except in the rare cases—such as some corporate structure fraud cases—where a defendant simply cannot offer any exculpatory explanation for its conduct.

C. Trials in No-Fault Anti-Fraud Litigation

A full trial manual is beyond the scope of this book. Indeed, state and federal procedures, individual local civil rules, and judges' individual preferences make it difficult to generalize the pretrial and trial procedures that may be followed in a no-fault insurance fraud case.

Nonetheless, there are certain pretrial and trial issues that will arise in virtually any anti-fraud case, and they merit some discussion.

First, most courts will schedule a trial of an action shortly after the close of fact discovery and expert discovery, will convene a pre-trial conference a few weeks before the scheduled trial, and will require the parties to file either joint or separate pretrial memoranda in advance of the conference. These pretrial memoranda can be massive documents, as they usually are required to identify any pretrial proceedings—such as motions in limine—that the parties expect to pursue, proposed stipulations of undisputed fact, potential witnesses and exhibits that the parties might introduce, proposed voir dire questions, and proposed jury instructions, among other points. The preparation of these pretrial memoranda are an essential first step in preparing for trial as they help to organize the presentation of the plaintiff-insurer's case and provide an essential preview of the defendant's defenses.

Second, an anti-fraud litigator will want to consider whether, and to what extent, to file any motions in limine seeking to exclude or limit any evidence that the defendant proposes to present at trial. In some cases, courts will direct that motions in limine be filed in advance of the pretrial conference, and the court will rule on the motions during the pretrial conference. In other instances, the court will set a briefing schedule on motions in limine during the pretrial conference and will rule on the motions at some point in advance of trial. The most common motions in limine that will arise in the context of no-fault insurance anti-fraud litigation will be *Daubert* motions, which will seek to exclude expert testimony proffered on behalf of one or more of the parties.

As discussed previously, the issues courts typically consider on *Daubert* motions center on whether the expert's proposed testimony is relevant and rests on a reliable foundation and whether the experts' theories or techniques are generally accepted or have been peer reviewed. In most cases, *Daubert* motions will not pose much of a problem for plaintiff-insurers because they will be presenting experts to testify as to generally accepted standards of care and to opine that a defendant's treatment practices failed to meet those standards. More commonly, it will be the defendants in a medical necessity case whose experts will be subject to a *Daubert* challenge because they will be attempting to justify patterns of treatment that fall far outside the norm.

Third, plaintiff-insurers will not be in a position to independently determine whether their anti-fraud lawsuits will be tried before a judge or a jury. While a case may be tried before a jury on the demand of any party,[7] an insurer will not be able to secure a bench trial over a defendant's jury demand unless the defendant has waived its right to a jury, for instance by failing to make a timely demand. While in some cases a bench trial may be preferable from an insurer's perspective—especially in venues known for indulgent jury pools—as a practical matter a plaintiff-insurer should expect its no-fault fraud cases to be tried before juries.

With that in mind, anti-fraud litigators should remember the importance not only of narrative and concision, but also of being respectful to everyone in the courtroom, even the defendants and adverse witnesses. When an attorney is presenting evidence of a massive insurance fraud scheme, there will usually be no need to put a gloss on that evidence with snarky remarks or a snide tone. While it can be tempting to indulge in this type of conduct, especially in the face of dissembling or brazenly false testimony from a defendant, it tends to alienate the jury and lower the attorney to the defendant's level.

[7] *See*, e.g., FED. R. CIV. P. 38.

Conclusion

No-fault insurance fraud rings have shown a considerable ability to adapt their schemes, not only to the constantly developing case law, but also to insurers' fraud detection and deterrence efforts.

When it became clear that a healthcare practice's bank records would be discoverable in a corporate structure fraud case, unlicensed individuals who illegally controlled healthcare practices began to authorize themselves as signatories on the practices' accounts and found other ways to unlawfully siphon the practices' revenues to themselves.

When the great weight of professional authority held a given healthcare service to be medically useless, they created phony professional societies to falsely extol the supposed virtues of the service.

When it was apparent that a professional entity could serve as a racketeering enterprise for purposes of a civil RICO claim, some no-fault fraud rings stopped submitting billing through professional corporations and started submitting their billing through unincorporated, putative sole proprietorships.

These are only a few examples of the ways in which corrupt healthcare services providers have attempted to thwart anti-fraud litigation. There are many others, but the upshot is that no-fault insurance anti-fraud litigation is a constantly developing field. Any of the practices or cases described in this book could change over time, or in a very short period of time, if a state alters its no-fault insurance regime, a court takes a different view on the scope of discovery in the typical no-fault fraud case, or if no-fault fraud evolves into some different, previously unknown form. The point is that it is impossible to foretell every possible issue that might arise in the context of no-fault anti-fraud litigation—it is only possible to present as complete a picture as possible of how it exists and is practiced today.

Table of Cases

Index

N